Cleaning
Plain & Simple

DONNA SMALLIN

Cleaning
Plain & Simple

The mission of Storey Publishing is to serve our customers
by publishing practical information that encourages personal independence
in harmony with the environment.

Edited by Nancy D. Wood
Copyedited by Nancy W. Ringer
Art direction and cover design by Cindy McFarland,
   based on original design by Wendy Palitz
Text design and production by Erin Dawson
Production assistance by Jennie Jepson Smith
Cover art and illustrations © Juliette Borda
Indexed by John Hulse

   The information in this book is true and complete to the best of our knowledge. All recommendations are made without guarantee on the part of the author or Storey Publishing. The author and publisher disclaim any liability in connection with the use of this information. For additional information please contact Storey Publishing, 210 MASS MoCA Way, North Adams, MA 01247.
   Storey books are available for special premium and promotional uses and for customized editions. For further information, please call 1-800-793-9396.

Printed in the United States by CJK
10 9 8 7 6 5 4 3 2 1

Library of Congress Cataloging-in-Publication Data

Smallin, Donna, 1960-
   Cleaning : plain & simple / Donna Smallin.
      p. cm.
   Includes index.
   ISBN-13: 978-1-58017-607-1; ISBN-10: 1-58017-607-0 (pb : alk. paper)
   1. House cleaning. I. Title.

TX324.S53 2006
648'.5—dc22
                                                              2005027657

With love for Laurie Bain Wilson,
my forever friend,
and for her son, my godson, Alex.

CONTENTS

ACKNOWLEDGMENTS

THIS IS MY FAVORITE PART OF THE BOOK — the part where I get to thank the people who helped bring this project to its completion with their contributions, suggestions, warnings, reviews, encouragement, and plain and simple friendship.

First, I have to thank Gerry Adcock for steering me in the right direction when I was trying to explain the difference between sanitizing and disinfecting. Gerry knows a lot about germs, but he also provided valuable information from leading germ experts, which not only clarified but also helped shape my thinking. Gerry, I want you to know how much I appreciate the time and energy you put into this project on my behalf. You are a kind soul.

For one of the most unique tips in the whole book, I have my carpet cleaner, Jason Stout, to thank. He showed me how to remove urine stains, using hydrogen peroxide and an iron. If that doesn't work, nothing will. Jason, thanks for making me a believer. Another great tip for cleaning the glass on a wood-burning stove came from a former book editor, Robin Catalano. Thanks for sharing, Robin.

In researching this book, I came across so much contradictory advice that sometimes I just had to get a second opinion. I thank Frank Barr, a jeweler at Sami Fine Jewelry here in Fountain Hills, Arizona, where I live, for graciously reviewing my advice on cleaning jewelry. I also want to thank my local computer guy, Ron Robertson of Robertson Consulting, for reviewing the section on cleaning computers and offering some of his own proven tips.

A big thank-you goes out to all my friends at Storey Publishing for their faith in me, but especially to my editor, Nancy Wood. My readers would have had a lot of questions if you had not already asked them. Thanks for helping me fill in those gaps. It's been my pleasure and honor to work with you.

Now that the book is done and I can breathe again, I look back and realize that the biggest contributions of all came from friends and family who pulled me through some of the more difficult times. Thank you for your loving support and encouragement.

INTRODUCTION

INTO EVERY LIFE A LITTLE DIRT WILL FALL. Add a layer of dust, a few stains, a dash of greasy grime, and a bazillion germs, and now you have a real job on your hands. The problem is that you also have a busy lifestyle, which doesn't leave much time or energy to deal with everyday grunge. You end up spending a good chunk of your free time cleaning (or feeling guilty that you aren't cleaning). Or you attempt to keep up as best you can, hoping all the while that you will someday have time to catch up.

Housekeeping is one of those jobs that's never done. In fact, in many homes it's a job that's barely begun. Working women have all but abandoned the traditional role of head housekeeper. Spouses and children have taken up some of the workload, but still, not everything that should get done is getting done. By choice or necessity, standards have been relaxed to accommodate busy schedules that frequently force domestic responsibilities to the bottom of the to-do list.

The simplest solution is to learn how to get your housecleaning done faster, so you can spend more of your free time doing what you'd rather be doing! That's the purpose of this book — to provide plain and simple cleaning tips, techniques, and strategies that make quick work

of housework. Of course, you want to do it right, too. I believe that even veteran cleaners will learn a thing or two in the following pages. Did you know, for example, that liquid chlorine bleach has a shelf life of just three to six months? Or that you should launder underwear last of all your washer loads? Or that the population of germs on your kitchen sponge doubles every 20 minutes? Look for Know and Tell sidebars throughout this book for other interesting facts worth knowing and sharing.

About This Book

Cleaning Plain & Simple is written for busy people who want a clean home *and* a life. It's the ideal cleaning guide for people who don't know the first thing about cleaning, as well as people who want to become better housekeepers and people looking for confirmation that they're doing it right. You'll find tips for cleaning everything in and around your home, from kitchen counters to barbecue grills to toilets to septic tanks. And because it takes lifestyles and special needs into consideration, this book also includes cleaning tips for allergy sufferers, strategies to ensure the safety and well-being of children, helpful advice for living with pets, simple ways to clean up the great outdoors, and plentiful information about "green" cleaning with natural, nontoxic products. This book is intended to be a useful, easy-to-read handbook as well as a comprehensive reference.

If you have picked up this book, I have to assume that you *want* to have a cleaner home. You may even enjoy cleaning. I know I've always found cleaning to be therapeutic for the body, mind, and soul. I believe that many of us are striving harder to maintain a clean house in an attempt to cope with a chaotic world. We can't do anything about terrorism, war, or earthquakes, but we can clean up our own little corner. And that little bit of control gives us a sense of peace.

You may never become a super cleaner. (See the test on page 6 to determine what type of cleaner you are.) That's okay. Whatever your cleaning goals, know that the only standards that matter are the ones you set for yourself. My goal is to help you learn how to care for your home in plain and simple ways that will help you achieve your goals in less time and with less effort than you ever imagined possible. So what are you waiting for? The quicker you get to it, the quicker you can say it's done.

A BRIEF HISTORY OF CLEANING

CLEANING HAS ALWAYS BEEN A DIRTY, never-ending job. But before running water and electricity, it was physically harsh labor that required incredible amounts of time, energy, and effort.

Way Back When

Before the industrial era dawned in America, women were responsible for all the household chores, including food production, cooking, laundry, spinning wool and flax, sewing clothes, soapmaking, and candlemaking. As industries grew, there was a huge exodus to cities as men went to work in factories and offices. These very same factories began to produce soap, candles, and clothing that were previously produced on the homestead, thereby eliminating these chores from the daily routine. Earned income also provided the means for people of all classes to hire out at least some of their laundry, which was by far the most dreaded chore of all.

Twentieth-Century Inventions

The introduction of electric power to homes eliminated the need for kerosene lamps and coal- and wood-burning stoves that blackened walls and dirtied furnishings with soot and smoke. It also eliminated all the work associated with maintaining a fire and cleaning out the stove, which was typically work that fell to housewives. The electric washing machine was undoubtedly the most labor-saving invention in the history of cleaning. Introduced around 1900, the washing machine eliminated the need to haul and heat gallons of water and to scrub, wring, lift, and hang heavy, wet clothes and linens. By the early 1930s, mass production and distribution made it possible for nearly every middle-class household to have a washing machine. Other twentieth-century inventions included the electric iron (1903) and the electric vacuum cleaner (1907). By the early 1950s, electric-powered appliances such as washing machines, clothes dryers, and vacuum cleaners were no longer luxuries, but necessities in the average American home.

Today and Tomorrow

Labor-saving devices such as the washing machine, dishwasher, and vacuum cleaner have made the work of cleaning easier. Still, the average full-time homemaker today actually spends about the same, if not more, time on housework as her grandmother did. While technology has taken the drudgery out of housework, it has also caused us to raise our standards of cleanliness. Because the work is easier, we do it more often. Instead of doing a couple of loads of laundry each week, some families wash and dry a couple of loads per day. So there is a constant parade of laundry from dirty clothes hampers to the washing machine and dryer and back. There's a similar procession of dishes and silverware from cupboards and drawers to the table to the dishwasher. And, in between all the marching, we are cleaning and recleaning floors, countertops, and appliances. It's no wonder that we are continually searching for ways to cut the time we spend on household chores.

Working Women

According to the Bureau of Labor Statistics, only 20 percent of men do housework, versus the vast majority of women. A study by the Ohio State University Extension Service reports that men would need to perform 60 percent more housework to catch up to the current household workload of women.

PART 1

The Basics

Ready or not, you're about to get a crash course in cleaning. What you read here may answer a lot of questions you've always wanted to ask, or it may simply confirm that you know what you're doing or explain why you need to do it. Either way, you're bound to find at least one "Aha!" or suggestion that will make your life easier. You may also discover some alternative solutions that can save you money.

Whether you enjoy cleaning or do anything you can to avoid it, there's no point in making it any harder than it has to be. Armed with proven tips, techniques, and strategies, you'll be able to accomplish every cleaning task — from disinfecting to decluttering — in record time and with the least amount of effort. Consider the next three chapters your marching orders: clean up and clear out!

CHAPTER ONE

GETTING READY

You don't need a degree in housekeeping to maintain a clean home. A little know-how goes a long way. You also don't need to spend all your spare time cleaning. What you do need are the basics, which include not only the right tools and supplies but also an understanding of how to use them — along with a clear idea of what you are trying to accomplish and why. Most people would probably enjoy living in a clean home — if only they didn't have to do the work! Guess what? It might not be as hard as you think.

Benefits of Cleaning

Why do you clean? What's in it for you? Would you like to be able to eat off the floors? Or would you be happy just to be able to fix dinner without first having to clean up the kitchen or empty a sink full of dishes?

There are some obvious benefits of cleaning. First and foremost, a clean home is a healthier home. Germs are everywhere. But some germs, especially germs in the kitchen, bathroom, and nursery, can create and spread illness. While it is impossible to eliminate all germs, cleaning and disinfecting is the best offense against them.

Regular upkeep can also help carpets and furnishings last longer. Frequent vacuuming, for example, can extend the life of carpets by preventing dirt from being ground in, which can destroy carpet fibers. If you can't keep up a regular cleaning routine, hiring a professional cleaning service could save you money in the long run. Plus, if the need arises to sell your house, a clean home that's obviously been cared for is more likely to sell quickly — and at the best price.

For many people, cleaning is its own reward. The look and smell of a freshly cleaned home produces a sense of accomplishment, satisfaction, and pride. Many people find cleaning to be good therapy — an opportunity to let your mind wander and ponder your current state of affairs. Even if you don't enjoy cleaning, you can look at the results of your labor and see the return on your investment. Besides, isn't it nice to come home to a clean house or apartment?

What, Exactly, Are We Cleaning?

DIRT. This is the stuff we track in on the bottom of our shoes and on our clothes and hair. It's also the stuff that blows in through open windows, which might include plant debris, pollen, and insects. Dirt also includes food crumbs, pet hair, excrement from household pests, and any other undesirable matter that can be wiped, swept, or vacuumed up.

DUST. *Dust bunny* is a cute name for something that's really pretty disgusting. Dust is actually made up of a mixture of things, including tiny fibers shed from feathers and fabrics, pet dander, food particles, bacteria, mold and fungus spores, and insect parts. It also contains dust mites, the microscopic creatures that feed on dust, and their waste products. Yuck. Think about that the next time you are tempted to skip cleaning under your bed.

GERMS. Like it or not, you share your home with billions of microscopic beings known as germs, some of which can cause you to become ill. Refer to the Q&A sidebar on page 8 for more information about cleaning up germs.

MOLD. Like germs, mold is a natural part of our environment. Still, we don't want to look at mold growing in the shower. Although it is not typically a huge health risk, mold often causes allergic responses such as sneezing, runny nose, and red eyes and can trigger asthma attacks.

What Type of Cleaner Are You?

Do you love to clean, or do you go out of your way to avoid it? The way we approach cleaning depends on our attitudes, preferences, experience, time, energy, and goals. Most of us tend to fall into one of four categories: super cleaner, speed cleaner, green cleaner, or catch-up cleaner. Knowing what type of cleaner you are will help you choose the best cleaning products, tools, and techniques for you. Since many of us have traits from more than one category, it might be helpful to read the plain and simple advice for each one.

The Super Cleaner

- ❏ You attack dust and dirt with a vengeance.
- ❏ You are adept at germ warfare.
- ❏ You put cleaning high on your list of priorities.
- ❏ You take pride in your ability to maintain and present a clean home.
- ❏ You find that cleaning helps relieve stress and even consider it therapeutic.
- ❏ You tend toward a more traditional approach to cleaning; for example, you may scrub floors on your hands and knees and/or use tried-and-true cleaning products.
- ❏ You are always cleaning something.
- ❏ Your home is considered immaculate by most standards.

Plain and simple advice: Go easy with harsh cleaning products that can damage surfaces over time. It's always best to start with the least harsh cleaning solution first. Since you spend a lot of time wiping counters and whatnot, be sure to disinfect kitchen sponges and dishcloths after use or you will just spread more germs every time you wipe. As a housekeeper extraordinaire, you can and should take pride in your work, but if cleaning starts to feel like an obsession, recognize that you may be using it as an excuse to avoid dealing with something else.

The Speed Cleaner

- ❏ You enjoy a clean home, but it's not one of your top priorities.
- ❏ Cleaning frequently gets postponed for one reason or another.
- ❏ When you have free time, you don't want to spend it cleaning toilets.
- ❏ You seek quick and easy solutions to your cleaning challenges.
- ❏ You may have a tendency to purchase the latest and greatest cleaning products and tools.
- ❏ You may have a whole cupboard or closet full of products you've tried that may or may not have lived up to their promises.
- ❏ If you could afford it, you would hire a professional cleaning service. If you have a cleaning service, you wish you could afford to have them come more often.

Plain and simple advice: If you want to spend less time cleaning overall, clean more often. Start with a thorough cleaning, and then get into the habit of doing a little cleaning each day. Keep cleaning supplies handy to where you use them or put them in a bucket or caddy that makes it easy to tote them to the job. Consider ready-to-use cleaning products such as disinfectant wipes for quick cleanups in between weekly or biweekly cleanups. Give away or discard cleaning supplies that did not work as well as you had expected or that you dislike for any other reason.

The Green Cleaner

❑ You prefer a softer, gentler approach to cleaning.

❑ You are not willing to trade dirt and germs for chemicals, nor do you believe that it is necessary to do so.

❑ You have a better-than-average knowledge and awareness of the ingredients in cleaning products.

❑ You prefer "natural" cleaning products and are willing to make your own cleaning solutions with natural ingredients.

❑ You or someone in your home may have allergies to some cleaning products, or you may be concerned about the use or storage of chemical-based cleaning products because you have children or pets or are expecting a child.

❑ You consciously choose nontoxic products in recyclable or refillable packaging and minimize your use of disposable products.

Plain and simple advice: There are some excellent commercial cleaners that contain natural ingredients on the market. But there are also products in your kitchen that will do the job just as well. White vinegar and water, for example, can be used to clean kitchen counters and floors.

Baking soda is the perfect nonabrasive cleaner for the kitchen and bath.

The Catch-up Cleaner

❑ You have a fairly high tolerance for dust and dirt.

❑ You put off cleaning until it becomes something that you absolutely must do.

❑ By the time you decide you need to clean, it's a monumental job that requires huge amounts of time and effort.

❑ You tend to accumulate clutter, which makes the task of cleaning seem even more overwhelming.

❑ You may have discovered that the only way you can keep your home clean is to hire the services of a professional cleaner. But even then, your home quickly falls into disarray between cleanings.

Plain and simple advice: It's a lot easier to keep up than to catch up. Consider hiring help to get your house clean, or arrange a work trade with family members or friends — their cleaning help in exchange for your cooking or babysitting, for example. Once your home is clean, get in the habit of everyday cleaning. Set a timer for 10 minutes in the morning and 10 minutes at night. Spend 10 minutes on everyday cleanup in your kitchen and bath and 10 minutes on one bigger chore, such as vacuuming. Offer yourself a daily reward for your efforts.

Q & A : The Lowdown on Germs

Q *What are germs?*

A *Germ* is an umbrella term for any potentially harmful microorganism. The three types of germs encountered most often in the average household are bacteria, viruses, and fungi and molds. All of these germs need to be cleaned up.

- Hot zones for bacteria include the kitchen, bathroom, and nursery. Raw eggs, dairy products, and the juices from raw meat, poultry, and fish can harbor harmful bacteria such as *Salmonella*, *Staphylococcus*, *E. coli*, and *Listeria*, which can cause food poisoning. Fecal matter from animals and humans is another common source of bacteria that can cause infection or illness. This is why food handlers in restaurants are required to wash their hands after using the bathroom.

- While viruses can cause illnesses such as chicken pox, measles, and flu, these germs can survive only a short time on surfaces and are more likely to be transmitted through the air.

- Fungi and molds are actually plant-like organisms that thrive in warm, moist conditions and cause ailments ranging from athlete's foot to asthma and other respiratory problems.

Q *How often should I disinfect surfaces?*

A A regular habit of washing your hands after using the toilet helps prevent the spread of disease; likewise, regular disinfecting of commonly used household surfaces can help keep you and your family healthy. Always disinfect kitchen countertops and cutting boards before and after preparing foods that may contain harmful bacteria. In most homes, the highest concentrations of bacteria are found on moist surfaces, such as dishcloths, sponges, and cutting boards, and on frequently touched surfaces, such as faucets.

Q *Are antibacterial products effective against germs?*

A Antibacterial products have been extremely effective in helping to prevent the spread of disease among hospital patients, but no health benefit has been proven for household use. In fact, the Centers for Disease Control and Prevention urges prudent use of antibacterial products in the home. The concern is that overuse of these products may cause strains of bacteria to become resistant, much like the overuse and misuse of antibiotics has caused some germs to develop resistance to standard antibiotic treatment.

Cleaning Terms and Definitions

There's more to cleaning than meets the eye. Sure, vacuuming and dusting get rid of visible dirt. But what about germs that cause illness? The only way to tackle germs is to sanitize or disinfect surfaces. Sometimes you need to deodorize also. And decluttering makes the job of housecleaning a lot easier. Let's look more closely at the definitions of these terms.

Cleaning. This is the process of removing dust, dirt, grease, and grime, which also reduces the number of germs. Cleaning is accomplished with some sort of detergent, which can be plain old soap and water, dishwashing liquid, or a commercially prepared cleaning solution. When you clean something, you can see the results of your labor, whether it's a full dustpan or vacuum cleaner bag or a dirty dusting cloth or sponge. And, depending on the products you use, cleaning can also leave your home smelling clean. It's this look and smell of clean that is probably the most satisfying aspect of housecleaning.

Disinfecting. While cleaning with soap and water will *remove* most germs from surfaces (just as washing your hands removes most germs from them), disinfectants effectively *kill* germs. It's always a good idea to disinfect surfaces in the kitchen, bathroom, and nursery. Disinfecting is also an extra precaution recommended to protect younger and older members of a household and persons with suppressed immune systems. If a household member is sick, you can reduce the risk of spreading viruses and bacteria by disinfecting frequently touched surfaces such as light switches, doorknobs, remote controls, and telephone receivers.

- **Destroy germs.** Household disinfectants are designed to destroy harmful bacteria and viruses, including *Rhinovirus*, the leading cause of the common cold. Only products with an Environmental Protection Agency (EPA) registration number on their label are approved germ-killing disinfectants. Read the product label to ensure that you are getting the type of disinfectant you want; the label will state what type of germs the product kills.

- **Clean before disinfecting.** For a disinfectant to be effective, soils should be removed from the surface of the object to be cleaned before the disinfectant is applied. Disinfectant cleaners remove soils and kill germs in one time-saving step. The label of such a product will state that it "cleans and disinfects."

- **Disinfect with bleach.** A commonly used disinfectant is sodium hypochlorite, more commonly known as liquid chlorine bleach. Diluted bleach solutions are extremely effective against many types of microorganisms, including bacteria, fungi, and viruses. For bleach to be effective as a disinfectant, you first need to clean the surface you'll be using it on. Afterward, swab down the surface with the bleach solution and let it air-dry. Be aware that bleach loses strength rapidly, so the solution needs to be made fresh each time you use it.

Sanitizing. Often confused with disinfecting, sanitizing does not *kill* germs but reduces the number of harmful germs to a safe level to create a more healthful, hygienic environment. Generally, that's all that's needed. Sanitizing basically renders most germs harmless, and those that are left will die a natural death. Cleaning with soap and water not only removes dirt from surfaces but also reduces most germs to less than an infectious dose. White vinegar is another nontoxic agent that's been proven to destroy or reduce to an acceptable level a broad range of bacteria, yeast, molds, and other microorganisms. And, of course, there are commercial sanitizing products available in many forms, including sprays and wipes.

Deodorizing. There's a difference between air freshening and deodorizing. Air freshening simply masks unpleasant household odors; deodorizing kills odor-causing bacteria to completely eliminate odors. Cleaning and disinfecting often remove odors by killing the germs that cause them. Odor around the toilet, for example, is a sign that bacteria are present and a thorough cleaning is needed. Odors that linger after cleaning require deodorizing. Effective deodorizers

KNOW AND TELL

Liquid chlorine bleach has a shelf life of only three to six months. Buy only what you can use up in that time period, taking into consideration that the bottle sat on the store's shelf for some time before you bought it.

include baking soda and vinegar, which absorb odors, and certain commercial products that kill bacteria in the air.

Decluttering. Clutter can make the cleanest home look dirtier than it is. Decluttering is the act of finding a home for those things you love and use, and letting go of everything that's just collecting dust. The less clutter you have, the quicker and easier it is to clean your home and keep it clean. Regular decluttering is an important step in the cleaning process that can save time and energy while improving the appearance of your home.

How To | **DISINFECT SURFACES**

There's a right way to properly disinfect a surface, such as a countertop, sink, high chair, or floor. You first need to clean it with soap and water or another detergent. If there are any crumbs or dirty residue left on the surface, you will not be able to properly disinfect it. Once the surface is clean, spray or wipe it with a diluted solution of liquid chlorine bleach or a ready-made disinfectant. Let the surface air-dry or wipe it dry with a clean cloth or paper towel. For a simpler alternative, use a commercial disinfectant cleaner that does the job of cleaning and disinfecting in one step.

What's in Your Cleaning Closet?

If you bought every cleaning tool and product on the market today, you would need an entire house just to store them. While many of these items are worth a look and a try, the only tools and products you need to keep around are the ones you actually use.

Take a look at what's in your cleaning closet or wherever you keep your cleaning tools and supplies. First, look at your tools. The right tools make any job easier. Is your vacuum cleaner in good working order? Is your mop head worn out? Make a note to repair or replace cleaning tools or purchase replacement accessories as needed. Remove any tools that are broken or unnecessary, such as the dust mop for hardwood floors that you no longer need in your all-carpeted home. Donate usable tools to Goodwill or The Salvation Army, or sell them at your next garage sale.

Recommended cleaning tools to have in your closet include:

- Vacuum cleaner
- Broom and dustpan (plus an outdoor broom if you have a garage or deck)
- Wet mop
- Dust mop for noncarpeted floors
- Two 10-gallon buckets for use in washing floors and windows
- Cleaning caddy or another 10-gallon bucket for toting cleaning supplies
- Rubber gloves to protect your hands from dirt, germs, cleaning solutions, and hot water
- Microfiber cloths or cloth diapers for dusting and cleaning

- Cellulose scrub sponges in different colors for different jobs: dishes, kitchen counters, bathroom
- Toilet-cleaning brush (best kept near the toilet for use as needed)
- Brushes for the floors and your shower/tub
- Old toothbrush(es) to clean grout and hard-to-reach areas
- White paper towels
- Trash bags
- Spray bottles for mixing homemade cleaners

Next, take a look at your cleaning products. Get rid of all the products you don't use or need. If you haven't used them in the past year, you probably won't ever use them. Read and follow the directions on each product's label for proper disposal. Do not mix cleaning products when disposing of them; some products, such as ammonia and liquid chlorine bleach, create harmful gases when combined. For more tips on disposing of household cleaners, turn to the end of this chapter (page 19).

Basic cleaning products you need include commercial or homemade versions of the following:

- All-purpose cleaner for floors, walls, countertops, and toilets
- Disinfectant
- Glass and mirror cleaner
- Nonabrasive scouring powder
- Tub and tile cleaner
- Oven cleaner
- Wood cleaner
- Furniture polish

The Perfect Vacuum Cleaner?

There are so many vacuum cleaner makes and models available that it can be difficult to choose the right one. When buying, first choose the category of cleaner that best suits your needs. There are five basic categories:

UPRIGHT VACUUM. Uprights are a good choice for a home with lots of carpeted floors and for anyone who prefers to push the vacuum cleaner rather than pull it. Easy to carry and store, many uprights have an easy-to-use pile height-adjustment feature, which is important if you have carpets of varying thicknesses to clean.

CANISTER VACUUM. Generally a little heavier and pricier than an upright, but also quieter, the canister vacuum is a good choice for homes with lots of bare floors. It's also ideal for vacuuming under beds and for cleaning a variety of surfaces, including carpeted and noncarpeted stairs, upholstered furniture and draperies, and automobile interiors. Backpack models can be comfortably carried around your home — even up a ladder for easier cleaning of pot shelves and tall furniture such as bookcases and armoires.

CORDLESS VACUUM. A cordless model may be either handheld or upright, but it is designed to be lightweight, portable, and easier to pull out when needed. The cordless handheld vacuum is the perfect choice for cleaning up after everyday messes. Keep one in high-traffic areas for spills, tracked kitty litter, animal hair, and quick touch-ups. Upright models are preferable for quick cleanup of larger areas.

SWEEPER/STICK VACUUM. This "electric broom" is most often used for quick cleanup of carpeted and noncarpeted floors in the kitchen, bath, and entryway but can be used anywhere to pick up debris. Smaller and lighter than a regular vacuum, it's great for getting kids into the vacuuming routine because it's so lightweight and easy to use.

CENTRAL VACUUM SYSTEM. The most powerful and priciest choice, a central vacuum is a built-in system that consists of a motor, a dirt canister, PVC tubing in the walls, centrally located floor or wall receptacles, a vacuum hose, and cleaning attachments. There's no heavy unit to push or pull and no electrical cord; simply plug the hose into any central vacuum receptacle to turn it on. Because the motor is installed in your basement or garage, operation is quiet. Unlike portable vacuum cleaners, the central vacuum system carries dirt and debris away from your living area, which also makes for cleaner operation. And the dirt canister generally requires emptying only several times a year.

When choosing a vacuum, you are likely to gravitate toward the kind your mother used. There's nothing wrong with that. If you like it, you're more likely to use it.

Once you know what type of cleaner you want, choose a brand and model based on other features such as warranty, ease of use, and quiet operation. Other factors to keep in mind include the following:

- Allergy sufferers should look for a high-efficiency particulate air (HEPA) filtration system, which is designed to trap 99 percent of harmful allergens, including mold spores, pollen, and pet dander.

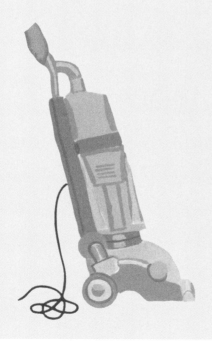

- Bagless models eliminate the need to purchase, store, and change bags; when the collection cup is full, you simply empty it and then put it back in the vacuum. Be aware, however, that emptying the collection cup is a messy process that tends to spew dust into the air; if you are sensitive to dust, you'll want to wear a dust mask. Also, bagless models need emptying more often than models with bags.

- Choose a vacuum cleaner that includes tools you can use: a telescoping wand and dusting brush for cleaning high up, a crevice tool to clean along carpet and floor edges, and an upholstery brush for cleaning furniture and heavy draperies.

- If you suffer from arthritis, choose a model with an ergonomically designed handle to reduce hand and wrist stress. You might also consider a self-propelled upright if pushing or pulling a heavy vacuum cleaner is a problem.

- A vacuum with a rotating brush or combination beater/brush bar is good for most carpets. A suction-only vacuum or one with an adjustable brush lifted away from the carpet is better for wool or wool-blend carpets with thick loop pile construction, which may become fuzzy with too much brushing or rubbing.

Once you declutter your cleaning closet, organize it by grouping together items by use, including any specialized cleaners for your car, laundry, shoes, silver and other metals, leather, and so on. Install hooks and wall-mounted holders for hanging mops, brooms, and dustpans. Store your clean rags, cloths, and towels in a hanging bag or a basket on a shelf. If you don't have a cleaning closet, here's an idea: hang an over-the-door shoe bag with clear plastic pockets behind your garage or laundry-room door, and use it for storing cleaning supplies. Just make sure the bag you purchase is compatible with your door and won't prevent it from closing all the way.

Put your basic cleaning supplies in a cleaning caddy or bucket for easy carting from room to room. Add cleaning cloths, sponges, paper towels, and rubber gloves and you're ready to clean anywhere, anytime. You might even consider stocking separate caddies for the bathroom and kitchen that you can store in those rooms. That way, you are ready for quick cleanups, without having to fetch what you need. Or hide cleaning supplies in strategic spots, such as behind books on a shelf, so if you get inspired to clean, you can dust off your books or polish your coffee table right then and there.

Selecting Cleaning Products

Simplify your life by choosing to use cleaning products that do double duty, such as disinfectant cleaners or all-purpose cleaners that can be used to clean toilets as well as countertops,

The Right Sponge for the Job

CELLULOSE. The good old standby; excellent for Formica and tile floors and walls.

ALL-SURFACE. A cellulose sponge with an abrasive scrubber on one side for tough cleaning jobs like pots and pans and barbecue grills.

NATURAL. Harvested from the sea, these soft, highly absorbent sponges are recommended for washing windows and cars.

NYLON SCRUBBING. A nonabrasive sponge for scrubbing without damaging Teflon-coated cookware and other surfaces that cannot withstand abrasive sponges.

METAL. A curly metal sponge (not steel wool, which can scratch) for all types of tough scouring jobs on surfaces that can withstand an abrasive scrubbing.

DRY CLEANING. A cellulose foam-latex pad that is used dry to remove dust and pet hair from upholstery, lampshades, and walls.

CLEANING "ERASER." A soft sponge designed to be wetted with water and used to "erase" marks and smudges from walls, floors, and other hard surfaces.

floors, and walls. You may also wish to consider using cleaning products that will not harm the environment. Look for "environmentally friendly" products, or make your own household cleaning solutions from nontoxic materials such as vinegar, pure soap, baking soda, washing soda, and borax. Cut down on waste by making conscious choices about your purchases. Consider using concentrated laundry detergents, which provide more cleaning power with less packaging. Also look for refillable containers and for containers made from recycled materials. Buy in quantities you will use soon, so products don't end up going to waste.

Traditional Disinfectants and Cleaners. These are the big guns: liquid chlorine bleach, ammonia, and pine-oil disinfectants and cleaners. The benefit of using these products is that they can be used for more than one purpose and they are very cost-effective. The disadvantage to these products is that they need to be diluted before use, which means having to mix up solutions. Also, misuse can discolor or damage finishes.

Ready-to-Use Products. It's a little more expensive to buy cleaning and disinfecting products in ready-mixed form, but it's far more convenient. Many product manufacturers have added fragrances and other ingredients that leave behind a fresh, clean scent. If you are allergic to fragrance, you can usually find unscented options.

Disposable Products. New disposable cleaning products have revolutionized the way we clean by combining tools and products and eliminat-

ing the need to mix or spray anything. Instead of dripping buckets, bottles, and sponges, we have the option of using premoistened, disposable cleaning cloths. Use them to wipe up dirt and germs, and then toss them in the trash, along with the dirt and germs. Disposables include wipes for just about everything:

- Cleaning appliances
- Sanitizing sinks, countertops, toilets, light-switch covers, and faucet handles
- Dusting furniture, television screens, and other surfaces
- Washing windows
- Washing dishes (lathering wipes) and cleaning baked-on foods in microwaves (heat-activated wipes)

Popular disposable products also include wet mops that utilize an onboard dispenser for liquid cleaning solution, as well as a disposable

EVERYDAY SOLUTION
Microfiber Cleaning Cloths

Microfiber cleaning cloths are a must for every household. Originally designed for clean-room applications in the electronics industry, microfiber is a nonabrasive synthetic material that effortlessly removes dust, dirt, and grease from any hard surface, from mirrors to countertops to floors. Machine washable and reusable, microfiber cloths, mitts, and mops require no cleaning products to be used with them. Simply wet, squeeze, and wipe for a streak-free, lint-free clean without chemicals.

cleaning cloth for the mop head. Flushable toilet-bowl cleaners are another disposable product designed to make a dreaded chore more pleasant.

Portable and easy to use, disposable cleaning products are very popular with today's busy housekeepers who are willing to pay a little more for convenience. The downside of disposables is the fact that they add unnecessary waste to already-crowded landfills. For this reason, exclusive use of disposable cleaning products is not prudent.

Green Cleaning Products. More and more people are choosing natural or environmentally friendly cleaners, which not only are more effective than early green products, but also have become more widely distributed and price-competitive in recent years. Organic and biodegradable products are the least toxic and most earth-friendly cleaning products. Look for the Green Seal or (in Canada) EcoLogo symbol on product labels. Or make your own eco-products. Green cleaning tools, such as pumice and microfiber cloths, also clean surfaces without chemicals.

Cleaning Naturally

There are natural alternatives that you may prefer over commercially purchased cleaning products, especially if you have allergic reactions to strong scents and chemicals. Baking soda and vinegar have been used for years to effectively clean, freshen, and deodorize homes naturally. And, because both cleaning agents can be purchased in bulk, they make for inexpensive cleaning formulas. The biggest drawback to these homemade cleaning solutions is that they may require a little more effort to get the job done. Do be aware that even natural cleaning products can be harmful if ingested. Be sure to label homemade solutions and keep them out of reach of children and pets.

● **Baking soda** makes an excellent nonabrasive scouring powder that cleans, freshens, and removes stains. You can mix it with enough water to form a paste that you apply to the surface to be cleaned, or you can wet the surface and then sprinkle it with baking soda. Use baking soda to scrub sinks, countertops, showers, tubs, and more without scratching. For heavier-duty applications, use it with a nylon mesh

make your own

All-Purpose Cleaner

Combine 1 teaspoon of a vegetable-oil-based laundry detergent, 1 teaspoon of borax laundry detergent, and 2 tablespoons of white vinegar with 1 quart of hot water.

sponge. Baking soda also absorbs and eliminates odors on contact. Use it in garbage cans, diaper pails, litter boxes, garbage disposals, and drains, or sprinkle it on carpets before vacuuming. *Helpful hint:* Buy baking soda in 10-pound containers at a discount club, and pour it into a large metal salt shaker for easy sprinkling. It's a good idea to label the shaker.

- **White vinegar** is a versatile, economical cleaner and sanitizer that cuts through grease, prevents mold from building up, and cleans glass. Buy it by the gallon. Fill a spray bottle with equal parts of white vinegar and water, and use the mixture to clean and sanitize surfaces and remove odors. (If you find the vinegar smell unpleasant, add a splash of lemon juice to the solution.) Add 1 cup of vinegar to 1 quart of water to make a cleaning solution for windows. Pour 1 cup of vinegar into the toilet to clean the bowl. Vinegar can also be used at full strength to sanitize wooden cutting boards or around doorways and windowsills to repel ants.

- **Lemon juice** is another natural cleaner and deodorizer. Fill a handy spray bottle with equal parts of water and lemon juice (you can use presqueezed juice from a bottle); use it to freshen the air in your home. Rub a cut lemon over a wooden cutting board to sanitize it. Or rub the cut end of a lemon over a faucet to remove lime scale. You can also put lemon peel and baking soda in your vacuum cleaner bag to deodorize it.

- **Salt** can be used as a cleaning agent and deodorizer. A strong brine solution poured down the kitchen drain can prevent grease

make your own

Natural Disinfectant Cleaner

Mix 15 drops of grapefruit seed extract with 2 cups of warm water (or use 1 teaspoon per gallon of water). Pour the solution into a spray bottle. Double the amount of grapefruit seed extract to create a super-strength cleaner for more extreme jobs. Grapefruit seed extract also whitens sinks, tubs, and tiles.

formula courtesy of Pure Liquid Gold

buildup and eliminate odors. Other uses suggested by the Salt Institute include using a paste of salt and vinegar to clean tarnished brass or copper or a solution of salt and turpentine to restore whiteness to yellowed enamel bathtubs and toilets. You'll find more uses for salt sprinkled throughout this book.

- **Hydrogen peroxide (3 percent)** is an excellent and inexpensive stain remover for carpets; refer to page 67 in chapter 4 for tips on using it to clean carpets. Readily available at drugstores and supermarkets, 3 percent hydrogen peroxide can also be used with vinegar to disinfect kitchen counters, cutting boards, and other hard surfaces: Spray a mist of hydrogen peroxide onto the surface and then a mist of vinegar. Allow to sit for a few minutes, and then wipe with a paper towel or a cloth.

Use Cleaning Products Responsibly

Sensible cleaning includes sensible use of household cleaning products. Take the time to read product labels so you know what you are buying and how to use it. Whenever possible, avoid the use of any products that are labeled as corrosive, reactive or explosive, flammable, toxic, or poisonous. Pregnant women should avoid overuse of household cleaning products, especially

For Safety's Sake

Accidental poisoning of children is a very common health hazard associated with cleaning products. Children can also be exposed to risk through inhalation of fumes from a product such as oven cleaner or air-freshener spray, through direct skin contact with cleaning products, or by touching surfaces that have been recently cleaned.

In the bimonthly newsletter *Cleaning Matters*, the Soap and Detergent Association offered the following tips for the safe use and smart storage of cleaning products around children:

- Schedule cleaning around the kids' routines, such as nap time or when they're not around.
- Don't be distracted when you are cleaning. Children act fast and can get hold of a product and swallow it in a surprisingly short time.
- Never leave cleaning buckets containing liquid unattended. Besides the obvious dangers of spilling, slipping, and sipping, there's the fact that toddlers are "top heavy." If they toppled into a bucket, they could drown, even in a very small amount of liquid.
- Close the caps and lids of cleaning product containers securely. Products with more potential hazard, such as some oven and drain cleaners, come with child-resistant packaging, but they don't come with someone to close the cap properly! It's up to adults to provide a safe environment.
- Store cleaning products in locations that are away from children, pets, and food. Install childproof locks on the doors of all storage locations.
- Keep cleaning products in their original containers. If a child accidentally ingests or spills something on him- or herself, the label provides information concerning the product's contents and advice on what immediate first aid to perform.
- Carefully dispose of empty cleaning containers. To protect children, pets, and garbage handlers, replace the lids on the containers first, and then place them in a sealed recycling bin or garbage container.

liquid chlorine bleach, disinfectants, air fresheners, aerosols, and carpet cleaners; they also should take care to avoid any products containing ammonia, benzene, formaldehyde, mercury, or phosphates.

- **Read product labels.** Always read and follow the manufacturer's instructions carefully to ensure that you are using a product correctly, particularly with regard to ventilation. If the label says to use the product in a well-ventilated area, open windows or turn on a fan to ensure that the space being cleaned has plenty of fresh air.
- **Do not mix products.** Never mix liquid chlorine bleach and ammonia, or any products that contain bleach and ammonia. This combination results in a dangerous, even lethal gas. As a general rule, never use two or more types of products in the same room at the same time unless you know for a fact that the two products are compatible.
- **Ask questions.** When it comes to the use of household products, there are no stupid questions. Check with the product manufacturer if you have any questions about the use or effectiveness of a product. If you are prone to allergies, or if you or anyone in your house has a diminished lung capacity, check with your doctor about household product use.
- **Avoid skin contact.** Many household cleaners contain chemicals that can cause skin irritation. Get in the habit of wearing rubber gloves for household cleaning. Gloves will also protect your hands and nails from the drying effect of water and chemicals. It's a simple, inexpensive precaution.

- **Remove jewelry.** Prolonged contact with water and chemicals can permanently damage gemstones. Always remove jewelry before you start to clean.

Disposing of Cleaning Products

Use up cleaning products before disposing of them, or give products you no longer have a use for to a friend, family member, or neighbor who will use them. The right way to dispose of cleaning products is the way that is best for the environment. Read the product label for disposal instructions. Generally, you will be instructed to use one of the following three methods, depending on the type of product.

Down the Drain. The proper way to dispose of water-soluble products (that is, products that mix with water) is to flush them down the toilet or pour them down the drain with running water. Most liquids, powders, and gels fall into this category. When disposing of powders, dispose of small amounts at a time to prevent clogging the pipes. When you are flushing products in a toilet, be sure that the toilet has not been just cleaned; you want to avoid potential interaction with residue from a toilet-cleaning product. Do not under any circumstances mix products during the disposal process.

Water-soluble cleaning products include:

- Liquid and powdered laundry detergents
- Liquid chlorine bleach
- Liquid fabric softeners
- Dishwashing liquids and powders
- Multipurpose cleaners

- Powdered cleansers
- Glass cleaners
- Disinfectants
- Ammonia
- Tub/tile/sink cleaners
- Carpet cleaners
- Floor cleaners

If you live in a home with a septic tank, do not flush or pour down the drain any unwanted cleaning products, to avoid the possibility of contaminating well water. Unlike city septic services, private septic systems are not capable of fully treating chemical waste. Instead, use up the products or give them to others.

In the Trash or Recycling Bin. Most solid cleaning products and empty product containers can be thrown in the trash. Plastic, paperboard, and metal containers (even aerosol cans) may be recyclable. Check with your community recycling center for local guidelines. "Trashable" cleaning products include:

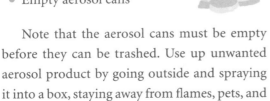

- Fabric softener sheets
- Stain remover sticks
- Premoistened towelettes
- Disposable mop pads
- Scouring pads
- Empty aerosol cans

Note that the aerosol cans must be empty before they can be trashed. Use up unwanted aerosol product by going outside and spraying it into a box, staying away from flames, pets, and children. Avoid breathing the fumes. If the aerosol spray is clogged, shake the can for a full 2 minutes. Then turn the can upside down and press the spray nozzle to release air. Turn the can right-side up again and spray until empty.

As Household Hazardous Waste (HHW). Products that fall into the category of household hazardous waste (HHW) require special disposal. Call the manufacturer's toll-free number for disposal recommendations, or check with your local waste-disposal facility. This category includes, but is not limited to, the following types of cleaning products:

- Polishes and waxes that harden on surfaces (including furniture, metal, and shoe polishes)
- Solutions for removing difficult stains or greases
- Flammable products
- Crystal drain openers
- Dry-cleaning fluid

An alternative to HHW disposal is to evaporate small amounts (less than ½ gallon) of the product. Move the container to a sheltered, secure outdoor area that is away from the activities of children and pets. Open the lid. The liquid in the product will evaporate over time. When the product has hardened into a solid material, discard it in the trash. But before undertaking this disposal technique, check to find out whether your community incinerates trash. If it does, do not dispose of the hazardous material in the trash, because burning will release the chemicals it contains.

CHAPTER TWO

CLEANING STRATEGIES

Cleaning is a dirty job, but someone's got to do it. Even if you hire a housecleaner, you still have some cleanup to do between visits. Everyday cleaning is the simplest way to minimize housework. In this chapter, you will learn proven systems and techniques to get the most common household chores done quickly and easily, with professional-looking results.

If you live in a household full of people, you probably have extra cleaning challenges — but you also have extra hands to help out. When you learn simple strategies for prompting your family to pitch in, everyone will wonder how you manage to keep your home so clean and tidy.

Everyday Cleaning

When you save up all your housecleaning for the weekend, it seems like a lot of work because it *is* a lot of work. The trick is to do a little cleaning every day. The payoff is that you will never again feel overwhelmed by housecleaning and your home will be cleaner than ever. Also, by incorporating everyday cleaning into your schedule, you'll have more time for rest and relaxation on your days off. Use the following everyday to-do list as a starting point, and modify it to suit your needs and lifestyle:

- Make all the beds.
- Check trash cans and wastebaskets; empty as needed.
- Round up dirty laundry and put it in the hamper.
- Wipe bathroom sinks.
- Sweep the kitchen floor.

- Vacuum carpets in high-traffic areas as needed.
- Clean the kitchen table and countertops.
- Hand-wash dishes or load, run, and unload the dishwasher.
- Start a wash, load and start the dryer, or fold laundry as needed.
- Sort your daily mail into categories: to pay, to file, to read, to call, or to trash or recycle.
- Pick up clutter.

Spend five minutes here and there throughout the day and you'll be done with your everyday chores before you know it. Challenge yourself to make your bed in under 60 seconds. Wipe bathroom sinks in the morning before leaving the room. Clean up the kitchen after dinner. Carry a trash bag from room to room and empty all the wastebaskets. Pick up clutter before heading to bed. Get the idea?

Helpful hint: Take advantage of convenience products, such as disposable wipes and shower-cleaner sprays, for these 5-minute cleaning sessions to make the job even easier.

My theory on housework is, if the item doesn't multiply, smell, catch fire, or block the refrigerator door, let it be. No one else cares. Why should you?

— Erma Bombeck

THE QUICKIE CLEAN: UNEXPECTED GUESTS

Got company on the way? Here's how to clean up your act in a hurry:

- Load any dirty dishes into the dishwasher, or put them in a dishpan and stash it under the sink.
- Wipe the kitchen counters and the stovetop.
- Give the toilet a quick brush and flush.
- Grab a roll of paper towels and a bottle of glass cleaner and use them to wipe down mirrors, countertops, and the toilet seat (top and bottom) in the bathroom.
- Hang fresh hand towels in the bathroom and kitchen.
- Pick up stray items and toss them in a laundry basket; store the basket temporarily in a closet.
- Close doors to bedrooms and other rooms not intended for guests.
- Light scented candles or spray some air freshener.
- Dim the lights.

The Weekly Routine

Everyday cleaning will go a long way toward keeping your home clean and tidy. But it's not enough. You need to develop and implement a systematic cleaning plan for those chores that require time and effort on a regular basis, such as mopping floors or cleaning your refrigerator. Most homes can be maintained with once-a-week cleaning. However, how often you tackle regular cleaning chores largely depends on how many people are living in your home. If you have children or pets, you probably need to vacuum and mop more than once a week. If you live alone without pets, you might be able to squeak by on a biweekly cleaning schedule provided you do everyday cleaning.

Following are three ways to approach weekly cleaning chores. Choose the one that best fits your personality, lifestyle, and goals.

Schedule A: All at Once. This is the traditional approach to weekly cleaning. It works well for people who have two or more days off each week and either enjoy cleaning or enjoy the satisfaction that comes from cleaning the whole house from top to bottom. With the all-at-once approach, every room in your home gets cleaned once a week. Here's the basic routine:

Bathrooms
- Clean the toilet.
- Sanitize the sink and countertop.
- Clean the tub and/or the shower and shower door.
- Wipe mirrors clean.
- Sweep or vacuum and mop the floor.
- Hang fresh towels.

Kitchen
- Sanitize the sink, drain, and disposal.
- Clean the oven or the refrigerator (alternate every other week).
- Sanitize the countertops.
- Clean the microwave.
- Sweep and mop the floor.

Bedrooms
- Change the linens.
- Put away clean clothes.
- Launder dirty clothes.
- Clean the floor.

Room by Room
- Clean the floors in all rooms (periodically move large items and sweep or vacuum beneath them).
- Sweep away any cobwebs.
- Dust and polish the furniture.
- File or toss paper clutter.
- Pick up other clutter.

Schedule B: 30 Minutes a Day. This could be the best approach for people who might otherwise put off weekly chores. Basically, it requires spending 30 minutes each day on one room or one whole-house cleaning task. The following example lays out one possible room-by-room daily schedule. Refer to chapters within this book for specific cleaning recommendations and instructions for each area.

- **Day 1** Kitchen
- **Day 2** Bathroom
- **Day 3** Living room, family room, dining room
- **Day 4** Bedrooms
- **Day 5** Office, den, entryways
- **Day 6** Laundry room and laundry
- **Day 7** Rest

As an alternative you could arrange day-by-day cleaning around a task-oriented schedule:

- **Day 1** Clean all mirrors, glass tabletops, and windows as needed.
- **Day 2** Clean the bathroom sink, tub/shower, toilet, and countertops.
- **Day 3** Clean the kitchen countertops, the sink and drain, the microwave, and the refrigerator or oven.
- **Day 4** Do the laundry, change the bedclothes, and put out clean towels.
- **Day 5** Dust and polish the furniture.
- **Day 6** Vacuum, sweep, and mop all floors.
- **Day 7** Rest.

The beauty of this schedule is that you need to get out only the cleaning tools and supplies for a particular chore instead of lugging around a whole caddy full of stuff.

Schedule C: One Task a Day. Make a list of the cleaning tasks that need to be done on a regular basis and post the list on your refrigerator. Pick one task each day and do it. This is a good approach for people who don't like routines. You get to choose what you feel like doing each day. The key to making this approach work is to do something every day and to complete every task on the list at least once every two weeks. Keep track of your progress by writing next to each item the date when you did the work. If you generate a master list on your computer, you can print clean copies as needed.

Deep Cleaning

You can do a deep cleaning of your home once or twice a year. Or you can break up that really big job into smaller monthly jobs by deep-cleaning room by room. Once a month, plan to do a thorough cleaning of one room. In a bedroom, for example, you might wash the walls, windows, curtains, floors, and bedding. You might also declutter and organize the closets and drawers. When all the rooms have been cleaned, start over with the first room.

If you do an extra-thorough cleaning of one room one week, you can usually get by with a quick clean in that room the following week or maybe even coast for two weeks with just everyday cleanup. Alternating deep cleaning with quick cleanups will buy you a little extra time to put toward the monthly cleaning.

Also once a month or so, dust ceiling fans, tops of bookcases and cabinets, and the top of your refrigerator. Disposable electrostatic dusters with extendable handles and pivoting heads help you reach high places for which you might otherwise have to get out the ladder to reach. Other favorite tools for dusting include lamb's-wool dusters, microfiber cloths, and cloth diapers.

Getting the Job Done

Do you have a hard time getting motivated to clean? Make housecleaning more enjoyable by putting on your favorite music or listening to a book on tape. Or motivate yourself with a reward, such as relaxing afterward in a hot tub, watching your favorite TV show, going out to the movies, or reading a book or magazine. Once you get started, try these proven tips for getting the job done faster and more efficiently.

- **Declutter first.** Remove clutter from floors, coffee tables, and other horizontal surfaces before you start cleaning. It's easier to do this if you have something to put things into, such as a basket or tote bag.

- **Clean from top to bottom.** Get out a broom and start with those cobwebs along the edges of the ceiling. Then dust the ceiling fans, tops of bookcases, and other higher-up surfaces. Allow the dust to fall to the floor. Work your way down by shaking out curtains, dusting surfaces, polishing furniture, and anything in between. Clean the floors last.

- **Clean from side to side.** Instead of removing everything from shelves or cabinets, move everything to the right to clean the left side, and then move everything to the left to clean the right side.

An Ounce of Prevention

The simplest way to cut your cleaning time is to prevent dirt and dust from accumulating.

- Place good-size doormats inside and out to absorb moisture, trap dirt, and minimize tracking. Clean the mats regularly.

- Institute a "no shoes" rule for your house, but do wear slippers or socks, because the oils on the bottom of your feet may dirty the carpets.

- To reduce the growth of mildew in bathrooms and other moist environments, use a paint with mold inhibitor added when refinishing the walls. You can have cleaner walls and minimize allergy symptoms at the same time.

- Change the filters in your furnace and air conditioners once a month during the heating and cooling seasons for better air cleaning.

- Ban food from bedrooms.

- In your kitchen and children's rooms, refinish the walls with a semigloss, rather than flat, paint. This will make it easier to clean grease, stains, fingerprints, and crayon marks that accumulate in high-use areas.

- Choose a carpet with built-in stain resistance for high-traffic areas.

- Use liquid or glycerin soap in the shower to reduce soap-scum buildup.

- **Let cleaners do the work.** After spraying on a cleaning product, wait a few minutes to allow the product to do its job. Use that time to clean something else. For example, spray your shower and tub with a "scrub-free" cleaner and let it sit while you wipe countertops and clean the mirror. You can also pretreat a rug stain while you dust the family room or clean rings in jewelry cleaner while you wash dishes.

- **Save steps.** Use a bucket or caddy to cart cleaning tools and supplies from room to room. A larger home might require two cleaning caddies strategically stored for easy access and a vacuum cleaner on each floor.

- **Focus.** Try not to get distracted when you are cleaning. You might not realize it, but when you really get into cleaning, you gain some momentum that works in your favor. Pick a room or task and stick with it until you are done. If the telephone rings, let your answering machine or voice mail service take a message.

- **Work your plan.** Clean each room in a clockwise direction, starting from the door, to ensure that every corner gets cleaned.

- **Take shortcuts.** Let dishes air-dry. For a quicker, easier way to make your bed, replace a top sheet and quilt with a duvet and cover. Look for other ways to save time on home chores. If you're a perfectionist, consider lowering your standards a little to create some free time.

- **Don't make work.** Don't waste time washing an entire wall if all you really need to do is spot-clean. If your clothes aren't noticeably dirty after one use, wear them an extra time to cut down on laundry. Also, if you habitually iron your sheets, don't feel you absolutely must. Take whatever time you save and do something for yourself or with family and friends.

- **Develop routines.** When you clean in an organized fashion, you clean more efficiently. If you do jobs in the same order each time, cleaning becomes automatic. You get to a point where you don't even have to think about what you are doing, and it feels less like work.

- **Go easy.** Always start with the least harsh cleaners first. You'll be less apt to ruin things in the process of cleaning. For example, in trying to remove a stain or soil, try water first. If the stain or soil doesn't budge, then try something stronger, such as dishwashing liquid or an all-purpose cleaner. Do the same with cleaning tools. If a cellulose sponge doesn't do the job, try a nylon scrubbing sponge.

- **Clean up spills immediately.** It's far easier to clean up spills when they are fresh rather than when they have dried, whether they're on a kitchen counter, in your oven, or on your clothes.

- **Trash the trash.** Place wastebaskets wherever trash accumulates: bathrooms, bedrooms, living room, and so on.

- **Buy easy care.** When purchasing furnishings or clothes, look for items that resist stains and are easy to clean and care for.

Pet Dander Everywhere

Dog and cat allergens are found in almost every home in the United States, whether or not dogs or cats live there. The highest concentrations are found on sofas, especially upholstered sofas. In July 2004, the National Institute of Environmental Health Sciences and the United States Department of Housing and Urban Development conducted a national survey to measure levels of indoor allergens that might trigger asthma. Dog allergen was detected in 100 percent of homes, and cat allergen was detected in 99.9 percent of homes, even though most households don't own a dog or cat. In homes with dogs and cats, the levels of allergens are almost always high enough that they could trigger allergies or asthma. Even 36 percent of homes without dogs had dog dander levels high enough to provoke symptoms. And 16 percent of homes without a cat had similarly high levels of cat dander. Where does this come from? Presumably it is tracked into the home on clothes and rubs off where people commonly sit. It also gets into the air. HEPA filters can help reduce exposure levels.

Allergies, Asthma, and Cleaning

Frequent cleaning can help reduce allergens and irritants that cause allergic reactions. When you wipe countertops, for example, you are wiping away more than germs. You also wipe away pollen, pet dander, dust mites, and mold spores — the four most common indoor allergens. If you're a long-time allergy sufferer, you already know more about the subject than we can possibly cover in this book. However, if you're new to living with an allergic person or suspect that you or other members of your household may be developing allergies, here are a few pointers.

Allergic reactions can range from being mildly uncomfortable to being life-threatening, as in a severe asthma attack. Some common signs and symptoms are watery eyes, runny nose, sneezing, nasal congestion, itching, coughing, headache, and fatigue. Obviously, symptoms like a sudden onset of wheezing and difficulty breathing should be addressed immediately by your doctor.

While regular and thorough housecleaning is recommended for allergy sufferers, the act of cleaning itself can aggravate symptoms. It's important to avoid cleaning in the presence of someone with allergies. If possible, clean while he or she is away, and allow at least an hour after cleaning before that person returns to the home. That way, any remaining stirred-up allergens and dust (you can't possibly remove it all!) can settle down and the air will clear.

If you are the one who suffers from allergy symptoms, wearing a face mask during cleaning might help, as could following the Schedule B plan (on page 23), where you clean a bit at a time rather than everything all at once. If your allergies are serious, find some way to hire a cleaning service or barter with someone who can do the big cleaning jobs.

There are three things you can do to manage allergens in your home and lessen allergy symptoms, as detailed below.

Control Dust and Dander. Every home has dust mites. These microscopic creatures live off human and animal dander and other particles that make up household dust. Dust mites thrive not only in dust but in sofas, stuffed chairs, carpets, and bedding. You can never entirely get rid of them, but regular cleaning will minimize their population. Following are some tactics that should help if you suffer from an allergy to dust mites:

- Dust with a damp cloth. Dry cloths and feather dusters just stir pet hair and dust mites back into the air.
- Mop or vacuum hard floors rather than sweeping.
- Vacuum all of your carpets, draperies, and upholstered furniture frequently to remove surface dust.
- Cover upholstered furniture with slipcovers that can be washed often.
- Use vacuums with high-efficiency filters or a central vacuum.
- Dust mites live deep in carpets and are not removed by vacuuming. Have carpets deep-cleaned regularly.

- If you can't bear to give up your pets, at least try to keep them off the furniture. Bathing dogs weekly will help minimize dander.
- Choose shades or washable curtains over other window coverings that tend to collect dust, such as horizontal blinds.
- Seriously consider replacing wall-to-wall carpets with smooth flooring and washable area rugs, especially in bedrooms.
- Use a mattress cover, and wash it and your sheets in hot water every week.
- Choose hypoallergenic pillows or use pillowcase covers designed to prevent dust mites from collecting in your pillows.

Control Moisture. Follow your nose and use your eyes. A musty odor, moisture on hard surfaces, or water stains may indicate the presence of mold — or at the very least, the ideal environment for mold to grow. The primary locations for mold in the home are basements, bathrooms, refrigerators, and garbage cans. Some strategies for mold control include the following:

- To clean and kill mold on hard surfaces, use a solution of ¾ cup of liquid chlorine bleach to 1 gallon of water, or an EPA-registered cleaning solution containing a low concentration of bleach (check the label). Dry the surface thoroughly to help prevent the regrowth of mold.
- Prevent mold by keeping drip pans in your air conditioner, refrigerator, and dehumidifier clean and dry.

- Fix leaky pipes, windows, and roofs to limit moisture in your home.
- Use a dehumidifier to keep relative humidity indoors under 60 percent and, ideally, between 30 and 50 percent. You can measure relative humidity with a hygrometer (humidity meter), available at many hardware stores.
- Have heating and cooling ductwork cleaned once a year.
- Use exhaust fans or open a window when showering, cooking, or using the dishwasher. Vent clothes dryers to the outdoors.
- Replace or wash moldy shower curtains.

Control Pollen. Pollen is not just an outdoor problem — it also gets tracked indoors on clothing and hair.

- Taking a shower and washing your hair before going to bed will help reduce allergy symptoms in the morning, because you won't be rolling around in pollen all night.
- Pollen counts are highest between 5:00 A.M. and 10:00 A.M. Saving outdoor activities for later in the day will help minimize exposure.
- Air conditioners allow you to keep the windows closed, which reduces the entry of allergy-causing pollen. Be sure to have air conditioners cleaned and serviced regularly by a professional, especially just before the cooling season. Change filters monthly when in use.

KNOW AND TELL

According to an article by Keoki Williams, MD, MPH, in the February 2004 issue of the *Journal of Allergy and Clinical Immunology,* mounting evidence supports the theory that exposing children to microbes and potential allergy triggers early in life helps shape their immune system, lessening the likelihood that they will developing allergies later on. So go ahead and get that puppy or kitten!

Getting Help from Family

Research shows that women with children spend more time cleaning than everyone else, "not because they want to but because the kids make more of a mess" ("Let's Talk Dirty," *American Demographics,* November 1998). The antidote is to enlist the help of family members, even if it means lowering your standards, because the fastest way to get cleaning chores done is to divide the work among household members. Two people can get the job done in half the time. Three people can accomplish even more in less time.

Sure, kids would rather play than work. But chores help teach children about shared responsibility, teamwork, and cooperation. It also teaches them skills they will need to live on their own someday. If you think about it, chores also provide an opportunity for family members to spend time together. Whenever possible, make cleaning time a group activity. At the very least, do a chore together occasionally, whether it's preparing the house for guests or cleaning out the garage. The added bonus of getting family members involved in the cleanup effort is that they might be more inclined to keep things cleaner.

Even small children can help. While one family member is vacuuming, a younger one can follow along behind, cleaning baseboards with socks on his or her hands. If you have two or more little ones, make it a contest to see whose sock puppet gets dirtiest. The older the child, the more complex the tasks he or she can be expected to do. Generally, here's what you can reasonably expect from children at various stages of development:

- Preschoolers (3 to 5 years of age) can pick up toys and help clear the table. Children at this age generally enjoy "helping" and imitating their parents in other tasks as well.
- Younger elementary-school children (6 to 8 years of age) can clear and set the table, empty the garbage, put away clean clothes, feed pets, and pull weeds in the garden.
- Older elementary-school children (9 to 11 years of age) can wash and dry dishes, load and empty the dishwasher, sort laundry, help wash the car, and do simple yard work.
- Teenagers can and should be expected to do laundry and other regular housekeeping chores as well as yard work.

Make a list of the chores that need to be done regularly. Hold a family meeting to talk about the concept of each family member having a job to do that helps out the family as a whole. Outline daily responsibilities and expectations. You might assign only one or two chores in the beginning, including one daily chore such as each person making his or her own bed. This will help establish a routine. Expect that children of all ages may need some gentle reminders about doing their chores: a posted checklist, notes, or verbal reminders. It's important to consistently enforce whatever was agreed upon. For example, whoever has laundry duty needs to check the dryer each day after school and fold whatever clothes are in there. Stand your ground; do not give in to whining and moaning.

One effective strategy is to tie privileges to getting work done. If assigned chores don't get done, no privileges are awarded. Privileges may include television or computer time, going to a friend's house after school or overnight, or going to the movies or to the mall. You might consider offering children a per-job salary or weekly allowance as an incentive. This can be a way of teaching money-management skills as well. Or offer to take the family out to the movies on Saturday nights or schedule family outings to the park, beach, or mountains for Sunday afternoons when the team works together to complete its goals.

In the process of getting children and partners involved in the cleaning process, you may need to demonstrate how to do a job. Also be prepared to communicate what constitutes "done." In the beginning, inspect each chore as it's done, and give praise to help reinforce good habits and build self-esteem. Younger children will need to be supervised as they learn to do their chores. As children mature and become more competent, they will not require your direct involvement except for the demonstration of new tasks that may be assigned. For any age, however, it's important to show your appreciation for household members' help so that they can see the value of their efforts and contribution to the family.

ENCOURAGING FAMILY CHORES

One Challenge:

If what you ask of family members seems to go in one ear and out the other, or if you're tired of repeating yourself about what needs to be done, put your chore list in writing. Choose one of the following systems of visual reminders.

Three Solutions . . .

1 Use a dry-erase board to write a chore list every Saturday morning. Have family members write their names next to the chores they will do. Make it a rule that if they don't volunteer for something, you will sign them up for something.

2 Make a list of routine chores that need to be done on a daily or weekly basis. Once you have your list, break it down into categories, such as cleaning up after meals, doing laundry, vacuuming, dusting and general cleaning, yard work, and garbage and recycling. Then assign chores to each family member for one week. At the end of the week, rotate the schedule.

3 Create a job jar. Write jobs on slips of paper and assign a wage or points for each job. Put these slips of paper in a large jar or empty coffee can. One night a week, have each family member draw a chore from the job jar. Hang a dry-erase board on which kids can keep track of their weekly wages or points. If you like the idea of a point system, assign a reward for various point levels. For example, so many points might earn a special privilege or the option to skip one weekly chore the following week. Let kids know that they can earn additional wages or points by doing additional chores.

Kid Clutter Patrol

Of course, with kids around, the extra work of putting away toys and other kid things needs to be done before you can clean. But you shouldn't be the one to do it. Teaching children to pick up after themselves is a lesson in personal responsibility that will follow them into their adult lives. Picking up after them not only makes more work for you but also can lead you to feel resentment and anger toward those you love.

Get tough if you have to. Let your kids know that whatever you find lying on the floor at a pre-designated time will go into the garbage. Then do it: throw out or donate the first thing that gets left out. A variation that works well for younger children is to tell them that whatever the vacuum cleaner touches either gets vacuumed up or goes in the garbage. Once they see that you mean business, they'll scramble to pick up their things when you get out the vacuum cleaner.

It also helps to establish playtime rules. Teach children to take out only a few toys at a time. If they already have two or three toys out, they must put one away before they can take out another. Help them find a place for everything, and then train them to put everything in its place when they are done playing. Consider restricting toys to one room of the house or establishing no-toy zones. Cutting down on the clutter will make your home look cleaner.

Get creative. The key to getting kids to clean up after themselves is to make it more like a game than work. Following are a few plain and simple game plans:

- **Shooting hoops.** Do your kids "forget" to put dirty clothes in the hamper? Make it more enticing by setting up a laundry basket under a wall-mounted or freestanding basketball hoop. This makes picking up clothes a little more interesting. Show them how it's done! If kids share a room, they can even challenge each other to see who can make the basket more often.

- **Pick up or pay.** Okay, this is not as fun as shooting hoops, but it can be very effective. Establish the rule that family members must pick up after themselves. If a parent has to pick up something one of the kids left out, that item will be forfeited until Saturday morning. To reclaim the item, its owner must pay a penalty of one extra household chore. If anyone chooses not to do the chore, you know that the item isn't important to him or her, so you can give or throw it away without guilt.

- **Beat the clock.** You know how it is: the quicker you can get an unpleasant job done, the quicker you can feel better about it. Playing "beat the clock" is a great way to speed up the process of cleaning up a messy bedroom or playroom. Assign a "put away" basket or pillowcase to each child. Set a timer for 30 seconds and see who can pick up the most stuff before the bell goes off. Repeat as necessary and keep score. Reward the winner with a simple indulgence.

- **Play "Coach Clutter."** Play a 15-minute game of pickup. Here are the rules: Players take up positions in the first room. When the coach blows the whistle, players start picking up and putting things away. When that room looks good, blow the whistle again and yell out the name of the next room. Players will then run to the next room and start picking up there. Wrap up the game with praise for a job well done and a special team reward at the end, such as a bowl of popcorn and a movie.

What about the Spouse?

In a household with two adults and no children, it's not reasonable for one person to be expected to do all the housework, especially if both adults work. Sharing in the responsibility is a show of support, caring, and respect for each other.

Try this: Make a list of chores that need to be done on a regular basis and then have your partner check off which chores he or she would be willing to do. You do the same. Plan to take turns doing those chores you both dislike. Or you and your partner can each write up your own chore list and then negotiate for the jobs that haven't been covered.

You may discover that your partner doesn't mind doing a chore you absolutely hate, and vice versa. However, if your partner doesn't do a job quite the way you would do it yourself, don't make the mistake of criticizing, or you might end up doing it yourself from then on! It helps to have a standard you can agree on, and like many other things in a partnership, this may require some compromise. The impor-

KNOW AND TELL

In "Dad: Grab a Dust Rag" (an article for Prevention.com, the Web site of *Prevention* magazine), Lori Nudo reports that a University of California sociologist found that wives find their husbands more sexually attractive when they pitch in to help clean, cook, and run household errands. Husbands' participation in household management also sets a good example for children and goes a long way toward countering traditional attitudes and roles regarding housework.

tant thing is to talk things over and reach an agreement about what's fair. The bottom line is this: when both partners share in the responsibility, you have more time and energy for each other.

Hiring a Housecleaner

Housecleaners aren't just for the wealthy anymore. More and more working women and dual-income families are hiring outside cleaning help. If you can afford it, trading money for time is worth every penny. Instead of coming home from work to housework, you can spend your free time on activities that are more important to you or simply rest, relax, and recharge. But that's not the only reason to hire a professional cleaner. It could be the best way to tackle those jobs that you can't keep up with or jobs that you may not be able to do safely,

such as washing windows or cleaning ceiling fans and fixtures. Hiring a professional cleaner may also be the answer if you have allergies to cleaning products, dust, dander, or mold. Of course, you'll still need to do some everyday cleaning, but that beats having to do the all-out regular cleaning that's required to maintain a clean home.

The first step to hiring a professional cleaner is to determine what type of cleaning services you need. Do you want a professional cleaner to come every week or every other week? Or do you just need help with occasional deep cleaning or seasonal tasks? If you decide you need regular services, what services do you need? Are there tasks you would prefer to continue doing yourself? Make a list of regular cleaning tasks that you wish to have done.

When you meet with a prospective cleaner to get an estimate, ask what services are included. Most cleaners have a set routine that includes basic cleaning tasks, such as vacuuming, cleaning, shining, dusting, disinfecting, and straightening. Some services, such as folding or ironing laundry, may be additional. You may, however, be able to negotiate a trade of one or more routine services for a customized service. If the cleaner provides all the cleaning products and equipment he or she will use, that savings could help justify the cost of the service. According to a government survey, the average homeowner spends $248 on laundry and household cleaning supplies and other household products for housekeeping. Your vacuum cleaner should also last longer if it is used less frequently.

The best way to find a professional housecleaner is to ask around. If you don't have a referral and instead cold-contact a housecleaner, be sure to ask for references. It's important that you feel comfortable with the person or persons you are hiring to come into your home. Discuss how you will handle letting them in your home. Will you provide a key? Is the service guaranteed? Can you reach the cleaner during regular business hours? If cleaning dates fall on holidays or if cleaning dates must be changed for some other reason, how will that be handled?

You should be aware that many individuals who hire out their services as professional cleaners are not properly insured. Professional insurances include bonding, liability, and worker's compensation. Bonding is insurance that will compensate you if an employee steals from you. Liability insurance covers your belongings in the event of damage. Worker's compensation insurance covers medical costs and lost wages if an employee is hurt or disabled on your property. Ask to see all certificates of insurance from a prospective housecleaner. At the very least, before hiring an independent contractor, review your home insurance to make sure it covers domestic employees. (Yes, you are considered that person's legal employer.) For peace of mind, you may wish to hire a company that uses employees rather than independent contractors, pays all employment taxes, and carries the proper insurances for its employees.

There's no need to clean house for your housecleaner. However, there are some things you can and should do before your cleaner arrives. Pick up and put away toys and any other clutter on the floors. Remove clutter from bathroom and kitchen countertops and any other flat surfaces. Put soiled towels and clothes in laundry hampers, and put away clean clothes. A quick uncluttering of your home will enable your cleaner to concentrate on doing his or her best work. It will also help keep clutter from building up around your home. As you pick up clutter, think about what habits may be causing it and look for solutions.

Green Cleaning Services

An independent, nonprofit organization called Green Seal has taken on, as its mission, the work of achieving a healthier and cleaner environment by identifying and promoting products and services that cause less toxic pollution and waste. In 2005, the organization developed a "gold standard" for green cleaning-product certification. Through this program, cleaning companies that are committed to a green cleaning program can become "Green Seal Certified." Most independent cleaners are not likely to become certified. However, if you are concerned about the use of toxic chemicals in your home, you can ask your cleaner to use green cleaning products. You may need to supply these products yourself.

CHAPTER THREE

CLEARING CLUTTER

Less clutter makes it a whole lot easier to clean your home. Think about it: all that stuff you no longer use or need or want is just collecting dust and grime. In the back of your mind, you're always thinking about the fact that you ought to do something about it. If you don't do anything, this stuff can accumulate over time to such an extent that it becomes difficult to clean under and around it without a great deal of effort. Even if you manage to keep your home clean, it just doesn't look clean when papers and things are piled up on tables, counters, and floors.

Unclutter First

You can really speed up the process of cleaning by uncluttering your home. If you have a lot of clutter, it will be well worth your time to purge your home of those things that are simply taking up space. You'll find lots of ideas in this chapter about how to decide what to keep and what to toss and what to do with the things you declare "tossable." Although uncluttering ultimately gives you the opportunity to do a thorough cleaning, don't worry too much about cleaning during the uncluttering process. If you try to clean as you go, it might slow you down, and you

don't want that. The cleaning will go much more quickly once the uncluttering is done, which is one of the benefits of organizing that you're sure to appreciate.

Uncluttering gives you the perfect excuse to get rid of all those things you really don't want or use anymore — everything from hair accessories to books to furniture. Just because you bought it or someone bought it for you doesn't mean you have to keep it forever. Give yourself permission to give away those things that no longer suit your tastes or lifestyle.

The hardest part about getting organized is getting started. Clutter won't disappear overnight. But if you commit to spending 15 minutes a day on uncluttering activities, you will begin to see noticeable improvement almost immediately. Start today and keep at it. The reward is well worth the wait. Following are seven ways to get started without having to put your life on hold:

- Make an uncluttering appointment with yourself. Write it in your daily planner, and honor that appointment as you would any other.
- Unclutter one shelf, one drawer, or one small area until you are done.
- Set simple daily goals. Example: "Tonight, I'm going to clean out my junk drawer."
- Plan little rewards for getting things done. Example: "I am going to unclutter my kitchen counter, and then I am going to read a magazine for a half hour."
- Focus on finding a simple solution to the one thing you find most frustrating each day. For example, if it takes you 10 minutes to find a matching set of earrings each morning, organize your jewelry.
- Make a list of organizing projects and write each one on a separate piece of paper. Put them in a jar or basket. Put aside some time

to get started, then reach in and pull out one project. Get that project rolling and do as much as you can in the allotted time. Keep coming back to it until that project is complete. Then start over with a new project pulled from the jar.

- Set a ticking timer or play your favorite CD. When the timer bell rings or your CD stops playing, it's quitting time. There may be days when you want to continue on for another hour. But if you've had enough for one day, just walk away. The clutter has been there for a while, right? It will be there when you come back to it tomorrow.

Pick a Mess — Any Mess

When clutter has been allowed to accumulate, it's discouraging to think about cleaning up. You might look around and ask yourself, "Where do I start?" The answer is that it really doesn't matter. Choose one of the following three options:

1. Start in the room where you spend the most time. This may help you begin to feel more in control of your environment and your life.
2. Start in the room that is most difficult to clean because of clutter and disarray. This could help reduce the stress that comes from continually looking at a job that needs doing.
3. Start in the room that is least in need of cleaning up and clearing out. This lets you reap the rewards of cleaning up quickly and may be just the motivation you need to unclutter the rest of your home.

Whichever option you choose, make it your goal to start with the most visible clutter first and then work your way down to uncluttering the stuff that's out of sight.

The clearing-out process is far less daunting and more manageable if you determine in advance how much time you will spend uncluttering in any given day. Keep in mind that your home didn't get cluttered overnight, and it's probably going to take some time to get it organized. If you can spare a whole day here and there, that's great. But you don't have to put your life on hold to get organized. Just setting aside 15 minutes to an hour each day can quickly add up to a job well done. In fact, 15 minutes a day adds up to 7 hours a month.

One Drawer at a Time

Uncluttering is a job that's best accomplished by focusing your time and attention on one area. If you try to unclutter a whole room all at once, you'll likely end up creating a bigger mess than what you started with. Instead, start with a clearly defined space, such as a countertop, a

Time to A-C-T

Got clutter? Uncluttering is the act of restoring balance to your life by eliminating the stuff you don't want or need anymore to make room for the things you love and use. With a little effort, you can transform chaos into order and free up time, energy, and space for the more important things in life. Try the ACT formula to get started:

A — **Assess your situation.** Ask yourself, "How did it get like this?" Before you can change anything, you have to accept responsibility for your role. Don't beat yourself up about it. Clutter happens. But if clutter is causing you stress, upsetting your relationships, or interfering with your job, it's time to do something about it.

C — **Commit to change.** If you keep doing things the same way in which you've been doing them, you're going to keep getting the same results. Change one thing, such as what you do with your bills when they arrive in the mail. Instead of leaving them on the counter, where they are bound to get lost in the paper shuffle, create a folder or large envelope labeled "Bills," and put all your bills into it as they arrive.

T — **Tackle one area at a time.** Have you ever attempted to unclutter your home or office and ended up with a bigger mess than you started with? Next time, start small. Start with a single drawer or shelf or section of your closet. Focus on just that one area, and don't move on until you have finished uncluttering it.

table or desktop, or a shelf. Remove everything, and wipe or vacuum the surface to clean it. Before replacing the items you just removed, sort them into five categories, using labeled boxes or bags to collect the items that belong in categories two through five:

1. **Things you love and/or use.** Obviously, things you love are things you want to keep, even if you never use them. Those things you do use (even if it's only once a year) are also things you'll want to keep.
2. **Things you could give away.** You might not need it or want it, but it's still perfectly useful. Don't trash it; donate or give it away to someone you know.
3. **Things that belong in the trash.** This includes everything from irreparable items to outdated papers to stray staples and lint. Toss it all.
4. **Things you could sell.** This category is optional. You could just donate or give away those things you don't need. But some people are more inclined to let go of things when they can get at least some return on their initial investment. If you decide to go to the effort of selling items online or at a garage sale, set them aside and designate a holding place in your home for that purpose.
5. **Things that belong elsewhere.** In the process of cleaning up, you will come across things that belong in another room or somewhere else altogether, such as books and videos that need to be returned or something you borrowed from a friend.

Deposit these items in a box or bag labeled "Store Elsewhere." When you are finished organizing for the day, take these items to the rooms where they belong. If items belong in the room you are organizing, but not where you found them (on the kitchen counter, for example), just give them a temporary home somewhere in a space that you have not yet uncluttered.

What about parts and pieces that you find? Or things that have parts and pieces missing? Set up a "Lost and Found" box somewhere, and put these items into it as you find them. You might also put in the box items that don't yet have a home or that you can't identify. When you finish uncluttering your entire home, go through the box to see whether you are now able identify and find a home for any of these things. Discard the junk.

EVERYDAY SOLUTION
Time to Unclutter

Use television time to get organized. Pull a drawer out of its cabinet and set yourself in front of the television. When the commercials come on, dump the drawer and sort the contents into four categories: throw away, give away or sell, put away (somewhere else), and put back in the drawer. When you're finished, put back what goes in that drawer and go get another drawer. At the end of the evening, throw away the trash, put give-away items and things to sell in a box for distribution, and put away what belongs elsewhere.

Keep or Toss?

What if you're undecided about what to do with a particular item? It's probably something you could give away, throw away, or sell, but for whatever reason, you're not quite ready to part with it. Ask yourself:

- Have I used this item in the past year? **Yes/No**

- Has anyone else in my home used it in the past year? **Yes/No**

- Do I have a definite use for this in the foreseeable future? **Yes/No**

- If it's broken, is it worth fixing? **Yes/No**

- Does this item serve a worthwhile purpose in my life? **Yes/No**

- Do I need to keep it for legal or tax purposes? **Yes/No**

- Is it more important to me to keep this item than to have the space it occupies? **Yes/No**

- Do I love it? **Yes/No**

- Does someone in my household love it? **Yes/No**

- Would it be difficult or expensive to get another one if I/we needed it? **Yes/No**

Scoring: There are no right or wrong answers, but a "Yes" answer to any of the above questions provides a sound reason to keep that item. A "No" answer, on the other hand, gives you good reason to toss it.

If you're undecided about an item, take the "Keep or Toss" quiz on this page. If you're still undecided, ask yourself, "What's the worst possible thing that could happen if I got rid of this?" Still undecided? Then go ahead and keep it for now, along with the things you love and use. Or put that item in a box or bag labeled "Undecided." When you finish uncluttering, seal the box, write the current month, day, and year on it, and put it in storage. If you haven't had a need to open that box one year from now, then you know that you don't need what's inside, and you can let it go.

Letting Go

For many people, uncluttering is scary and uncomfortable, because it means letting go of things that have become a part of their lives. It helps to realize that the most important things in life are not things. If you are reluctant to let go of things, start with the easy stuff. Walk through your home with a large trash bag. Throw out anything that is clearly garbage:

- Candy and gum wrappers
- Expired coupons
- Outdated flyers and calendars
- Spoiled food
- Expired medicines
- Socks with no mate
- Stretched-out socks
- Permanently stained clothing
- Worn-out shoes
- Rusted tools and utensils
- Broken items that aren't worth fixing
- Cracked coffee mugs

All of these items have outlived their usefulness. They're just taking up valuable space in your home. The same can be said of anything you do not love or use regularly. If you can bring yourself to let go of these things, you will create more space for the things you really love and use. You won't miss the other stuff. In fact, you will likely enjoy the feeling of freedom that comes from letting go. And once you clear out your space, it will be a whole lot easier and quicker to clean it and keep it clean.

Following are some plain and simple tips to help you let go of material possessions you no longer love or use and clear out valuable space in your home.

- **Do it scared.** It's normal to feel some anxiety about letting go of things; most people, do to some extent. Do it anyway. You may find that letting go of material possessions helps you let go of emotional clutter, because the physical act of letting go can trigger a release of frustration, anger, guilt, and other emotional garbage.

- **Weigh the pain.** When you weigh the pain of letting go against the pleasure of living a less cluttered life, the choice becomes clear. All you need to do then is make a commitment, and the rest will take care of itself.

- **Imagine that you're moving.** Ask yourself, "Is this item worth the effort of packing up, carrying out to the moving van, and unpacking at the new place?" If not, give it a new home.

- **Don't touch it!** Instead of picking up each object as you try to decide what to do with it, have a family member or friend hold it. Holding it yourself emphasizes your attachment to it. This is precisely why a good salesperson will encourage you to touch something or try it on!

Start with Today's Stuff

It's a lot easier to keep up than to catch up.

- Put new photos into an album instead of adding them to the pile that's been accumulating for the past 10 years. Even if you never get around to organizing the backlog, at least your most current photographs will be organized from today forward.

- Hang up clothes or put them in a drawer or laundry hamper as soon as you take them off.

- Sort your new mail every day; immediately toss anything that is junk.

- Spend 5 minutes at the end of each day picking up clutter and putting it where it belongs. Make it a family affair and a household requirement; everyone picks up their own stuff. To make it more fun for young children, give them a pillowcase in which they can collect errant belongings.

- Resist the urge to just put something down at the spot where you happen to be when you are finished with it; instead, take a moment to put things where they belong.

- **Think about your abundance.** If you have more than one of a particular item, be honest with yourself. How many do you really need? If you're uncluttering a junk drawer, for example, and you find that you have an exorbitant number of pens or rubber bands, ask yourself how many is enough. Keep what you can use and give away the rest.

- **Kick out the strangers.** Judith Kolberg, the director of the National Study Group on Chronic Disorganization, developed an uncluttering game called Friends, Acquaintances, and Strangers that you can play with your belongings. As you look at each item, ask yourself whether it is a friend, an acquaintance, or a stranger. An outfit you wear often is a friend. Something you bought but never wore is an acquaintance. Clothes that don't fit or that you haven't worn in a year or more are strangers. Find a new home for acquaintances that have overstayed their welcome. Kick out the strangers.

- **Give up the caretaker job.** The more stuff you have, the more stuff you have to take care of and the more space you need to store it. Make a conscious decision to let someone else take over the caretaker job.

- **Come back to it.** If you've been doing pretty well with letting go but get stuck trying to decide whether to keep a particular item or not, set it aside for a day. You may simply be too tired to decide, or there may be other things going on in your life that are interfering with your decision-making ability.

The Great Giveaway

Clutter is physical proof of our abundance. If you have clutter, you are richer than you think. Sharing your abundance can be a joyful experience, knowing that others are benefiting from things you have held close to your heart but no longer need. Stuff you're hanging on to in case you might need it someday could do immediate good in the hands of someone who really needs it right now.

Think of someone you know who might need or enjoy having what you no longer want. Ask whether that person would be willing to come and get whatever you are giving away. One thing you don't want is a box full of stuff that you have to deliver to every corner of the world, because you know what will happen: the box will just sit there and become a source of frustration.

It may be more convenient to donate your whole box of giveaways to one charitable organization and be done with it. The simplest way to unload your unwanted, unneeded belongings is to find one charity that accepts all types of things, from clothing and shoes to furnishings. That way, you don't have to think about what should go where. All you have to do is put it in a box and take it to that one place. Some organizations even schedule regular neighborhood pickups. If you prefer, you can separate your giveaways into several bags for delivery to different donation stations. Refer to the following section for a partial list of where to donate what. If you itemize on your income tax returns, you may be able to use your donation as an income tax deduction. Just be sure to keep a list of the items you donated, including the thrift store value of each item, and ask for a tax receipt from the charitable organization.

A Second Chance for Clutter

When you donate things you consider clutter, you give those things a second chance to be useful and valuable once again. Old towels, for example, can become comfortable bedding for rescued animals at a shelter. A cell phone can become a lifeline for a victim of domestic violence. Several organizations specialize in the collection of certain types of things that are very much needed by people in your local community and beyond. Following is a partial list of where to donate what:

• **Eyeglasses.** Donate used prescription eyeglasses and prescription or nonprescription sunglasses to the Lions Recycle for Sight program. Look for a drop-off box at your eye doctor's office or the retail store where you shop for eyeglasses. Your glasses will be shipped to regional recycling centers, where they will be cleaned, categorized by prescription, and prepared for distribution to needy people around the world.

• **Women's business clothing.** Donate those suits, blouses, and slacks you no longer wear to Dress for Success, an organization that distributes clothing to low-income women who are trying to get jobs to support themselves and their children. Larger sizes are in high demand. Log on to their Web site (see Appendix B) to find a drop-off point in your area.

• **Period clothing.** A local theater might love to have your grandfather's old suits.

• **Computers.** If you have a newer desktop or laptop, you may be able to donate it to the National Cristina Foundation, a nonprofit organization that distributes used systems to disadvantaged children. For more information, log on to their Web site (see Appendix B). Other nonprofit organizations that accept donations of working computer equipment include reBOOT Canada and Techsoup.

• **Magazines and newspapers.** Many schools and other organizations put out dumpsters for collecting magazines, newspapers, and phone books for recycling, which keeps all that paper out of our already-crowded landfills. You can also take magazines (or forward an unwanted subscription) to doctors' and dentists' offices, hospitals, and prisons. First, be sure to cut out your address label for protection of your privacy.

• **Scrap fabric.** Fabric might be useful at a senior citizens' center, grade school, or community theater.

• **Books.** Take a look at your bookshelves. Books you haven't read for years (and probably won't read again) can go to a local literacy project, library, school,  or community center. Or bring a box of books to work to share with coworkers.

• **Textbooks.** Chances are no one wants your used textbooks, including most libraries. However, these might be appreciated at a prison. You may be able to make your donation through a local church.

• **Sheets, blankets, and towels.** Take worn items to an animal shelter or a homeless shelter.

Donate those in better condition to a domestic violence shelter. Again, if you are unsure about making contact, try a local church.

- **Home furnishings.** Furniture, lamps, wall hangings, and artwork of all kinds can be donated to a domestic violence shelter, the Salvation Army, or Goodwill.

- **Toys, games, and stuffed animals.** Donate gently used items to a children's hospital, domestic violence shelter, or community recreation center.

- **Cell phones.** Several organizations collect and recycle used cell phones and then distribute them to victims of domestic violence. Franklin Covey stores, for one, participate in the nationwide Donate-a-Phone program. Your local police station might also accept cell phones for the same purpose. Collective Good (see Appendix B) is another resource for recycling cell phones. Find more recycling centers by doing a quick online search. If you prefer, search for sites where you can sell your old cell phone.

It Pays to Unclutter

You can clear out your closets and drawers and make some cash by selling things you no longer want or need. You won't get rich uncluttering your home, but you may end with enough to pay for something you really want. The primary outlets for selling secondhand items are consignment shops, classified advertising, Internet auction sites, and yard and garage sales.

Selling on Consignment. Consignment shops usually accept your secondhand belongings with an agreement to sell them and give you a percentage of the selling price — something in the neighborhood of 40 percent. Items remain in the shop until they sell or until the end of a specified contract period (usually 60 to 90 days), after which you can collect your earnings. Most shops will offer to donate unsold items to charity. Take them up on their offer! There's no sense in bringing things back home.

To find a shop near you, look in your yellow pages under "Consignment Shops" or "Secondhand Shops." To maximize your earnings, you may want to check out a few stores before choosing one. Compare policies. Also take location into account. Don't choose a store that is off the beaten path unless you are sure that it does a lot of business.

Online Bulletin Boards

A really simple way to find a new home for reusable items is to post them on an online bulletin board such as Freecycle. Join your local freecycling community by signing up at www.freecycle.org. Then send an e-mail to other members offering the item(s) you wish to give away. Once an item is claimed, you can make arrangements for the taker to come and get it. Another online bulletin board can be found in the free category in the "For Sale" section of the Craigslist Web site at www.craigslist.org. (Be sure to post in your local area.)

Some consignment shops accept only clothing, but many will accept all kinds of things, including:

- Clothing and accessories
- Furniture
- Kitchenware
- Decorative household items
- Sporting equipment
- Toys
- Infant furniture and items
- Videos and books

Some stores specialize in specific items, such as used sporting equipment, books, or children's clothing. Clothes must be in excellent condition, with no loose or missing buttons, no falling hems or tears in the material, and no stains. Newer clothes, designer labels, and classic styles sell best. Bring them to the store cleaned, pressed, and on hangers. Bear in mind that consignment shops want seasonal clothing that is coming into season. The proper time to bring seasonal clothes to a consignment shop is:

Spring/summer	mid-February
Fall	mid-August
Winter	end of September/ early October

If it's too late in the season to bring in your clothes, put them in storage and put a note in your calendar reminding you to get them out before the beginning of the next season.

Selling Direct. You can sell larger items directly to buyers by placing a classified advertisement

Cleaning Up

An informal March 2004 poll of members of the National Association of Professional Organizers (NAPO) found that an impressive 78 percent had found cash or uncashed checks for their organizing clients. In terms of how much money they turned up:

- 4 percent had found less than $5
- 7 percent had found $5 to $50
- 5 percent had found $51 to $100
- 24 percent had found $101 to $500
- 12 percent had found $501 to $1,000

AND

- a fairly remarkable 26 percent had found $1,000 or more.

in one of your local newspapers or weekly circulars. Items you might consider advertising include furniture sets, large appliances or power equipment, exercise and sports equipment, and computer equipment. While selling direct will generally yield the best price, you do have to pay a fee for the advertisement. Also be prepared to spend time on the telephone and in person with prospective buyers.

For selling valuable items such as jewelry, antiques, coin collections, musical instruments, and the like, look for stores that specialize in buying and selling these items. The yellow pages of your telephone book are a good place to start. You may wish to get more than one estimate to ensure that you're getting a fair price.

Selling Online. You can sell just about anything on the Internet. The world's largest online marketplace is eBay (www.ebay.com). People use eBay to buy and sell all sorts of things, including:

- Antiques and art
- Books, movies, and music
- Business, office, and industrial items
- Clothing and accessories
- Collectibles
- Computers and peripherals
- Dolls and teddy bears
- Home and garden items
- Jewelry, gemstones, and watches
- Photo and electronic equipment
- Pottery and glass
- Sports equipment and memorabilia
- Tickets for events and travel
- Toys and hobby items

For its services, eBay assesses two selling fees: a nominal insertion fee for the listing of each item (or a quantity of same items) and a final value fee, which ranges from 1.25 to 5 percent of the final sale price. Additional fees apply for optional services, such as an online payment service that allows eBay to collect payment from a buyer and deposit it into your bank account.

LiveDeal (see Appendix B) is a similar service that is free and lets you buy and sell locally, giving you an opportunity to try before you buy. And you avoid the hassle and high cost of shipping by closing the deal in person.

Local and national "drop and ship" services will sell items for you on eBay. One such national service is AuctionDrop (see Appendix B). After calling for authorization, you bring unpacked items to any UPS Store location to be professionally packed and shipped to AuctionDrop's centralized processing hub. AuctionDrop's staff handles the necessary steps for selling an item on eBay, including photography, testing, research, listing, customer service, payment processing, repacking, shipping, and returns. For basic service, no prepayment is necessary, as AuctionDrop takes a variable commission on the sale.

Recycling

Rather than add to the landfill, recycle things you don't need, such as plastic grocery bags and wire hangers, by taking them back to where you got them, in this case to the supermarket and the dry cleaner. You can also recycle used ink and laser cartridges through the manufacturer, office supply stores, and school fund-raising programs.

Organizing a Garage Sale. One time-proven way to get rid of unwanted stuff, and make a few bucks in the process, is to hold a garage or yard sale. Planning ahead will minimize time and effort while maximizing sales. Following are seven simple steps for a successful garage sale.

1. Set a date. Check first to find out whether your municipality requires you to have a permit to hold a garage sale or puts any restrictions on garage sales. Then pick a date for your garage sale. Friday is a busy garage-sale day, as is Saturday. One day should be sufficient, but if you have a great deal of stuff to sell and you don't mind spending an extra day selling it, make it a two-day sale. Most buyers will be there in the morning, so you may want to end your sale by 2:00 P.M. rather than wait around for stragglers.

2. Write and place an advertisement for your sale. List your big-ticket items and some of the more desirable things. Specify "no early birds" in your ad unless you are willing to start selling at the crack of dawn. Also include the hours of your sale. Run the ad three days before and on the day of the sale.

3. Designate a collection spot. Set up one area of your garage or home for collecting, sorting, and pricing items to be sold. Keep similar items together — for example, furniture, sporting equipment, books and videos, infant clothing and toys, kitchenware, or linens.

4. Put a price on everything. Use stickers or signs. It's best when prospective customers don't have to ask, "How much is this?" If you are unfamiliar with garage-sale pricing, go to a garage sale or two and look for items similar to those you will be selling. As you collect items for your garage sale, price them.

5. Make garage-sale location signs. Post signs pointing the way to your sale at strategic locations, including the nearest intersection with a main road, the end of your street, and the end of your driveway. Write in large capital letters with black marker on brightly colored card stock. Keep it simple:

```
GARAGE SALE
FRI-SAT-SUN
9:00–2:00
99 ANYWHERE ROAD
```

Post the signs up to one week prior to your sale. Check local community restrictions first. And make a note to yourself to take them down after the sale.

6. Arrange your wares attractively. To display smaller items, lay them on tables or on a sheet of plywood laid over two sawhorses and draped with a tablecloth. Put all clothes on hangers, then hang them on a length of clothesline or secure a long pole or broom handle between two stepladders to serve as a clothes rod. Separate men's, women's, and children's clothing and accessories and put out a mirror. If you're selling electrical appliances, make sure you have an outdoor outlet available so customers can test them; if necessary, run a heavy-duty extension cord out to the garage-sale area. The more you can set up your sale along the lines of a retail store, the easier it is for customers to browse and find things. Remove from the garage-sale vicinity any items that are not part of the sale, or attach to them a sign that reads "Not for Sale." If you have items that you simply want to give away, put them in a box out by the road with a "Free" sign.

7. Be prepared. Think about how you will handle money. Will you wear a fanny pack or apron or use a cash box? Will you need a helper? Be sure that you have enough coins and bills to make change for at least two $20 bills — five fives, thirteen ones, and two dollars in loose change geared to your pricing system (for example, if you price everything in increments of 25¢, you will need only quarters). Have a calculator or paper and pencil handy for quick addition. You'll also want some shopping bags and a few boxes, as well as newspaper for wrapping breakables. Set up as much as possible the night before your sale. If you are setting up in a garage or barn, make sure you have enough light so your wares can be seen. If you are having the sale outdoors, be prepared for rain: either have space ready in your garage or another enclosed space in case you need to move everything inside, or predesignate a rain date. Consider reducing everything to half-price in the last hour of your sale.

To encourage your children to clean up their rooms, offer to let them keep whatever they make from selling their stuff at the garage sale. If you don't have quite enough stuff to attract customers or can't stand the thought of going it alone, invite friends and family members to join you in your garage-sale effort, with the understanding that they do all their own pricing and setup, that they help you on the day of the sale,

and that they take all unsold items with them when they leave. You'll need a system for tracking who sells what to keep proceeds straight; you might think about using color-coded price stickers. If you're working with just one other person, you can simply direct buyers to the appropriate money-taker.

Another idea is involve your immediate neighbors. Let them know that you are planning a garage sale and ask whether anyone is interested in having a garage sale on the same day as yours. Then you can advertise the block sale together and split the cost of advertising. Be sure to give your neighbors plenty of advance notice (at least one month) so they have time to go through their homes and set aside stuff they want to sell.

The Online Yard Sale

Selling clothing, accessories, sporting goods, and other items on the Internet is often a simpler and more lucrative alternative to the traditional yard sale. Auction sites include eBay, LiveDeal, and Yahoo! Auctions. You can also search online for possible sale sites, using the keywords "for sale" and "newsgroups" in the search box to find local newsgroups. Describe your items honestly and in detail, making sure to mention brand names. Posting photographs of sale items will also help to sell items.

Getting Organized

Uncluttering is half the battle. Organizing is the other half. Without organizing, uncluttering is a job you'll have to do over and over again. Organization puts you in control of your belongings by systematizing or putting your things in order. Getting organized shouldn't be complicated. In fact, the more complicated your organizational system, the less likely it is that you will be able to maintain it. While there are some basic guidelines for getting organized, only you can figure out what works best for you. If it works well enough for you to keep it up, it's good!

More often than not, the reason why things don't get put away is that they are homeless. How can you put everything in its place if you don't have a place for everything? The key to getting organized is to find the best possible home for all of your belongings, from measuring cups and spoons to memorabilia.

When choosing a home for an item, don't think, "Where shall I put this?" Instead, ask yourself, "Where am I most likely to look for this?" Ideally, the home you create will be close to where the item gets used and in a spot where others might be apt to look for it if they need it. As you look at where your belongings are stored in a particular room, consider the following questions to help you determine whether each item is in the best location:

- How often do I use it?
- Where do I use it?
- How accessible is it? How accessible should it be? Do I need easier access?
- Does it belong in this room or somewhere else? Where would be a better place?

Life is denied by lack of attention, whether it be to cleaning windows or trying to write a masterpiece.

— Nadia Boulanger

Things you use often should be either visible or easily accessible. Store those things you use most often between neck and knee height and toward the front of a closet or cabinet. Store things you rarely use on higher or lower shelves or in a long-term-storage area. You may find that the best place for some items, such as a broken lamp or outdated event flyer, is in the trash. Still other items, such as a suit you no longer wear, might best be located in someone else's home! Donate it!

If you already have a particular item stored in a certain location but it isn't being used, figure out why. Perhaps it is not conveniently located. A good example is the hamper. If your kids get undressed in the bedroom but the hamper is in the bathroom or the laundry room, it's no wonder their dirty clothes always wind up on the floor. Instead, put a hamper in each bedroom or wherever it makes sense.

Favorite Organizing Products

Half the job of organizing is having the right tools. There are some terrific products you can buy to help organize your possessions. But be careful that you're not just organizing clutter. You want to keep it pared down. Also, resist the temptation to buy organizing products until you

Contain Yourself

Use containers to organize your belongings. In addition to boxes, crates, baskets, and bags, think of drawers, shelves, and clothes rods as containers. Keep like items together in separate containers. This makes it easier to find what you're looking for, even if you never get around to organizing the contents of the container. Another good reason to "containerize" belongings is that there's a limit to the amount of stuff any one container can hold, which puts a limit on clutter.

Group items together in whatever way makes sense to you. In your closet, clothes can be sorted by type (shirts, pants, skirts, dresses, and suits) or by color and hung accordingly in these categories. In the kitchen, small items such as cookie cutters can be collected in zip-sealed plastic bags to keep them separate from other small kitchen gadgets in a drawer.

To maximize existing storage space, think vertical. Think about what you might be able to hang on walls, from the ceiling, and behind closed doors. A shoe rack hung over the back of a door, for example, takes up less space than a standing shoe rack. Use same-size storage boxes so that you can stack them on shelves to make use of unused space at the top of closets. In cabinets, you might be able mount hooks or narrow shelves to the inside of the door to hold spices or pot lids.

If you have a lot of dead space at the top of your cabinets, raise or lower the shelves so that you can make better use of space. You also could install freestanding shelving or hanging wire baskets under the shelves to create additional storage space. Consider replacing fixed shelves with adjustable shelving or pull-out drawers so that even things in the back of the cabinet are accessible. You can buy a do-it-yourself kit for this project at most hardware and home stores.

Designate temporary storage areas for items that you plan to sell at a future garage sale, gifts purchased in advance of the occasion, clothing to go to the dry cleaner, and library books and rented videos that must be returned. Store a marker and stickers with your garage-sale items so that you can price them as you put them into storage.

Don't just toss things into storage. Take the time to put them where they belong or to create a place for them so that you don't have to spend hours or days reorganizing your storage at a future date. Keep an open catchall box in your storage area for catching all those things you find throughout the year that belong in a packed box. Instead of getting everything out just to put away one item, keep it in the catchall box. The next time you pull out all the boxes, you can put away everything in the catchall box.

know exactly what you need to contain. And be sure to measure your space so that you buy the right-size product.

Sometimes the best organizing product is something you have in your home that you acquired for some other purpose but are not using. A magnetic knife holder can be mounted inside a cabinet door to hold nail clippers, tweezers, and scissors. Hat boxes, decorative tins, and woven baskets have a wonderful way of containing clutter on shelves while adding to the decor of any room.

While a filing cabinet or bookcase is probably a worthwhile investment, you don't have to spend a lot of money on most organizing products. Check out your local dollar store for inexpensive jewelry organizers and shoe bags. Following are some ideas for recycling everyday items into free organizers:

- In the medicine cabinet or under the sink, empty diaper-wipe containers can come in handy as airtight containers for storing first-aid supplies, makeup, pain relievers, and vitamins. *Helpful hint:* Label the boxes so you know what's inside without having to open them.
- To store odds and ends in the kitchen junk drawer, workshop, or office drawer, use recycled microwave food trays, check boxes, margarine tubs, aerosol-can tops, or other small containers to collect like items such as batteries, rubber bands, and bag clips.
- Stack plastic milk crates or wooden produce boxes face out against a wall or in a closet and use them to store books,

binders, and notebooks in a kid's room or college dorm room.

- Use cardboard copy-paper boxes or cardboard produce boxes with lids as long-term storage boxes.
- Use a liquor carton with interior dividers to store rolled-up artwork. Or use one in your coat closet to store dry umbrellas.
- Empty egg cartons can be quite useful for storing small items, such as small crafts supplies. Or you can remove the lid and place the carton in a desk drawer to hold paper clips and other small items.
- Use a shoebox to store photos temporarily or as a dresser-drawer organizer.
- Film canisters are very useful for storing small items like buttons, safety pins, and, in the toolbox, screws and nails. Use masking tape to label each container, or use a piece of clear tape to attach a sample item to the outside of the container.

EVERYDAY SOLUTION
Stair Basket

Keep a basket at the bottom of the stairs for collecting items that need to go upstairs. Make it a habit to pick it up on your way up and bring it down on your way down.

Help Is on the Way

Don't be afraid to ask for help if you need it. For example, when you get ready to clean out your closet, invite a friend to help you determine what does and does not look good on you. And minimize distractions during the time you've set aside for uncluttering. Let the answering machine take your calls, and let housemates know that you don't want to be disturbed.

But what if you are so overwhelmed that you can't even get started or you get overwhelmed in the middle of organizing your closet? Professional help is available, in the form of professional organizers who can help you get and stay organized. These organizing experts can provide ideas, information, structure, solutions, and systems to help you regain control over your time and space. To find a professional organizer near you, look in the yellow pages under "Organizing Services." Request a free referral through the National Association of Professional Organizers (NAPO) (see Appendix B), whose members have pledged to follow a strict professional code of conduct that includes complete client confidentiality. When contacting a professional organizer, ask about his or her experience with situations similar to yours. Don't hesitate to ask for references. And do choose someone you feel comfortable with, since you will be working together closely.

Avoid Tough Decisions

If you find it difficult to get rid of junk, think about that before bringing anything into your home. Learn to say "no thanks" to things you don't want or need.

> *Have nothing in your houses that you do not know to be useful or believe to be beautiful.*
>
> — William Morris,
> nineteenth-century English designer

There are at least three support-group programs for people who are chronically disorganized:

- **Clutterless Recovery Groups** is a nonprofit self-help organization run by clutterers for clutterers. In addition to providing online information and support, this group offers workshops and meetings in cities throughout the United States.
- **Messies Anonymous** provides educational and motivational aid to chronically disorganized individuals and sponsors 12-step support groups in which participants set goals, discuss problems, and celebrate victories.
- **Clutterers Anonymous** also offers a 12-step program and other resources for recovery.

Another group, the National Study Group on Chronic Disorganization (NSGCD), can help you find a professional organizer who specializes in working with individuals who are chronically disorganized. The organization's Web site (see Appendix B) offers a list of graduates from its programs with links to their e-mail addresses as well as an opportunity to request a referral to a NSGCD member organizer in your area.

Staying Organized

Getting organized isn't easy, but then, nothing worth doing is easy. Staying organized is even more challenging, because you have to retrain yourself to do things differently. Did you know that it takes 21 consecutive days to establish a new habit? That means you have to make a conscious effort every day not to do the same old thing. Once you've uncluttered your home and found a place for everything, staying organized comes down to picking up, putting away, and getting rid of excess stuff on a regular basis.

The best way to stay organized is to take care of today's things today. Resist what might be your natural inclination to put things off. Procrastinating usually results in more work later, not to mention more time, more stress, and sometimes even more money. Following are some simple everyday strategies for staying organized by taking care of the little things.

- **Don't put it down — put it away!** Before you put something down, ask yourself, "Is this where it belongs?" In the beginning this will feel like work, but if you keep after yourself, it will become second nature to put things away. Take dressing and undressing, for example. Even when you're in a hurry, remind yourself that it takes just a minute or two to put away clothes after undressing — far less time than it takes to pick up and put away several weeks' worth of clothing. And it's not just that time and work you save when you put away clothes right away. How often have you had to launder or iron an article of clothing because it had been left on the floor overnight or for a week?

- **Lay down the law with household members.** Whoever makes a mess is responsible for cleaning it up — now, not later. That means all household members are responsible for cleaning up their own bathroom mess, their own kitchen mess, and their own bedroom mess. Set minimum standards at first, especially for younger family members, and then raise the bar.
- **Pick up every day.** Set aside a specific time each day for a quick walk-through of your home with a basket or tote bag in hand, collecting stray items and returning them to their rightful homes. Do it while your morning coffee or tea is brewing or just before you go to bed. If it takes longer than 15 minutes, let that be your early warning system that you may be falling back into old habits. When you catch yourself thinking, "I'll do it later," stop and do it now.
- **Unclutter as you go.** When you go to the basement, to the attic, to the garage, or up or down the stairs, take something with you to put away. A few minutes here and there every day can add up to uncluttering in no time flat!
- **Leave your "campground" cleaner than you found it.** Make it your mantra never to leave a room without improving its appearance. Toss the old newspaper in the recycling bin. Straighten pictures and lampshades. Close

doors, cabinets, and drawers. Put dishes in the dishwasher. Get in the habit of making your bed after your morning shower or after breakfast. A made bed not only makes the room look nicer but also feels nicer to get into. If you share a bed, make it a rule that the last one up makes the bed. Get up earlier every day, and you may never have to make the bed again!

- **Make it easy to stay organized.** Designate a "drop off" box for library books and videos that need to be returned. Keep a "put away" basket in a central location, or even one in every room, for collecting things that belong elsewhere. Make putting away a daily family chore. (And as an added bonus, if you get unexpected visitors, you can use these baskets to pick up and stash clutter in a hurry!) If you find yourself picking up the same areas over and over again, see if you can come up with a simple, practical solution for preventing or reducing future messes. For example, if your kitchen counter is littered with empty beverage bottles and cans, move the recycling bin closer to that area.

- **Make standard "to do" or "to remember" lists.** Prepack your gym bag with a list of what you need to take with you. That way, you won't have to waste energy rethinking what you need every time. And you'll never end up at the gym without your sneakers or a towel for your shower! Make lists for anything you do on a regular basis, such as closing up your summer home or packing to go to the beach. File all of your lists in the same folder in your filing cabinet. Or, if you prefer, keep individual lists with related items so that you'll be sure to find the appropriate list when you start looking for your stuff.

- **Set limits on recyclable items.** How many plastic shopping bags do you need to save? How many empty margarine tubs and yogurt containers are enough? Being frugal is one thing, but if you have more than you need, you are actually wasting valuable space. Keep just a few and recycle the others. Do the same with cardboard boxes, rubber bands, twist ties, and similar items you've been collecting. One way to keep this kind of clutter to a minimum is to find a container that holds only the amount you have decided to keep.

- **Consider buying less.** Do you really need more stuff? Think twice about buying things that require extra maintenance and upkeep, such as knickknacks that have to be dusted and clothing with special washing instructions. Think three times before buying souvenirs; take photographs or keep a journal instead.

- **Simplify your life with the 80/20 rule.** Most people use only about 20 percent of what they own. The other 80 percent is just taking up valuable space, getting in the way, and causing more work than is necessary. In other words, it's clutter. Keep your home clutter-free by making a conscious decision to surround yourself with only those things you love and use.

One of the advantages of being disorderly is that one is constantly making exciting discoveries.

— A. A. Milne

The Price You Pay for Clutter

The modern-day Libertarian Harry Browne once said, "Everything you want in life has a price connected to it. There's a price to pay if you want to make things better, a price to pay just for leaving things as they are, a price for everything."

What is the price you pay for clutter and disorganization? "Leaving things as they are" is most likely costing you one or more of the following:

- Space that could be put to better use

- Time and energy lost in looking for misplaced things

- Stress from knowing that you really should get organized but not knowing where or how to start

And, of course, there are the financial costs:

- How many times have you bought something you needed, only to realize later that you already had it?

- How many times have you bought something on sale (or on a whim) that ended up a permanent fixture in your closet or collecting dust somewhere?

- Have you ever discovered that something valuable was ruined because you didn't put it away properly?

- Are you considering a move into a larger, more expensive apartment or house largely because you need more room for your stuff? How much will it cost to move? What will be the additional housing cost each year?

- What items are you hanging on to that you could sell at a garage sale, on eBay, or on consignment to recoup some of your initial investment?

- What items could you give away as non-cash, tax-deductible donations? Do the math. If you are in a 28 percent tax bracket, a $600 donation of clothing you aren't wearing is a $168 tax savings.

Weigh the "price to pay just for leaving things as they are" against the "price to pay if you want to make things better." Yes, you will need to invest some time and energy to get organized, but you don't need to put your life on hold to do it.

Commit to spending 15 minutes a day organizing one area or task until it is done. Don't get discouraged about how much remains to be done. Just focus every day on doing something toward your goal, and eventually you *will* realize a substantial return on your investment in every aspect of your life.

Periodic Purges

The easiest way to maintain a clutter-free home is this: for every one item you bring in the front door, send one packing out the back door. Apply the one-in/one-out rule to everything from household items to clothing to paper — and even organizing products. Decide before you go shopping what you intend to let go to make room for your purchase. When you receive a gift, do the same. Keep in mind that what goes out does not have to be equal in value or size to what comes in.

When your child receives a new toy, donate an old one to charity. A good time to ask kids for a donation is just before or just after Christmas, their birthday, or another occasion on which they typically receive gifts. Keep a cardboard box in each child's room for collecting outgrown toys and clothes. When the box is full, take it to your favorite charity, a consignment shop, or even the nearest yard sale.

At least once a year, host a party. Getting ready for a party is fun and gives you extra incentive to do a thorough uncluttering. This is also a good time to rearrange your knickknacks and framed photographs and eliminate any that are no longer meaningful.

In January of each year, clean out your filing cabinet to make room for the new year's files. Save only what you need to save for legal or financial reasons, and discard the rest. Throughout the year, as you file papers, flip quickly through the folder to see whether it contains any papers that can be tossed.

Part 2

Room-by-Room Challenges

Some of the most challenging rooms to clean are those high-traffic areas where we work and play, such as the family room and office. The kitchen and bathroom present their own unique challenges, along with a particular need to disinfect to protect against the spread of harmful germs. And the laundry room should really be a much larger room for the work that gets done there, don't you think?

There's also the challenge of cleaning up those areas where we store all the stuff we don't know what do with. And finally, there's the great outdoors, which admittedly is not a room, but it can't be ignored in a book that's all about cleaning everything in and around your home. You get the picture. Now, here's how to deal with these challenges, room by room.

CHAPTER FOUR

FLOOR TO CEILING

Every room shares the common challenge of cleaning floors, walls, and windows. Thanks to the force of gravity, floors are pretty much an everyday cleaning challenge, while walls and windows are more of a once- or twice-a-year endeavor. With or without furnishings, clean floors, walls, and windows noticeably improve the appearance of any room while helping to maintain the value of your home.

Cleaning Floors

Most floors require only regular vacuuming or a light cleaning with a mild solution to keep them looking good. Use large, good-quality entry and exit mats at each exterior door to keep out dirt and other substances, such as oil or asphalt, which can cause premature wear on interior flooring. Encourage your family to remove shoes at the door, and wipe up spills immediately. Use mops with disposable cleaning cloths to make weekly cleanup fast and easy.

Follow the manufacturer's instructions on how to clean your flooring. If those instructions are not available, use the following care and cleaning instructions as a guide.

Hardwood Floors. As a preventive measure, consider placing mats at entrances to rooms with wood floors to prevent gritty dirt, which can mar a wood floor's finish, from being tracked in. As for keeping wood floors clean and glowing:

- **Sweep.** Sweep or dust-mop as often as you can. Use a wool dust mop to bring up the shine of hardwood floors. Do not use furniture polish on your dust mop or directly on wood floors, as it could leave your floors slippery.

- **Vacuum.** Vacuum wood floors as often as you vacuum your carpets. Use the hard-floor attachment, not the carpet beater brush, which can damage wood flooring.

- **Mop or buff.** Damp-mop polyurethaned floors occasionally with a mop that is completely wrung out, not dripping. Do not damp-mop waxed wood floors, as doing so will dull their finish. Instead, buff waxed floors occasionally to renew the shine, and rewax them every year or so with a wood cleaning/waxing compound.

- **Remove spills and spots.** Clean up spills immediately with a dry cloth or paper towel. Use a damp cloth to clean up a sticky spot. Use a clean white cloth moistened with acetone or nail polish remover to remove oil, paint, marker, lipstick, ink, or tar. To remove candle wax or chewing gum, harden the material with ice and then gently scrape it away with a plastic scraper, such as a credit card. After removing a tough spot, wipe the area clean with a damp cloth and then dry it with a dry cloth.

Wood Laminate Floors. Mop with a mixture of 1 cup of vinegar in 1 gallon of warm water, or with just plain water. As with hardwood floors, wring out your mop so it is only slightly damp.

Polyurethane or Wax?

If you're not sure whether you have a waxed or polyurethane-coated wood floor, sprinkle a few drops of water on the floor. If the water beads up, the floor is probably coated with polyurethane.

Ceramic Tile, Slate, or Stone Floors. Mop weekly (or more often in high-traffic areas) with a cleaner made for ceramic floors or a mixture of 1 cup of vinegar in 1 gallon of water. Do not use detergent or soap, which can dull the surface.

To remove surface stains from grout, rub the grout with a piece of folded sandpaper or a pink pencil eraser. For tougher stains, mix 1 tablespoon of bleach with 16 ounces of warm water in a spray bottle. Spray the bleach mixture onto the grout and use a toothbrush to scrub between the tiles. You can also try pouring peroxide on the grout line, covering it immediately with a towel, and letting it stand for 8 hours or overnight before wiping clean. If all else fails, you may need to remove and replace the grout. Sealing the new grout will help prevent future stains, and it's advisable to reseal the grout every two years to keep it looking good.

Vinyl or Linoleum Floors. Vacuum the floor and remove any spots from it before wet-mopping. You can remove a black scuff mark with an artgum or pink pencil eraser. Another trick is to spray a little WD-40 lubricant on a towel and lightly rub the mark. Wipe up any remaining oily residue with a sponge wetted with a solution of dishwashing liquid and water and rinse well. Then, on to the mopping.

- **New flooring.** Mop new flooring with warm water only or a mixture of 1 cup of white vinegar in 1 gallon of water. This may sound strange, but avoid using detergents or other cleaners, as they tend to leave behind a sticky residue that actually attracts dirt.

- **Older flooring.** To clean older linoleum or vinyl floors, try mopping with 2 cups of ammonia in 1 gallon of hot water. Be sure to ventilate the room well when using ammonia, and do not use ammonia on the floor if you recently used liquid chlorine bleach or a product containing any bleach, as the combination of bleach and ammonia can produce lethal fumes. Use a nylon-bristle brush to lift dirt buildup from grooves and dimples in the flooring. Follow up with a coat or two of acrylic floor wax to help keep the floor clean.

- **When all else fails.** If you can't get the floor clean by mopping, you may need to "strip" the floor with professional-strength ammonia or a vinyl-floor stripper/cleaner, which you can get at your local hardware store. Follow up by applying several coats of acrylic floor wax.

How To — CLEAN FLOORS LIKE A PRO

People who clean for a living know how to get the job done in the most efficient way. They also know how to extend the life of their cleaning tools through proper use and care. Here's how the pros do it.

SWEEPING. Holding the broom to one side, use short strokes to sweep debris into one or more piles, depending on the size of the room. An angled broom with synthetic bristles is your best bet because it gets into corners and picks up even fine particles.

DRY-MOPPING. Dry-mopping picks up dirt, dust, and other particulates from the floor and can renew the shine of your floor finish. Keep the head of the mop on the floor for the entirety of the mopping; picking up the dust mop during use will release particulates back into the air, and they will then settle back on the floor. When you're done, take the dust mop outside and gently shake out the dust before storing it, so that it's ready for the next use. Floor-cleaning tools that use disposable dusting cloths are a convenient alternative to traditional dry dust mops and can help reduce the amount of dust that ends up in the air.

WET-MOPPING. Always mop floors from the corners outward to prevent buildup in the corners of your floors. Before wet-mopping, use a vacuum, broom, or dust mop to remove dust and dirt from the floor. This makes mopping a much cleaner, easier task. To wet-mop, start at the far end of the room and mop your way backward out the door. Change the water in the bucket after mopping each room or, if rooms are small, after every two rooms. After wet-mopping, rinse the mop head well, using warm water. This is especially important if you used a diluted vinegar solution to wash the floors, because the acetic acid in the vinegar may cause the mop head to deteriorate. Also be sure to dry any metal parts on the mop when you are done with it, to prevent rusting. Change the mop head every other month or so, depending on usage. If the head is starting to fray or looks worn, it's time to replace it.

VACUUMING. Pick up toys, debris, and large pieces of trash before vacuuming. It's best to vacuum after dusting, or stirred-up dust will fall on your freshly cleaned carpets. Before vacuuming, select the height setting appropriate to the type of flooring: hard floor or level loop, shag, or plush carpeting.

Make slow passes on one section at a time. Use a push-pull stroke extending about 3 feet. Overlap strokes slightly until you have covered the area completely. Two or three strokes per pass are usually sufficient for light soiling; five to seven passes are necessary for heavily soiled areas. Work away from the wall where the vacuum cleaner is plugged in, to avoid getting tangled up with or vacuuming over the cord. Take care not to bump into moldings or walls with the vacuum, as it could leave black marks. Use the crevice attachment to clean along baseboards and other attachments as needed to clean hard-to-reach areas. *Helpful hint:* As much as possible, arrange furniture so that you can vacuum every last inch of floor without having to move anything.

Avoid vacuuming blind cords, string, coins, paper clips, gum, and electrical cords, as any of these could spell the end for your vacuum cleaner. Also do not attempt to vacuum up water or large pieces of debris. To clean rug fringe, use the dusting brush on the hose, and vacuum parallel to the fringes. The dusting brush can also be used to clean books, tabletops, lamps, baseboards, and drapes. To clean furniture, use the furniture nozzle (the small, wide tool that does not have brushes).

When you are finished, unplug the vacuum cord at the wall; pull only on the plug, not on the cord. Return the vacuum cleaner to your storage area. Check the filter bag. If it's more than half-full, empty it or replace it with a new bag, so that the next time you use the vacuum cleaner it will operate at maximum efficiency and will not release particles from the bag into the air. Also inspect the vacuum belts and replace them as needed (generally once a year). With a damp cloth, wipe the vacuum cleaner and cord clean of any loose dust or soil. Rewind the vacuum cord.

Carpets and Rugs. Vacuum carpets at least once a week. You may need to vacuum carpets in high-traffic areas such as hallways, stairs, and entryways as often as two or three times a week. See page 63 for tips on how to vacuum like a professional.

About 85 percent of the soiling in carpets is loose dirt. Frequent vacuuming will help prevent that dirt from becoming ground in and will extend the life of your carpets. The other 15 percent is oily, sticky stain that vacuuming can't remove. That's why it's important to deep-clean wall-to-wall carpeting every 12 to 18 months. You may need to deep-clean more often in high-traffic areas and in front of furniture or if you have pets or small children.

Don't wait until your carpet is heavily soiled to deep-clean. This shortens the life of the carpet and makes it harder and costlier to clean. In addition to making your carpets look better, deep cleaning will remove dust mites and other allergens and promote a healthier home environment. And hot-water extraction or steam cleaning, which is the preferred method of cleaning carpets, improves the stain resistance of your carpet by decreasing its ability to attract dirt.

There are a number of do-it-yourself methods for carpet cleaning. You can rent a professional-quality wet-extraction cleaner or buy a home cleaning system. But often the safest, fastest, and easiest way to clean carpets is to hire a professional. Some stains, such as rust, can be removed only by professional cleaning. Following are some helpful tips for hiring a reputable carpet cleaner:

- Ask for referrals from friends, family, colleagues, and neighbors, or ask a prospective cleaner for references.
- Beware of door-to-door solicitors or companies contacting you by phone.
- Find out whether the cleaner is bonded and insured.
- Look for a carpet cleaner who is certified by the Institute of Inspection, Cleaning, and Restoration Certification, a nonprofit certifying body for the flooring inspection, floor covering and specialized fabric cleaning, and disaster restoration industry.
- Check the contractor's record with the Better Business Bureau.
- Obtain an estimate from more than one company.
- Beware of pricing that is too good to be true.
- Do not sign a contract or make a payment without first receiving a written estimate.
- Read your contract before signing it.

KNOW AND TELL

Think twice before reaching for any carpet spot-remover product. If it does not remove the spot, you need to completely rinse the product out of the carpet before trying another stain-removal method. Even if the stain comes out with the commercial product, the chemicals in the product tend to reattract soil to that spot, making the stain seem to reappear.

CARPET SPOT TREATMENTS

Following are several simple formulas for removing most types of stains from carpets and rugs. The key to getting out stains is patience. Follow each step of the process. Some stains may require a second or even third treatment. Always blot; don't rub stains.

Water-soluble stains

alcohol • beer • milk • cola • berries • excrement • food dye • gravy • jelly • mud • washable ink • wet latex paint • ice cream • mustard

Treatment Formula	Instructions
Detergent solution	Absorb as much of the stain as possible with dry white towels. Then blot the stained area with white towels dampened with cool water until there is no more transfer of the stain onto the towels. If any of the stain remains, prepare a solution of mild liquid detergent (no more than ¼ teaspoon of detergent to 32 ounces of water). A clear, nonbleach liquid dishwashing detergent is recommended. Spray the solution lightly onto the spot and blot repeatedly with white towels, working from the outer edge in toward the center of the spot to avoid spreading the stain. Do not use too much detergent, because the residue will contribute to rapid resoiling. Rinse the spot thoroughly by spraying it with clean water, and then blot or extract the moisture. Absorb any remaining moisture by placing several layers of white towels over the spot and weighing them down with a heavy object. This step is necessary even when the carpet doesn't seem particularly damp.

Special water-soluble stains

blood • chocolate • coffee • wine

Treatment Formula	Instructions
Ammonia solution	Absorb as much of the stain as possible with white towels. Then blot the stained area with white towels dampened with cool water until there is no more transfer of the stain onto the towels. Prepare a solution of 1 tablespoon of household ammonia mixed with 1 cup of water. Dampen a white towel with the solution and use it to blot the stain, or spray the solution directly onto the stain. Absorb any remaining moisture by placing several layers of white towels over the spot and weighing them down with a heavy object until the carpet is completely dry. If any of the stain remains, follow the complete instructions for removing water-soluble stains with a detergent solution (above). *Caution:* Do not use this solution on a wool or wool-blend carpet.

Vomit and urine stains

Treatment Formula	Instructions
Vinegar solution	Scrape up the solid matter with a large spoon or spatula. Absorb as much of the liquid as is possible with white towels. Blot the stained area with white towels dampened with cool water until there is no more transfer of the stain onto the towels. Prepare a mixture of equal parts of white vinegar and water. Dampen a white towel with the solution and use it to blot the stain, or spray the solution directly onto the stain. Then follow the instructions for removing water-soluble stains (above).

Oil-based stains
lipstick • asphalt • butter • crayon • food grease • auto grease • permanent or ballpoint ink • oil paint • dried latex paint • shoe polish

Treatment Formula	Instructions
Spot remover	Depending on the stain, you may need to hire a professional cleaner. To try removing it on your own, start by blotting away as much of the stain as is possible with white paper towels. Apply a nonflammable spot remover formulated specifically for grease, oil, or tar to a paper towel and repeat the blotting. (**Note:** Be sure to wear protective gloves, as the solvent will quickly remove oils from your skin and could result in irritation.) Do not pour or spray the spot remover directly onto the carpet pile, as damage to the backing or adhesive underneath could result; use the towels to transport the solvent to the carpet. Repeat as often as necessary. Be sure that the room has adequate ventilation. If necessary, continue to blot the stained area with white towels dampened with cool water until there is no more transfer of the stain onto the towels. Then follow the instructions for removing water-soluble stains (above).

Nail polish

Treatment Formula	Instructions
Non-oily nail polish remover	Apply a small amount of polish remover to a white cloth and pretest it in an inconspicuous area of the carpet to make sure that the remover does not discolor or otherwise damage the carpet. Then work the remover gently into the stain, from the edges of the spill into the center to prevent the stain from spreading. Allow the remover to remain on the spill for a few minutes. Be patient. You may need to blot the area several times. Rinse thoroughly by spraying it with clean water to remove traces of remover, and then blotting to extract all traces of the remover. Absorb any remaining moisture as described in the instructions for removing water-soluble stains (above).

Candle wax or chewing gum

Treatment Formula	Instructions
Ice or freezing product	Freeze the gum or wax by applying ice or a commercially available freezing product in an aerosol can. Shatter the material with a blunt object and vacuum up the chips before they soften. Then follow the instructions for removing oil-based stains (above).

Note: Difficult stains — such as mustard, fruit juice, coffee, or tea — on a carpet made from polypropylene or other solution-dyed fibers may be removed with a mild liquid chlorine bleach solution (one part bleach to five parts water). But be careful. If you aren't absolutely certain your carpet is solution dyed, contact your carpet manufacturer to confirm.

courtesy of Shaw Industries, Inc., a Berkshire Hathaway Company

Spot-clean carpets as needed. The trick to preventing spots and spills from turning into permanent stains is to treat them immediately. Because many carpets are stain resistant, the quicker you act, the more likely you will be able to keep the spill from setting. Remove any solid soils by gently scraping the material off with a spoon, table knife, or spatula. Absorb wet spills by blotting them with white paper or cloth towels. Refer to the chart on page 65 for simple solutions to use for removing specific types of stains.

One of the simplest, safest, and most effective solutions for removing many types of stains (except greasy stains) from all kinds of carpets and rugs is 3 percent hydrogen peroxide, available at supermarkets and drugstores. It is the only solution for removing urine from wool carpets. Blot up as much of the stain as you can with a white towel. Don't rub; just lay the towel on the soiled area and step on it to help it absorb the liquid. Thoroughly spray or pour 3 percent hydrogen peroxide on the stain and cover it immediately with a white towel. Let sit for 8 hours or overnight. Do not lift the towel prematurely, as sunlight will turn the peroxide to water. Repeat as necessary.

For older or tougher stains, plug an iron into a nearby outlet and set it to "Cotton." Thoroughly spray or pour peroxide onto the stained area and then cover it immediately with a wet towel. When the iron is heated up, apply it to the wet towel and hold it in place for 15 to 20 seconds. Lift and repeat over the entire area of the stain to transfer the stain to the towel.

White Toweling

Always use white towels to blot and clean stains on carpets. Dyed towels may leave stains on carpets, especially lighter carpets.

Caution: Do not use a towel that is thin or has holes, and don't touch the carpet with the iron, or you may burn or melt your carpet. Also, because hydrogen peroxide becomes volatile at temperatures over 350°F (177°C), it's advisable that you turn on a fan or turn your face away from the rising steam. Blot the area dry when you are finished. Cover the treated area with a dry towel and lay a heavy object on top of the towel to remove any lingering traces of the stain as it dries.

Don't be afraid to try hydrogen peroxide. The 3 percent solution will not bleach your carpet. A 10 percent solution of hydrogen peroxide would do that, but it is available only in beauty supply stores. The only type of peroxide drugstores and supermarkets carry is the 3 percent solution. If you are at all hesitant about trying hydrogen peroxide on your carpet, first pour a little on the carpet in your clothes closet to test it for fading. If you do your own steam cleaning, try replacing half the recommended solution with 3 percent hydrogen peroxide for exceptional results.

Cleaning Walls

Some people like to wash walls every year whether they need it or not. Households with children or high occupancy and use may require more frequent wall cleaning. Also, if you allow smoking in your home or use a wood-burning stove or fireplace, your walls may start to look

CRAYON MARKS ON WALLS

One Challenge:

If you have a budding artist in residence, you may be faced with the dilemma of how to get crayon marks off the wall. Fortunately, it can be done.

Three Solutions . . .

1 Dampen a clean cloth with water and dip it in baking soda. Use the cloth to wipe the area firmly to remove the marks. This may take a little "elbow grease." Repeat as needed.

2 Spray the marks with WD-40 lubricant and wipe in a circular motion with a clean cloth. Wash away any remaining residue with a sponge wetted with dishwashing liquid and water.

3 Wet an eraser-type cleaning sponge, squeeze out the excess water, and use the sponge to wipe away the marks. This is by far the easiest, most effective solution.

make your own

Wall Cleaner

Dissolve ½ cup of borax in 1 gallon of warm water. Stir in ½ tablespoon of ammonia.

gray or dingy sooner rather than later. Generally all you have to do to keep walls looking good is to spot-clean finger- and handprints and smudges around doorways, on moldings, and on other frequently touched spots. But occasionally it may be necessary to clean entire walls.

Painted Walls. Semigloss and glossy paints tend to hold up to cleaning better than flat paint. Use a squirt or two of dishwashing liquid in a bucket of warm water to spot-clean or wash an entire painted wall. If a stronger cleaner is needed, mix 2 tablespoons of ammonia or 2 tablespoons of powdered laundry detergent in 1 gallon of warm water. This stronger solution is likely to remove some paint as well as dirt, so be sure to test the solution first in an inconspicuous area of the wall. If after the test the wall looks cleaner without having a changed color or finish, the stronger solution should be safe to use. Follow this procedure for the washing:

- Sweep, dust, or vacuum the walls first to remove cobwebs, dust, and loose soil. Before washing very dirty walls, wipe them down with a dry chemical sponge (available at hardware stores) to remove the top layer of grime.

- Fill one bucket with the washing solution and another with clean water.
- Begin with one small (2 feet by 2 feet) area at the bottom corner of one wall. Dip a large cellulose sponge in the cleaning solution and then squeeze it out; the sponge should be fairly wet but not dripping. Use the sponge to gently wipe the wall.
- Rinse the area you just washed with a second large cellulose sponge dipped into the bucket of clean water and squeezed out.
- Continue washing, working from the bottom to the top of the walls to prevent the cleaning solution from dripping down the dirty wall, which can leave streaks that are very difficult to remove. Work from one small area to the next.
- Wipe the moldings with a lint-free cloth, and allow the walls to dry.

Wallpapered Walls. It's always best to check with the wallpaper manufacturer for cleaning instructions. Clean spots as soon as you notice them, to prevent permanent staining. If the manufacturer's cleaning instructions are not available, add a squirt or two of mild dishwashing liquid to a gallon of water. Dip a sponge in the solution, squeeze out the excess water, and use the sponge to wipe away dirt from the wallpaper. Rinse with a sponge dipped in clean water and squeezed out. Blot the wallpaper dry with a lint-free cloth. If you need to use a stronger cleaning solution, test it first in an inconspicuous spot or on a remnant of your wallpaper. Never use an abrasive cleaner, and avoid rubbing, to prevent discoloration.

Paneled Walls and Woodwork. Dust the walls regularly with a soft cloth or the dusting brush attachment on your vacuum cleaner. To remove a buildup of soil, you may need to clean the wood with a special cleaner or cleaning wax made for wood paneling.

Washing Windows

When was the last time you washed your windows? In an ideal world, windows get cleaned — inside and out — once or twice a year. It's one of those jobs that many people dread doing and often hire out. If you decide to do it yourself, you can make the job a little less overwhelming by washing windows inside one day and outside another day. Break it down even more, if you like, by washing the windows on only one side of your house or in one room at a time. Whatever you decide, though, avoid washing windows on a sunny day, because they if they dry too quickly, they are likely to streak.

What You Need

- ❑ Bucket
- ❑ Cleaning solution (see page 71 for proven homemade formulas)
- ❑ Cloths or a sponge for washing
- ❑ Lint-free cloths (such as microfiber cloths or cloth diapers), paper towels, newspaper, or a squeegee for drying
- ❑ Chamois cloth (optional)
- ❑ Cloth rag

Newsworthy Window Washing

Many people swear by using crumpled-up newspaper to dry windows. Contrary to what you might expect, wiping with newspaper does not leave ink on the window. It is, however, advisable that you wear rubber gloves to keep the newsprint from leaving smudges on your hands.

Follow these simple do-it-yourself steps for professional results:

1. Outdoors, sweep the windows, tracks, and sills with a broom. Indoors, vacuum the windowsills and frames with a dusting brush attachment.
2. Dip a cloth or sponge into the cleaning solution. Squeeze it out gently; it should be wet but not dripping. Wash the windows, using circular strokes, working from the outside corners and edges in.
3. Starting in the top left corner of the window, wipe the glass with a squeegee, paper towels, a crumpled-up sheet of newspaper, or a lint-free cloth. Use vertical strokes on the outside of the window and horizontal strokes on the inside; that way, if there are streaks, you'll know whether they're inside or out.
4. If there are any drips around the edges of the window, wipe them away with a dampened chamois cloth or simply let them air-dry to avoid smearing.
5. Dry the windowsill with a regular cloth rag.

make your own

Glass Cleaner

No glass cleaner in the house? Sorry, that's no excuse for not washing windows. All you need is a bucket of warm water and a squirt of dishwashing liquid. Or you can try one of these proven formulas:

Formula #1. Add ¼ cup of white vinegar to a 16-ounce spray bottle, and fill the rest of the bottle with warm water.

Formula #2. Combine 3 tablespoons of ammonia, 1 tablespoon of white vinegar, and enough water to fill a 16-ounce spray bottle.

Formula #3. Combine 1 cup of rubbing (70 percent isopropyl) alcohol, 1 cup of water, and 1 tablespoon of white vinegar in a 12-ounce spray bottle.

Formula #4. Add ½ cup of ammonia and 1 teaspoon of dishwashing liquid to 1 gallon of warm water.

Grandpa's Best Window-Washing Formula

- ½ cup sudsy ammonia (a special formulation that has had a small amount of detergent added to it)
- 1 pint rubbing (70 percent isopropyl) alcohol
- 1 teaspoon dishwashing liquid

Combine the three ingredients in a bucket. Add enough water to make 1 gallon of liquid that will make for the cleanest windows you've ever had.

Cleaning Window Treatments

It's tempting to ignore the state of your curtains, blinds, shades, and other window treatments, but they should be cleaned once a year. With regular care, most window accessories will retain their good looks for a very long time. It's best to avoid using strong detergents or stain-removal products. Look for fabric care labels on drapes and curtains, or refer to the cleaning instructions that came with your window treatments. If you don't have care or cleaning instructions, following are some good general guidelines.

Drapes and Curtains. Gently pat and shake your drapes and curtains as part of your regular cleaning routine, to keep dust from building up on them. Vacuum heavy drapes with an upholstery attachment and lighter drapes with the dusting brush attachment. Wash sheer curtains in the washing machine on the delicate cycle; hang them while they are still damp, to help prevent wrinkles.

Horizontal Blinds (Aluminum, Faux Wood, Wood, and Vinyl). Dusting horizontal blinds regularly will help keep dust from building up on them. When dusting is not enough and a buildup of dust and soil needs to be removed, extend the blinds fully and turn the slats to the closed position. Wipe the slats from top to bottom with a slightly damp microfiber cloth, sponge, or lamb's-wool duster. Then open and reclose the slats in the opposite direction and repeat. Or, if you prefer, follow the same procedure, using a vacuum cleaner with a brush attachment.

The next step in cleaning depends on the type of blinds you have.

- **Aluminum, vinyl, faux wood, and painted wood blinds.** Wet a sponge with a solution of ¼ cup of wood oil soap or a few capfuls of dishwashing liquid in 1 gallon of warm water. Squeeze the excess water from the sponge and then use the sponge to wipe the blinds. Wipe the blinds dry with a clean, soft cloth.

You may find it easier to clean aluminum or vinyl blinds by hanging them outdoors on a wooden fence or outside wall, using a couple of strategically placed nails. Close the slats and spray the blinds with a garden hose. Open and close slats in the opposite direction and spray again. Squirt a small amount of dishwashing liquid into a dishpan or a bucket of warm water. Dip a sponge or soft-bristled brush into the suds and use it to clean the slats on both sides. Then rinse the blinds with a garden hose and allow them to dry.

- **Stained wood blinds.** Clean the blinds with a sponge or cloth dampened with a lemon-oil or other wood preservative. After cleaning the blinds, spray them lightly with an antistatic spray to help prevent them from reattracting dust, dirt, and hair.

Vertical Blinds (Vinyl, Fabric, and Sheer). Regularly dust or vacuum the louvers with a dusting brush attachment. Close the vanes in one direction and vacuum or dust, and then close the vanes in the other direction and repeat to get both sides.

• For Best Results

The squeegee is the best cleaning tool for windows and mirrors, because it doesn't leave streaks. If yours does, you need to either buy a new squeegee or perfect your technique. Start with the squeegee held at the top left corner and draw it straight down along the edge of the window. Then position the squeegee at a slight angle and use horizontal, overlapping strokes to pull it from left to right. (Left-handers will be more comfortable starting at the top right corner and then wiping from right to left.) Wipe the squeegee clean with a dry, lint-free cloth between swipes. Use the cloth to dry the edges of the glass.

When cleaning sliding glass doors, mirrored wardrobe doors, or very large windows, wash the top half and then use the squeegee to dry it before washing and drying the lower half. *Helpful hint:* Lay a towel on windowsills first to catch drips.

To remove light soil from louvers, sponge one vane at a time with a mixture of dishwashing liquid and warm water (one squirt in a gallon of warm water is sufficient), and blot dry with a clean white towel. If needed, individual vinyl louvers can be removed and immersed in a tub full of water with a few capfuls of dishwashing liquid mixed in. Lightly scrub the louvers with a sponge or soft-bristled brush; then drain the tub, rinse the louvers, and wipe the louvers dry with a lint-free cloth. Do not immerse fabric louvers in water, with the exception of sheer louvers, which can be removed and washed in the washing machine, using a mild detergent on the gentle cycle. Spin them dry and then rehang.

Roman or Pleated Shades. To start, fully open the shade, remove it from the window, and lay it flat on a clean, dry surface. In warm weather, it can work nicely to spread a vinyl tablecloth over a picnic table or on the lawn. Vacuum the shades with an upholstery attachment. To clean soiled spots, use an aerosol spray-foam upholstery or fabric cleaner. Spray the foam cleaner over the entire area to be cleaned. Gently scrub back and forth with a clean, damp sponge until the stains are removed. Remove excess water from the fabric by patting it with a clean, dry towel. Move the shade to a clean, dry surface to dry. Rehang the shade when it is completely dry.

KNOW AND TELL

Believe it or not, you can buy self-cleaning windows. They cost about 20 percent more than regular glass windows but need cleaning only about half as often. The glass contains titanium dioxide, which when exposed to the sun's ultraviolet rays sets off a chemical reaction that disintegrates organic matter. It also causes water to shed off the glass, taking dirt and debris with it.

Cellular Shades. Dust the shades with a feather duster or lightly vacuum the fabric with a dusting brush attachment. To remove soil, remove the shade from the window and lay flat on a clean, dry surface. Sponge the stain with warm water to which you've added a squirt of dishwashing liquid. Blot dry with a clean, dry towel.

CHAPTER FIVE

HIGH-TRAFFIC AREAS

This chapter covers high-traffic living areas — all the public rooms and areas in your home that get regular use, such as the entryway, family room, living room, den, home office, recreation room, and playroom. Regular use means that regular cleaning is required. One of the biggest challenges in cleaning these everyday living areas is all the stuff that gets dropped off and left behind. So, in addition to cleaning tips, this chapter includes a number of proven decluttering strategies.

Arrange for a Change

Organizing your home and possessions to fit your lifestyle can go a long way toward making it easier to clean. Walk through your home and look at what's lying around. Where do you tend to drop your keys when you come in the door? Where do you put things you need to take with you when you leave for work? Where do the kids leave notes and papers they bring home from school? Also consider how you use each room. Ask these questions:

- What, if any, items are not being used or enjoyed but are simply collecting dust? What could I do with those things?

- What items tend to get left out rather than put away? Why?
- Is there a space in this room that could be utilized for storage?
- What organizing products could I use here? Shelves? Baskets?

You may not be able to eliminate clutter completely, but you can work with it. For example, a very effective way to get family members to hang up their coats is to hang hooks in the entryway or hall closet. Hooks are easier to use than hangers. Having coats hung up gets them off the backs of chairs and the floor, which makes it easier to clean house.

PLAIN & SIMPLE ORGANIZING TIPS

- Place a shoe rack, stacked crates, or a bin near the door to collect shoes.

- Keep a tote bag or basket near the door as a temporary home for borrowed books and rented videos that need to be returned.

- Discourage the dumping of mail, books, and backpacks on the dining room table by keeping the table set with placemats, dishes, silverware, napkins, and candles.

- Put a wastebasket in every room to collect and minimize paper litter.

- Organize books, videos, DVDs, and CDs by category to make it easier for household members to put things away in their proper places.

- Store magazines and catalogs in an upright position, not horizontally. Not only will they look tidier, it will be easier to find and recycle older issues if you don't have to fish through a pile.

- Hide craft projects and other works in progress behind a decorative screen.

- Establish clutter-free zones in rooms where you entertain guests — no junk allowed!

- Lay down ground rules for everyday living areas; for example, "If you carry it in, carry it out."

Entryways

The simplest thing you can do to ease housework is to keep out dirt. Good-quality mats at each doorway, inside and outside, will greatly reduce the amount of dust, dirt, and grime coming in on the bottoms of shoes. A mat will also absorb moisture that would otherwise interact with dust and dirt to create spotting on carpets. During winter or wet weather, when mud is being tracked in, consider setting out a boot scraper. Also, don't forget to place a mat at the top of your basement stairs to keep basement dirt from being tracked into the main part of your home.

Use commercial-quality doormats, and train your household members to wipe each foot twice. Outdoors, use a coarse mat to remove as much dirt as possible from the shoes of anyone entering your home. Indoors, the best mat is one made of dense, level-loop, woven nylon pile with a nonslip rubber backing. A piece of level-loop or plush carpet is also a good option.

Shake out and vacuum the indoor mats as often as you can — at least weekly. Regular removal of the fine dirt particles that can lodge between the fibers will prolong the life of the mat. Vacuum the underside of the mat once a month. For best results, use a canister vacuum with a carpet brush attachment, or an upright vacuum with a beater bar. If a spill occurs on one of the mats, blot the area — do not rub it — with a clean, absorbent white towel.

Encourage family members and guests to remove their shoes upon entering the house by placing a shoe rack or a basket at each outside door. In winter or wet weather, set out rubber or plastic boot trays or bath mats to collect wet shoes, boots, and drippy umbrellas. This not only makes it easier to clean but also helps protect your flooring from water, mud, and salt.

PLAIN & SIMPLE ORGANIZING TIPS

- Remove everything that does not belong in the entryway.
- Store only in-season coats and accessories in the hall coat closet.
- If you have kids, put up hooks at kid height where they can hang their coats and backpacks.
- Keep a basket or tote bag handy in the entryway for collecting library books and rented movies that need to be returned.

Stash a supply of small towels near entryways to wipe your four-footed friends' wet or dirty paws.

The entryways you use most often should be cleaned along with your everyday living areas. In addition, once a month or so, clean dirty smudges off the door, especially in the area around the door handle. Also wipe down the moldings, any windowsills, the baseboards, and the switch plates. At least twice a year, inspect and clean light fixtures in the entryway and outside your home. Don't forget to clean the bulbs, too.

While you may not typically use the main entrance to your home, it is this entrance that provides guests with a first impression of your home. A clean and tidy entrance creates a warm welcome. Make maintaining the main entrance part of your regular cleaning routine. Vacuum, sweep, or shake out the outdoor mat. Sweep leaves, dirt, and debris from the entrance, including the porch, steps, and sidewalk. Use the broom to remove cobwebs from around the door and from light fixtures. Clean dust and dirt from the front door, and wash any entry windows as needed. Spruce up the entrance with a large potted plant on your stoop or a seasonal wreath on your door.

Living Areas: The Cleaning Routine

Declutter before you clean. Clear tabletops and all horizontal surfaces of items that belong elsewhere. Put away DVDs, CDs, and books. Straighten items on shelves. Toss old magazines, catalogs, and newspapers. Pick up toys. Return stray clothes and shoes to closets. *Helpful hint:* Grab a laundry basket in which you can toss everything that needs to be returned to a different room.

Everyday cleaning might include a nightly clutter pickup, the folding of throws and fluffing of pillows, and the spot-cleaning of furniture, carpets, and rugs. The weekly cleaning routine should include:

- Dislodging cobwebs from ceiling corners, light fixtures, windowsills, and door frames
- Dusting tabletops, bookcases, lamp shades, shelves, framed photos, and other items in your living space.
- Cleaning and polishing wood furniture
- Vacuuming and mopping

How often you need to clean everyday living areas depends on how much use they get and by how many people and what activities take place there. For example, eating and drinking can leave behind a mess that requires more frequent cleaning, whereas a formal living room that does not get much use may need cleaning only once or twice a month.

Cleaning Home Furnishings

Over time, without regular cleaning, furnishings will begin to look drab. Ground-in dust and dirt can stain fabrics and shorten the life expectancy of furniture, curtains and drapes, lampshades, and other home furnishings. When vacuuming floors, get in the habit of vacuuming upholstered furniture with the upholstery attachment on your vacuum cleaner. You'll need to do this at least once a week, and possibly more often if you have pets or if your furniture shows signs of needing a cleaning. Between vacuumings, remove pet hair, lint, and food particles from your furnishings with a tape-style lint remover or foam latex sponge.

Neutralize odors on furniture, curtains, and carpets with fabric refresher. Spray the refresher evenly on the fabric until the fabric is slightly damp, then let it air-dry. As the fabric dries, the odor fades away.

Treat stains on upholstered furniture immediately. Dab the stain with a clean white cloth wetted with lukewarm water. To avoid spreading the stain, work from the outside of the stain inward. If that doesn't work, try spraying 3 percent hydrogen peroxide on the stain and covering it immediately with a towel. Press the towel into the fabric and then allow it to stand for 8 hours or overnight. Repeat as necessary. Use caution when spot-cleaning older furniture; it's often best to clean the entire piece, to avoid creating spotty-looking fabric.

Following are additional cleaning procedures for specialized types of furniture coverings and materials.

Slipcovers. Slipcovers should be cleaned every six to eight weeks if you have pets or at least once every season. The challenge with cleaning slipcovers is to avoid shrinking them. The safest way to clean slipcovers, even machine-washable slipcovers, is to have them professionally cleaned. If you choose to do it yourself, don't try to wash slipcovers in your home washer. You'll get better results if you wash them in a larger commercial washer. Wash slipcovers in cold water and then use the air-dry or low-heat setting on a commercial dryer. To prevent shrinkage, remove the slipcovers while they are slightly damp, put them back on the furniture, and allow them to finish drying there. Always wash all of the pieces of the slipcover at the same time; otherwise, there will be differences in color over time, due to fading.

Leather. Clean smooth leather furnishings by dusting them regularly with a dry, soft cloth. Also vacuum any crevices regularly. Consider using a leather upholstery cleaner and conditioner occasionally to replace the leather's natural oils and restore its luster. To clean up a spill, wipe up the excess liquid immediately with a clean, absorbent cloth. Then use a clean cloth slightly dampened with lukewarm water to clean the entire area; for example, if the stain is on the seat, clean the entire seat cushion, and if it's on the arm, clean the entire armrest. Start at the outside of the spill and work your way toward the center. Never use saddle soaps, oils, abrasives, furniture polish, varnish, or ammonia on leather.

To clean nubuck leather, brush it occasionally with a suede brush to get rid of the flat and shiny areas caused by contact with skin. Some manufacturers offer special nubuck cleaning cloths to clean dirt and dust and raise the leather's nap. There are also products designed to clean stains without removing color or harming nubuck leather.

Microfiber "Suede." Sueded fabrics should be vacuumed at least once a month. Wipe up spills immediately. Dab — do not rub — at stains with absorbent paper towels or a nonabrasive cloth, and if they persist, use only colorless, mild soap suds or special cleaning products to remove them. Dry any damp spots with a hair dryer.

Wood. Clean and polish wood furniture weekly. Instead of using a feather duster, which just stirs up dust and moves it around, use an ever-so-slightly dampened microfiber cloth or clean cloth diaper and dust in the direction of the grain. The dampness collect the dust and also keep dirt particles from scratching the wood.

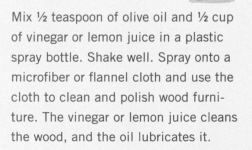

make your own

Wood Cleaner & Polish

Mix ½ teaspoon of olive oil and ½ cup of vinegar or lemon juice in a plastic spray bottle. Shake well. Spray onto a microfiber or flannel cloth and use the cloth to clean and polish wood furniture. The vinegar or lemon juice cleans the wood, and the oil lubricates it.

A white ring or milky spot on wood caused by exposure to heat or water is likely to be a stain in the wax and not the finish. Try one of these five simple solutions to remove it:

- Rub the ring with a flannel or cotton cloth moistened with denatured alcohol.
- Apply a small amount of toothpaste to the spot. Rub with a clean cloth.
- Apply a spoonful of mayonnaise to the stain and rub it in. Let it sit overnight.
- Moisten a cotton swab with saliva and wipe the stain away.
- Apply a mixture of equal parts of olive oil and white vinegar with a clean cloth.

Whatever method you choose, rub in the direction of the grain of the wood, remove the cleaning solution with a clean, dry cloth, and rewax if necessary. In any event, it's a good idea to wax wood every 6 to 12 months to help it retain its natural moisture.

Following are some plain and simple tricks for cleaning other home furnishings:

- **Lampshades.** Vacuum lampshades with the dusting brush attachment, dust them with a clean paintbrush, or wipe them gently with a foam latex sponge or lint-removal tool.
- **Lightbulbs.** A dirty lightbulb emits 20 percent less light than a clean one. And clean bulbs save electricity and last longer, because less heat builds up inside them. So make it a practice to dust bulbs regularly. If the bulb is downright grimy, clean it with a damp rag. But first make sure that the bulb is cool enough to comfortably touch. Otherwise, the thermal shock may break

the glass bulb. Also, do not touch a lightbulb with wet hands, or you might get an electrical shock.

- **Ceiling light fixtures.** Remove the glass casings and clean them periodically to remove dead insects and dirt. Dry the casings thoroughly before replacing them over the bulbs.
- **Ceiling fans.** Wipe the fan blades with a cloth dampened with white vinegar so that it will cut through grease and dirt. A specially designed ceiling-fan duster makes this job easy by eliminating the need to get out the ladder.
- **Books.** Clean the edges of the pages with a natural bristle brush, and clean the covers with a soft cloth. Align books with the outer edge of shelves to avoid dust buildup on those edges.
- **Live plants.** Spray plants' leaves thoroughly with water to simulate a cleansing rain. Put towels down on the floor before you start spraying. Do not clean hairy leaves this way, though, as they don't like getting a shower. Instead, wipe them gently with a cloth dipped in soapy water.
- **Artificial flowers.** Pour some salt into a paper bag and add the flowers. Shake vigorously. The salt will dislodge and absorb the dust and dirt on the flowers.

Q & A : "Burning" Questions

Q *What's the best way to clean a brick fireplace without using chemicals?*

A For the spot cleaning of concentrations of soot and smoke stains, use an art-gum eraser. For larger stained areas, use a stiff-bristle brush and a mild solution of dish-washing soap and water.

Q *What do you suggest for cleaning glass doors on a woodstove?*

A Dirty glass doors really spoil the beauty of a wood-burning fireplace. To clean, make sure that the fire in the stove has burned out, but the stove and door are still slightly warm. Coat the glass with a foaming glass cleaner or spray white vinegar on it. Wait at least 30 seconds, then use a paper towel to wipe it off. You may need to scrub any stubborn areas. If you used vinegar, you may need to repeat this treatment. When you're done, wet a paper towel with warm water and use it to wipe off the cleanser residue and any remaining soot. Wipe the surface dry with a clean, dry paper towel.

Q *What's the best thing to do with fireplace ashes?*

A Urban dwellers don't have much choice but to throw them in the trash. Country residents might be able to dump them somewhere on their property. If you're a gardener, you can use the ashes in your garden; just store them (outdoors in a sealed ash bucket) until you need them. Like lime, wood ash will make acidic soil more alkaline. Depending on what you're growing and the makeup of your soil, you might want to sprinkle ashes over your vegetable and flower gardens throughout the winter months. But check on the specifics first. For instance, lilacs and peonies grow best in alkaline soil, while azaleas do better in acidic soil.

- **Framed art and photographs.** Never spray cleaner directly on a framed piece, because it could seep underneath the frame and onto the painting. Instead, spray the cleaner onto a cloth and then use the cloth to wipe the glass and frame.
- **Candles.** Clean soiled candles with an absorbent cotton ball dipped in rubbing alcohol.

Cleaning Electronics

Clean the outside of electronic equipment weekly with a slightly damp microfiber cloth or other soft, lint-free cloth, and dry with another cloth. When you keep your electronic equipment clean inside and out, you protect your investment, optimize its performance, and prolong its life. Always read the manufacturer's suggestions before cleaning, to avoid doing any damage. However, here are a few general practices that are usually safe:

- **CD/DVD players.** You can periodically use a CD/DVD lens cleaner, a disk that you insert into the player. This will clean and remove dust and other airborne contaminants from the delicate laser lens. Remove fingerprints and dust from CDs and DVDs by wiping them with a dry or slightly damp lint-free or microfiber cloth in a straight line from the center of the disc toward the outer edge. Always hold CDs and DVDs by the edges to prevent finger smudges.

- **VCRs and videocassettes.** If your picture playback is blurred or interrupted, dirt may have accumulated on the video heads. Before you run to an electronics repair shop, try cleaning the video heads. Simply playing a good-quality blank videocassette is the safest method. If the playback has snow or noise, use a head cleaner — a videocassette that cleans the VCR as you play it. Head cleaners are available "wet" or "dry"; most technicians prefer the wet style, as it tends to be less abrasive. Keep in mind that cleaning video heads removes only the dirt and grease that is currently on the heads. As you play more cassettes, especially high-use cassettes from a video store, the heads will get dirty again. Using a head-cleaning cassette too often can cause premature failure of the VCR, so you might be better off having the heads professionally cleaned. Keep videocassettes in a dust-free, smoke-free environment and away from heat and direct sunlight. Plastic storage boxes are best for long-term storage. Store cassettes rewound and upright, rather than lying flat.

- **Audiocassette players.** Cassettes that jam, poor sound quality, and other problems may be due to dirty heads, capstans, or pinch rollers. Clean these parts with a cotton swab moistened with commercial head/pinch roller cleaner or rubbing (isopropyl) alcohol. Refer to your owner's manual if you are uncertain about which parts to clean, or have the player professionally serviced.

- **Speakers.** Dust your speaker covers frequently with a feather duster to prevent dust buildup. Periodically wipe the cabinet with a soft, damp cloth and wipe with a dry cloth.

- **Television.** Remove dirt and dust from exterior surfaces by wiping them with a soft cloth that has been immersed in lukewarm water and wrung out as much as possible. Even if the unit is heavily soiled, do not apply cleaner directly to it. Instead, soak a cloth in a solution of water mixed with just a drop of dishwashing liquid. Then wring out the cloth, wipe the unit clean, and finish by wiping with a dry cloth. Wipe the screen from time to time with a dry microfiber cloth or other soft, dry cloth.

Cleaning Your Computer

Have you looked closely at your computer lately? If you haven't cleaned it in a while, it's time to wipe away the accumulation of dust and dirt. Before getting started, though, be sure to turn it off and unplug it.

- **Casing (for monitor and hard drive).** Once a month or as needed, clean the computer casing. Never apply a cleaning solution directly to the computer casing. A microfiber cloth slightly dampened with lukewarm water is generally all you need to clean dust and dirt from the computer. To remove heavy soiling, soak a cloth in a solution of water mixed with just a drop of dishwashing liquid. Then wring out the cloth, wipe the unit clean, and finish by wiping with a dry cloth. Use a handheld vacuum or a vacuum attachment to remove any buildup of dust and dirt, especially at the back of the unit, but also around the disk drives. You can also use canned compressed air, available at any office-supply store, to blow away dust from those areas.

- **Monitor screen.** Due to its strong electromagnetic field, the monitor screen is a dust magnet. Get in the habit of cleaning it once a week, or keep your cleaning supplies handy and do it whenever you happen to think of it. To make it easier to see dust, fingerprints, and other grime, turn the monitor off. Dampen a microfiber cleaning cloth with lukewarm water, or spray a soft, lint-free cloth with glass cleaner that does not contain ammonia, and use the cloth to wipe the screen. Never spray any cleaning product directly on the monitor. To clean a laptop or liquid crystal display (LCD) screen, shut down the system and disconnect the power. Wipe the screen with a microfiber cloth. If additional cleaning is required, apply an LCD cleaning solution (or mixture of equal parts of rubbing alcohol and water) to the cloth and gently wipe the screen from top to bottom in single strokes to avoid redepositing soils back on screen. You can also purchase premoistened wipes for this purpose. Do not use paper towels or tissues, as they can be too abrasive. Allow the screen to dry before restarting the system or closing the laptop.

- **Keyboard.** To remove dust and debris from around and beneath keys, vacuum your keyboard with a special handheld keyboard vacuum or vacuum attachment. You might also try using a can of compressed air. Spray short blasts of air between keys to dislodge dust, dirt, and crumbs. Do not shake your laptop upside down in an attempt to remove debris from underneath the keyboard; because the central processing unit (CPU) and keyboard are all one unit, you're apt to damage the computer. To clean grimy key tops, wipe them with a soft cloth dampened with rubbing alcohol. If keys are sticky from a spilled beverage, you may need to take the keyboard apart (only if you know how!) to clean it, take it to a repair shop to have it cleaned, or buy a new one.

- **Floppy drive.** Clean the drive periodically with a floppy-drive-cleaning diskette. Follow the manufacturer's directions for use. Wait five minutes before using the drive, to allow it to dry.

- **CD and DVD drives.** Clean the drives periodically with a cleaning diskette designed for that purpose. Follow the manufacturer's directions for use.

- **Mouse.** It's time to clean your mouse when it starts behaving badly. The problem is that dirt and dust accumulated inside the mouse interfere with signals to your computer. If the mouse is connected to your computer, unplug it. Turn it over, twist the removable cover counterclockwise to release it, and take out the ball. (Some mouses allow you to just pop out the ball, without removing the cover.) Wash the ball with dishwashing liquid and water or glass cleaner, and allow it to air-dry or dry it with a lint-free cloth. Spray compressed air inside the mouse to dislodge dust and dirt. Dip a cotton swab in rubbing alcohol and use it to clean the roller wheels. Finally, put the mouse back together. Also clean the mouse pad, so that any debris or oil that is on it won't be transferred right back to the mouse. Most pads can be washed in the sink with dishwashing liquid and hot water. Dry overnight.

Cleaning Up Your Hard Drive

Regular cleanup of your computer's hard drive will help keep it operating at peak performance. Cleanup includes deleting unneeded files, archiving old files, reorganizing hard drive space, uninstalling unused programs, and checking for spyware. Different computers and operating systems have different ways of accomplishing these tasks, so check your user manual for the correct procedures. You might need to purchase special software that will take care of some of these functions. The time and research

you put into learning how to do some of these procedures will pay off, as you will enjoy a more efficient, faster system.

It's a good idea to perform these cleanup activities every three months or so. Write the task in your calendar now as a reminder. Always back up data before starting any computer cleanup activities, in case you accidentally delete something you did not intend to delete.

- **Uninstall unused programs.** Unused programs take up hard drive space and, in some cases, memory, which slows down your computer. However, deleting a software icon from your desktop does not remove the associated program. Check your owner's manual for the proper way to uninstall the programs you no longer use. If you change your mind later and want one back, you usually can reinstall it from the original owner's CDs that came with your computer, or you can download it from the Internet.
- **Defragment your hard drive.** When you save files, they are stored randomly on the hard drive; sometimes they are even broken into pieces to fit whatever space is available. Defragmenting your hard drive reorganizes those scattered pieces, allowing your computer to find a file more quickly when you ask for it. This process can take a while and is best performed when you are not using your computer, as it will slow the system down.
- **Delete temporary files.** Every time you go online, your computer saves the pages you visited in temporary Internet files, which reside on your hard drive until you delete them. If you

surf online frequently, you may want to delete temporary files once a month; less-frequent surfers can do this once every three months. Deleting temporary files is a very safe process that will not harm any of your other files.
- **Delete or archive files.** Nonprogram files such as text documents don't take up much space on your hard drive, but music and photographs do. If your hard drive is filling up, you may wish to delete files you no longer need or archive entire folders on a CD or other storage device.
- **Check for spyware.** Spyware and adware are deceptive advertising tools consisting of software that is remotely installed on your computer without your consent, while you are online. This software causes pop-up ads, redirects you to the advertiser's search pages, and generally decreases your productivity. Periodically run a spyware detection program to find and remove unauthorized auto-run software from your hard drive. Windows users can go to www.adaware.com to download free spyware software.

Minimizing Paper Pileup

If there's one thing that clutters up a home fast, it's paper in all of its many forms. The best strategy for avoiding paper pileup is a three-part approach:

1. Limit the amount of incoming paper.
2. Develop a system for storing paper items.
3. Recycle regularly.

Every day, open and sort the mail into five categories: for other family members, action items, to read, to file, and to trash. Immediately discard junk mail. (This is easiest to do if you open your mail near a trash can or recycling bin.) Don't even open it. You know what's junk. Place items to be filed in a folder labeled "To File." Place items to be read in a folder labeled "To Read," which you will take to your reading place later. If a piece of mail requires action, you don't have to respond immediately, but do try to minimize the number of times you handle it. For example, file mail you need to act on today in a folder labeled "To Do Today." Divide mail for other household members into stacked trays or vertical files, with each tray or file labeled with one person's name. This is also a good place to keep your "To File," "To Read," and "To Do Today" folders.

When you receive bills, save only the bill and payment envelope. Throw away the outer envelope and advertising inserts. If you can't bring yourself to just toss them, scan them quickly for information that may be interesting or relevant. Then toss them. Do be sure to read any important notices. Take bills to the place where you pay bills. Create a simple system for storing bills, such as a folder or large envelope labeled "Bills to Be Paid."

Don't let your "To File" folder get too full! File regularly to avoid the buildup of paper clutter. Do it daily, weekly, monthly, or quarterly, depending on the volume of paper. When you file something, flip through the folder to see whether it contains anything that can be thrown out. Once a year, purge old folders and papers from your filing cabinet. Put only what you really need to keep in long-term storage.

Just Say "No"

To reduce the amount of unsolicited mail you receive, send a postcard or letter asking to have your name removed from all lists to the Mail Preference Service, Direct Marketing Association, P.O. Box 643, Carmel, NY 10512. Be sure to include your name and address exactly as it appears on the mail you receive. Allow several months for the deluge to subside. Meanwhile, make a commitment to throw out every catalog and direct-mail offer without even looking at it.

If you want to stop telemarketers from calling, write to the Telephone Preference Service, Direct Marketing Association, P.O. Box 1559, Carmel, NY 10512, and ask to be removed from all national solicitation lists.

Beware of the paper clutter you create. Think twice before duplicating documents on the copier or printing out e-mails. Use the copier only when absolutely necessary. Store e-mail messages in folders on your computer instead, or simply make a note of the information you need from them and then delete them. Also think twice before bringing home free brochures and pamphlets. Read them on the spot if you can, and then put them back. Bring home just the information you need, in the form of a note jotted down in your daily planner or a small spiral notebook. Finally, throw away or recycle cardboard boxes, unless you have a definite or immediate use for them.

The Paper Plan

If you've got piles of paper everywhere — school papers, mail, financial statements, and the like — you need a paper plan!

- **Box it up.** Clean off your desktop or kitchen counter by gathering and putting all your papers in a box. Set a goal to go through the papers in that box to determine what to do with them. Meanwhile, if you are looking for something, you'll know it's in the box somewhere.

- **Fifteen minutes a day.** Plan to spend 15 minutes a day going through papers in piles and files. Pick a pile or box of papers — or tackle your filing cabinet. When your 15 minutes is up, mark where you left off and start there tomorrow.

- **Keep or toss?** When deciding what you need to save, ask yourself, "Do I need to save this for legal or tax reasons?" If the answer is yes, save it. If the answer is no, ask yourself, "Could I get this information again pretty easily if I needed it?" If so, toss it.

- **Clip and save.** Rather than keeping entire magazines for selected articles, clip and save just the articles and file them in binders by category, for example, home-decorating ideas or recipes. Insert the pages into three-hole-punched plastic sheet protectors. Use dividers to create subsections within the categories.

- **Dump the junk.** If you have piles of unopened junk mail offers, solicitations, and catalogs, dump them. Don't even give it a second thought, because you know you'll get more.

- **Shred personal information.** Be sure to shred preapproved credit card offers and blank checks, to reduce the risk of identity theft. Also shred bank statements and any other papers with account numbers or personally identifiable information.

CHAPTER SIX

KITCHEN

As the heart of the home, the kitchen gets more use than any other room. It should come as no surprise, then, that the kitchen is also the most challenging room to keep clean. There's everyday clutter to contend with, as well as grease, crumbs, and spills. But it's what you can't see that really creates a challenge in the kitchen — bacteria. Your floor may be clean and shiny and your cupboards organized, but a truly clean kitchen requires daily diligence against germs.

Fight Bacteria

It's virtually impossible to maintain a germ-free kitchen. However, you can get rid of 99 percent of germs with just soap and hot water. But you need to disinfect surfaces to kill the germs. (See the Q&A box on page 8 for more information about germs and disinfecting.)

When you're done preparing food, be sure to clean and disinfect everything that came in contact with raw eggs, meat, poultry, or fish or your hands, including cutting boards, countertops, and faucets. Use paper towels to wipe up raw egg and juices from raw meat, fish, or poultry, and then discard the paper towels (don't reuse them). Use a mild solution of liquid chlorine

KNOW AND TELL

According to a University of Arizona study, the average sponge has as many as seven billion germs on it. So disinfect those sponges!

bleach solution (1 tablespoon of bleach in 1 gallon of water) or a disinfectant kitchen cleaner; allow to air-dry or dry all surfaces with a clean cloth or paper towel. A nontoxic option is to spray the affected areas with a mist of vinegar, followed by a mist of 3 percent hydrogen peroxide. Let the combination sit for a few minutes, and then wipe with a paper towel. You can also use vinegar or a natural citrus-oil cleaner to sanitize surfaces.

Sponges and dishcloths are among the worst offenders for spreading germs around a kitchen. If you use a cloth to wipe down a surface contaminated by germs, the cloth itself becomes contaminated and will contaminate other areas when used again. Do not reuse cloths or sponges that were used to wipe up raw meat, fish, or poultry. It's also a good idea to use a designated sponge (in a different color from your regular sponge, so you can tell the two apart) for washing dishes and wiping counters that have come in contact with raw meat or eggs, to avoid cross-contamination. Replace sponges at least once a month.

Wash countertops, cutting boards, and your hands thoroughly with hot, soapy water before preparing foods and after handling raw meat, poultry, fish, or eggs. Maintain a separate preparation area for raw meats and poultry, with separate cutting boards, knives, and dishes, to avoid contaminating other foods with the juices. It's also important to wash any plates or utensils that have come in contact with raw meat before using them for cooked foods.

It's a good practice to fill the sink with hot, soapy water before preparing raw meat or produce. Toss cutting boards and utensils you use in the water as soon as you are done with them. Wash these items immediately and rinse them with clean hot water.

The best thing you can do to keep countertops clean is to keep them dry. Bacteria are everywhere, and they love moist environments. So wipe down countertops when you are done using them, and dry them with a clean cloth or paper towel afterward.

The Daily Routine

Start with today's stuff: Do the dishes as you finish with them, and wipe up all spills as they occur to prevent a tougher cleanup job later. It's also a good practice to clean up while you cook. Fill a dishpan with hot water and dishwashing liquid. Toss in used measuring cups and spoons, utensils, and other dirty items. Wipe pots and pans inside and out with a soapy sponge while they are still warm. Put away cooking supplies as you finish with them.

Make it a habit to wash the dishes every night, after dinner. Wipe any grease and food from your counters, backsplash, stovetop, and microwave with a soapy sponge. If you choose to disinfect surfaces, use an all-purpose disinfectant cleaner or a diluted solution of liquid chlorine bleach (1 tablespoon of bleach per gallon of water) mixed in a spray bottle to wipe countertops, faucets, cabinet and door handles, and other frequently touched surfaces. Sanitize sponges and dishcloths. Then sweep the floor and empty the trash and recycling bins if needed. *Helpful hint:* Keep a broom and dustpan handy, perhaps alongside the refrigerator.

If you start with a clean kitchen, it takes only a few minutes each day to keep it clean. You can even use a few minutes here and there to tackle weekly or occasional cleaning projects. For example, while you are waiting for water to boil or a casserole to cook, you can wipe cabinets or clean and disinfect the trash can.

Weekly Cleaning

Pick a day of the week on which to do your weekly cleaning so you can get on a regular schedule. Generally, here's what usually needs to be done.

- **Floor.** Your kitchen floor should be cleaned at least once week, and more often if you have shedding pets or crawling children or if you are a very messy cook. It's not necessary to sanitize the floors; just clean up the dirt. Most floors can be safely mopped with a squirt of dishwashing liquid in a bucketful of water, an all-purpose cleaner diluted as directed, or a solution of 1 cup of vinegar in 1 gallon of warm water, which works well even on sealed wood floors. For quick cleanups, try a mop that utilizes an onboard cleanser dispenser or a premoistened cleaning cloth.

How To DISINFECT YOUR SPONGES

Used sponges and dishcloths should be disinfected daily. Choose one of the following four simple methods of disinfecting.

1. Place damp sponges and cloths in the microwave oven, and "cook" them on high power for 1 minute. Do not microwave dry sponges and cloths; they could catch fire. Let them cool before using.

2. Soak sponges for 5 minutes in a dishpan containing a solution of 1 cup of liquid chlorine bleach and 1 gallon of water. Rinse them with clean water and hang them up to dry. (Bonus: This procedure sanitizes the dishpan at the same time.)

3. Launder sponges and dishcloths, using the hot-water cycle of your washing machine. Then dry them in the dryer to sanitize.

4. Toss sponges and dishcloths in the dishwasher with a load of dishes.

- **Garbage disposal and drains.** Food particles get trapped in the garbage disposal and drain, creating the perfect environment for the growth of bacteria and mold. Clean your kitchen sink drain and disposal once or twice a week by pouring ½ cup of baking soda followed by 1 cup of white vinegar down the drain. Plug the drain and let it fizz for a few minutes. Rinse with a pot of boiling water. Or mix 1 tablespoon of liquid chlorine bleach with 1 gallon of water. Pour the mixture into the disposal and let it stand for 5 minutes, and then flush with cool water. Freshen your disposal periodically by grinding lemon, orange, or grapefruit rinds with ice cubes and running water. You can also pour down the kitchen drain a strong brine solution of 2 tablespoons of salt in 2 cups of water to prevent and eliminate odors.

Spot-Cleaning Countertops

Moisture on your countertops can contribute to rust stains and ink stains from newsprint or packaging. If you do have an ink stain, you may be able to remove it with a splash of rubbing alcohol on a paper towel. To remove rust stains, make a paste of baking soda and vinegar and rub gently into the stain. The best solution for cleaning dirty grout is 3 percent hydrogen peroxide. Pour it on the stained grout seams and cover the area with a towel; let sit overnight.

- **Refrigerator.** One moldy item in the refrigerator can infect everything else with mold spores. Go through your refrigerator at least once a week and toss anything that is moldy or out-of-date.

Monthly Cleaning

Monthly cleaning is easiest to do consistently if you get yourself into a routine. Plan to do your monthly kitchen cleaning on or near the first of every month to help you remember to do it.

- **Refrigerator.** Clean the inside with a solution of 2 tablespoons of baking soda mixed in 1 quart of hot water. Clean the outside as directed in "Cleaning Large Appliances," page 94. Consult your owner's manual to determine whether the drip pan is removable; if it is, pull it out and clean and disinfect it.
- **Cabinet and drawer fronts.** Make up a mixture of ½ cup of vinegar or ¼ cup of liquid oil soap in 1 gallon of warm water. Dampen a clean cloth in the solution and use it to wipe each surface, but take care not to get them excessively wet. If necessary, use a solution of ½ cup of sudsy ammonia in 1 gallon of warm water to cut through grease.
- **Cabinet and drawer interiors.** Empty one cabinet or drawer at a time and use an old toothbrush to dislodge debris from the inside corners. Then vacuum up any crumbs, dust, and dirt. Spray the interior with an all-purpose cleaner or a mixture of equal parts of vinegar and water, and wipe up with a clean cloth. Use a damp cloth to rinse, and then be sure to allow the inte-

rior to dry thoroughly before putting back the items you removed. Shelf liners help keep the floors of cabinets cleaner and prevent black marks on pots and pans; if you have liners, check their condition during your monthly cleaning, and replace them as needed.

• **Trash can.** Take your trash can outside or stick it in the bathtub and clean it with hot, soapy water. Spray it with disinfectant and let it dry completely (to prevent the growth of mold) before returning it to its home and putting in a new trash liner. *Helpful hint:* Store extra trash liner bags at the bottom of the can or near the can for easy replacement.

• **Wood cutting boards and butcher-block counters.** Season all of your wood surfaces monthly to prevent staining and the absorption of food odors and bacteria. To season, warm up some mineral oil by heating it in the microwave for five to ten seconds. Wipe the warm mineral oil on the surface, in the direction of the grain, with a soft cloth. Wait for 6 hours, then blot up any excess oil.

• **Garbage disposal.** Clean the cutting blades by filling the garbage disposal with ice and running the disposal (with the water running) until the ice has dissolved.

- Take everything off your counters, clean each item, and then put back only what you use every day or at least twice a week. Find a new home for everything else.

- Move items you use only infrequently to the backs of cupboards or to another storage area.

- Put out a decorative bowl or basket to collect odds and ends.

- Pare down kitchenware to those things you have used within the past year. Give away or donate the rest.

- Store things closest to where they are used; for example, keep your pots and pans near the stove, and put the dishes and flatware near the dishwasher, the sink, or the table.

- Organize pantry items by category: pastas, cereals, soups, canned fruits, canned meats, baking items, sweeteners, and so forth.

- Hang a cork bulletin board inside your pantry or a cupboard door; use it to pin up notes, emergency telephone numbers, shopping lists, and stray coupons.

- Set limits on leftover yogurt containers, margarine tubs, and other plastics. Decide how many you really need. Toss the rest.

- Create a three-ring binder for collecting and storing recipes by category.

Cutting Boards

Recent studies prove that hardwood cutting boards are more hygienic than plastic boards. Knife cuts and scars in the plastic provide hiding spaces for bacteria that are nearly impossible to kill even with vigorous scrubbing. Hardwood actually absorbs the bacteria, trapping it inside. Any bacteria on the surface will die off within three minutes after the surface is washed and dried.

- **Cleaning.** After each use of your cutting board, scrape off any remaining food with a steel scraper or spatula and then scrub the board with hot, soapy water. It's generally safe to put high-density plastic boards in the top rack of the dishwasher. However, if the water does not get hotter than 165°F (74°C) in the dishwasher, all sorts of bacteria can survive. If you have an antibacterial cycle, use it. Otherwise, wash and dry the board by hand. If your wood cutting board or butcher block is stained, wet the surface and sprinkle it with kosher or sea salt. Let sit for 24 hours, then rinse it off. Make a paste of coarse salt and water and use it to scour the board or block to make the stain rise to the surface. Rinse the surface and then scour again, now with hot, soapy water. Alternate scrubbing with salt and soap until the surface comes clean. *Note:* Most bacteria cannot live in a high-salt environment, so cleaning a wood cutting board in this fashion also sanitizes it.

- **Sanitizing.** After cleaning them, sanitize wood and plastic cutting boards with a diluted solution of liquid chlorine bleach (1 teaspoon of bleach in 1 quart of water) or a solution of one part vinegar to five parts of water. Pour the solution over the board and allow it to stand for several minutes. Then rinse the board and dry it with a clean towel. Small wood cutting boards with no metal parts can be microwaved to kill any bacteria they contain inside and out: wet the board and then microwave on high for 5 minutes. Microwaving does not work for plastic, because plastic will not get hot enough in the microwave to kill bacteria.

- **Storing.** After the boards have completely dried, store them vertically. If you must lay them flat, prop up one corner to prevent moisture from accumulating underneath, which creates the perfect breeding ground for bacteria and mold. To remove mold from a cutting board, clean with a solution of 2 tablespoons of liquid chlorine bleach in 16 ounces of water and then rinse thoroughly.

Cleaning Small Appliances

Unplug appliances and allow them to cool completely before you clean them. Wipe them down with a damp cloth or sponge, and dry them with a soft cloth or paper towel. To clean appliances that come in close contact with food, such as mixers and food processors, wipe them with an all-purpose cleaner. To remove grease, use a sudsy microfiber cloth, followed by a clean damp cloth. Be careful not to get electrical parts wet. Do not immerse appliances in water. Avoid the use of abrasive cleaners, scrubbing brushes, and chemical cleaners.

Toaster/Broiler. Empty the crumb tray often to avoid the accumulation of food in the bottom of the appliance. Wipe down the outside of the toaster/broiler with a cloth or sponge and mild, soapy water and dry it with a clean cloth.

Coffeemaker. Wipe the outside of the machine after each use with a damp cloth or sponge and dry it with a clean cloth. Clean the hot plate as needed with a liquid cleanser (not an abrasive cleaner). It is generally safe to wash the carafe, lid, and filter basket in the top rack of the dishwasher, but check the manufacturer's instructions to make sure.

Over time, mineral deposits might build up in your coffeemaker, which will slow down the time it takes to brew the coffee. Decalcifying or removing these minerals from your coffeemaker can restore the flow rate to normal. If you have hard water, you may need to repeat this process as often as once a month, or whenever the brewing time begins to slow.

1. Pour 4 cups of white vinegar into the water container.
2. Set the glass carafe (with lid in place) on the hot plate
3. Snap the filter basket in place (without a paper filter in it), and switch on the appliance.
4. Let half of the vinegar flow through. Switch off the appliance and let it sit for about 10 minutes. Then switch it on again and allow the remainder of the solution to run through.
5. Repeat with a clean vinegar solution as many times as is necessary until the flow rate returns to normal.
6. Run two cycles of clean water through the unit to rinse it.

Blender/Mixer/Food Processor. Fully disassemble all removable pieces, and wash them by hand or run them through the dishwasher. If you're putting them in the dishwasher, clean the underside of food processor blades with a pipe cleaner or toothbrush and hot soapy water first. Wipe down the outside of the appliance with a hot, soapy cloth and dry with a clean cloth. Let all pieces of the appliance dry completely before reassembling it.

Electric Can Opener. Wipe the can opener with a sudsy cloth after each use. If you can remove the cutting part, immerse it in hot, sudsy water. If you can't remove it, use a soapy pipe cleaner or a toothbrush to scrub the cutting edge. (This is the way to clean a manual can opener as well.) Wipe the opener with a clean, damp cloth to rinse, and let it dry completely.

Cleaning Large Appliances

The big challenge when cleaning refrigerators, ovens, and stoves is to do the job without scratching them. As a general rule, clean all painted surfaces, door handles, and trim with an all-purpose cleaner or a cloth dampened with soapy water, white vinegar, or another nonabrasive cleaner. Rinse with a damp cloth and dry thoroughly with a soft cloth. Do not use paper towels, scouring pads, powdered cleaners, bleach, or cleaners containing bleach, because these products can scratch and weaken the paint finish. Clean stubborn grime with a paste of baking soda and water. After cleaning them, apply a coat of kitchen appliance wax or automobile paste wax to painted appliances to help keep them clean and shiny.

Microwave Oven. From time to time, wipe the inside of your microwave with a solution of 2 tablespoons of baking soda and 1 quart of hot water to keep it fresh. Some spatters can be cleaned up with a paper towel, while others may require a damp cloth. Remove greasy spatters with a sudsy cloth, then rinse with a damp cloth. Do not use abrasive cleaners, sharp utensils, or commercial oven cleaner on any part of your microwave. If you have a removable turntable, wash it carefully in warm, sudsy water or in the dishwasher. Be sure to replace the turntable before operating the microwave. If you have a

How To STEAM-CLEAN YOUR MICROWAVE

Here's an easy way to loosen food particles stuck to the inside of the microwave: Pour 2 cups of water into a microwave-safe container; for a fresh scent, add 1 teaspoon of vanilla extract or a few slices of lemon. Microwave on high for 5 minutes. Remove the container and wipe the oven clean. You can accomplish the same thing by microwaving 1 cup of vinegar in a bowl.

shelf and defrost rack, clean them with mild soap and water or in the dishwasher (use the top rack of the dishwasher for the defrost rack, to prevent the plastic from melting).

Clean the outside of the microwave, including the control panel and door gasket, where the door seals against the microwave, using a slightly sudsy solution of warm water and dishwashing liquid on a soft cloth or sponge. Do not use cleaning sprays or abrasive cleaners, especially on the control panel, as they can damage the finish. Even some paper towels can scratch the control panel.

Oven. Thoroughly cleaning your oven, whether gas or electric, is one of those dreaded tasks that can be avoided to a large extent by regular cleanup of spills and splatters. After every use, wipe out the cool oven with a cloth dampened with hot, soapy water or equal parts of white vinegar and water. If something has boiled over or spilled in the oven, clean up the mess, using one of the following easy-clean methods:

- Sprinkle salt on the residue while the oven is still warm. (If the spill is completely dry, wet it lightly first.) When the oven cools, use a spatula to scrape up the softened spill, and then wipe up any remaining residue with a soapy sponge. Rinse by wiping with a wet sponge.
- Pour vinegar directly on the residue and cover it with a damp towel until it has softened and can be removed easily.

When the oven has more residues and stains than can be removed by the above methods, or when it releases a smoky odor when you use it, it's time to clean it more thoroughly. Begin by using hot, soapy water and a nylon scrubby sponge to thoroughly clean the top, the sides, and the front of the oven door (except the glass). Then wipe with a wet sponge or cloth to rinse. To remove persistent stains on the door vent trim, use a soft abrasive cleaner and a nylon scrubby sponge. Use a glass cleaner to clean the glass on the outside of the door. Be careful in all cases not to let water drip into the vent openings on the sides of the door.

How you clean the inside of the oven will depend on what type of oven you have.

- **Non-self-cleaning oven.** Clean the door gasket and the area around it with a nylon scrubby sponge and hot, soapy water. To remove large amounts of oven grime, use an oven cleaning product. Keep in mind that oven cleaners are very potent. Be sure to protect your floor from permanent chemical damage by spreading several layers of newspapers in front of the oven and at least 1 foot beyond the drip line of the door when it is open. Wear rubber gloves to protect your skin, and use the oven cleaner only as directed on the product label. Or try one of the natural oven-cleaning methods described in the sidebar on the next page.

- **Self-cleaning oven.** Self-cleaning ovens use very high temperatures to burn off stains and spills. Before starting the self-clean cycle, use the oven-cleaning tips above to soften and remove burned-on spills. If your oven racks and broiler pan are silver-colored, remove them and clean them as directed below; if they're gray porcelain-coated, they can stay in the oven for the self-clean cycle. In either case, check your owner's manual for confirmation. Once the oven has cooled, use a wet paper towel to wipe up the white residue left behind, which is basically the ash of oven grime that has been exposed to extremely high temperature. *Helpful hint:* Because the oven gets so hot during the self-clean cycle and remains hot for several hours afterward, plan the self-clean cycle accordingly. A hot summer day is not the time to self-clean your oven. For safety reasons, it's also wise not to run the self-clean cycle while you are out of the house or sleeping.

After you've cleaned the interior of your oven, or while the self-clean cycle is running, clean the broiler pan and the oven racks. You can clean them with oven cleaner: Spray them with your choice of product and then put them in a trash bag; tie it up and leave it outdoors for at least 30 minutes. Remove the pieces from the bag and rinse them off with a wet sponge or towel. Then wash in hot, soapy water and dry. Or, if you prefer a less toxic approach to cleaning, try these simple solutions:

• **Broiler pan.** For easy cleaning, sprinkle the pan (including both the bottom tray and the grid that goes over it) with detergent while it's hot. Cover the whole thing with wet paper towels or a dishcloth, and let it sit for 30 minutes before washing as usual with hot, soapy water. There's never a need to clean the broiler element; any soil will burn off when the element is heated.

• **Oven racks.** Clean oven racks with an abrasive cleanser or steel wool. After cleaning, rinse each rack with clean water and dry it with a clean cloth. Or put the racks in the bathtub, cover them with hot water, sprinkle 1 cup of powdered detergent on top, and let soak overnight. (Place a towel underneath the racks to prevent them from scratching your tub.)

Natural Oven Cleaning

Start by wiping off all visible grease and removing any burned-on food, following the tips outlined in this chapter. Then try one of these natural solutions for cleaning your oven.

• Spritz the floor of your oven with water. Then sprinkle the contents of one small box of baking soda on the oven floor, until it is completely covered. Spray the baking soda with enough water to moisten it and let sit for at least 30 minutes. If the oven is very dirty, leave the soda on overnight; spritz it again with water before going to bed. The next day, use a wet sponge to remove the baking soda and grime. To clean the sides of the oven, make a paste of baking soda and water and use it to scrub with a nylon scrubbing pad. If necessary, use a nonsoapy steel-wool pad to gently scrub hardened spills.

• Preheat the oven to 200°F (93°C) and then turn it off. Place a small bowl of ammonia in the warm oven and leave it overnight with the oven door closed. (You can also do this immediately after using your oven, as it cooling.) The next day, wipe the interior clean with soapy water and a sponge. Use a nylon mesh sponge to remove baked-on residues. Rinse well with a wet sponge.

To minimize future cleaning ordeals, line the bottom of your newly cleaned oven with aluminum foil. Replace the foil when spills occur.

Ceramic (Sealed) Cooktop. If the cooktop or a stove beneath it has been used recently, allow it to cool. Clean the cooktop with a ceramic cooktop cleaner after each use, as follows:

1. Shake the cleaning cream well. Apply a few drops directly to the cooktop.
2. Use a damp paper towel to clean the entire cooktop surface.
3. Use a dry cloth or paper towel to remove all cleaning residue. There is no need to rinse.

To remove burned-on food, spread a few drops of the cleaner on the residue area. Scrub the area with a ceramic cleaning pad, applying pressure as needed. If any residue remains, repeat. Or use a single-edge razor-blade scraper at approximately a 45-degree angle against the glass surface to scrape it up. Then spread a few drops of the ceramic cooktop cleaner to the residue area and use a cleaning pad to remove any remaining material.

Traditional Cooktop (Electric or Gas). Allow the cooktop to cool. Clean the surface around the burners with a nonabrasive cleaner, then wipe the surface with a clean, damp cloth or sponge to remove all residue. To cut through grease on your cooktop, use a sponge soaked in white vinegar. Wash removable drip pans along with your pots and pans in hot, soapy water; soak them first and scrub them with a nylon scrubbing sponge if needed. For quicker cleanup next time, line the drip pans with foil; when the foil gets dirty, simply replace it. To remove stub-born, cooked-on spills, place the drip pans in the oven the next time you set it to self-clean. Buff non-ceramic drip pans gently with a steel-wool pad to remove any discoloration.

To clean the controls on your cooktop, check first to make sure that all the knobs are in the "off" position, and then remove them. Wash the knobs in hot, soapy water. Clean up spatters on the control panel with a damp microfiber cloth or a paper towel dampened with glass cleaner. Remove heavier soil with a sponge or cloth and warm, soapy water. Allow the controls and knobs to dry, then replace the knobs, making sure to properly align the "off" position indicators. Do not use abrasive cleaners of any kind, to prevent scratching the finish.

Exhaust Fan/Hood. Wipe off the hood of the exhaust fan with white vinegar to cut grease and dirt. Once a month, remove and wash the metal filter(s) in hot, soapy water or as directed by your owner's manual.

Dishwasher. Periodically clean the heating element by wiping it with a cloth dampened with vinegar. Then use the cloth to clean the soap and detergent buildup from the dispenser and spray arms.

Refrigerator/Freezer. Vacuum the coils on the bottom or back of the refrigerator at least once a year to keep the unit operating properly. At the same time, wash the refrigerator sides and the flooring underneath. Be careful when moving the refrigerator away from the wall. Pull it straight out, and return it to its position by pushing it straight in. Moving the refrigerator in a sideways direction may result in damage to the flooring or the refrigerator. Also make sure you don't roll over the power cord or icemaker supply line.

Unless you dust it regularly, the top of the refrigerator gets very grimy. For quick and easy cleanup, cover the top with plastic food wrap that you can simply peel off and replace every few months. Or cut a piece of fabric to fit the top of the refrigerator. Remove the fabric periodically, toss it in the wash, and then put it back in its place.

The best time to clean the inside of your refrigerator is before you go shopping or when it is more empty than full. First, toss out spoiled or out-of-date food. Remove perishables temporarily to a cooler and nonperishables, such as sodas and vegetables, to a nearby counter. Remove all parts of the refrigerator that can be removed and set them aside.

Dissolve 2 tablespoons of baking soda in 1 quart of hot water. The baking-soda solution will not only clean but also help neutralize odors. Wet a cloth with the solution and wipe the refrigerator walls, shelves, and floor. Rinse with a cloth or sponge dipped in clean water, and then dry with a paper towel or clean rag. You could also clean the interior by spraying it with an all-purpose cleaner, wiping away any residue with a cloth or paper towel, and drying with a paper towel or clean rag. Start at the top and work your way down. (Also wipe the bottoms and sides of jars, bottles, and containers before putting them back.) Never use liquid

chlorine bleach to clean the interior of the refrigerator, as it can damage seals, gaskets, and linings.

To remove dried-on food residue in the refrigerator, soak a towel in the baking-soda solution and lay the towel on top of the food residue. Close the door and let sit for 20 minutes, or until the material has softened enough that you can simply wipe it away.

Wash all the removable parts in hot, soapy water. Allow them to come to room temperature first, because the extreme temperature difference between the refrigerator-cold parts and the hot water may cause the parts to break when you immerse them. Another option is to place the shelves in the sink, spray them with an all-purpose cleaner, scrub, and then rinse. Do not wash any plastic refrigerator parts in the dishwasher unless the manufacturer states that is safe to do so. *Helpful hint:* Empty your dishwasher, pull out the lower rack, and use it as a place to drain and dry refrigerator drawers, shelves, and other accessories.

Use the same cleaning strategies for your freezer or the freezer compartment of your refrigerator. Wash and rinse the ice trays thoroughly before refilling them and putting them back in the now-clean freezer. Older refrigerators may also require defrosting. And don't forget to clean and sanitize the drip pan at the base of your refrigerator (provided it is removable) to prevent it from become a breeding ground for bacteria.

Finish up the job by placing an open box of baking soda in both the refrigerator and freezer compartments to absorb and prevent odors. Immediate cleaning of food spills will also help reduce odors. To combat a foul odor, soak a few cotton balls in vanilla extract (real or imitation) and place them in a small bowl in the refrigerator or freezer until the smell is gone.

Spotless Stainless Steel

For stainless-steel appliances that really shine, start by cleaning the exterior with a cloth soaked in a slightly sudsy mixture of hot water and dishwashing liquid. Wipe with a clean, hot, damp cloth to remove the soap residue. Dry with a clean cloth.

Starting at the top and working in one section at a time, spray the appliance with a furniture polish that contains orange oil. Wipe with a clean cloth in the direction of the grain (generally up and down for large appliances and from side to side for smaller appliances) until all streaks are gone. The oil not only removes water spots but also helps protect the finish against fingerprints and smudges. You can also wipe the surfaces between "oilings" as needed with a damp microfiber cloth.

Cleaning Sinks

Here's an unpleasant thought: according to Charles P. Gerba, a University of Arizona professor, there are more germs in your kitchen sink than on your toilet seat. Think about that the next time you are about to put produce in the sink to wash it. To sanitize your sink, use a commercial disinfectant, a solution of 1 part liquid chlorine bleach to 16 parts of water (except if you have a stainless-steel sink), or a cloth moistened with white vinegar. For regular sink maintenance and cleaning, read on.

Stainless-Steel Sinks. Always rinse the sink after use. Prolonged contact with salty and acidic food particles can cause pitting in the sink surface. Clean your sink by using a sudsy nylon sponge. Then rinse it and wipe it dry with a paper towel or soft cloth. Or spray the sink with an all-purpose cleaner or glass cleaner and use a soft towel to dry it. To bring out the shine and remove water spots, wipe with a cloth moistened with white vinegar.

Do not use abrasive cleansers, ammonia, or bleach, which can damage the finish of the sink. Also do not use steel wool. If you need additional cleaning power, wet the sink, sprinkle it with baking soda or another nonabrasive scouring powder, and rub it gently with a sponge. To prevent flatware and other hard items you toss in the sink from scratching up the finish, place a perforated rubber or plastic mat in the sink; wash this mat with soap and hot water at the same time that you clean the sink.

To remove white mineral residue that has formed as a result of water evaporating, line the sink with paper towels and saturate them with white vinegar. Also lay vinegar-saturated paper toweling on the faucet base. Let sit for at least 30 minutes. Then discard the towels, scrub the sink with a sudsy nylon-mesh sponge, rinse, and wipe dry.

For rust and other hard-to-remove stains, try an all-metal polish or stainless-steel cleanser. Apply the polish or cleanser, scrub the surface gently with a soft cloth, and then rinse all surfaces thoroughly and dry with a soft cloth.

SMART PURCHASE

If you're in the market for a child's high chair, look for one with a seat covering or entire seat panel that comes off, for easier cleaning. Choose patterns over solids for the seat cushion; patterns conceal stains better. And keep in mind that vinyl is easier to spot-clean than cloth. The new pop-out, tray-within-a-tray feature on some models is nice because it actually fits in a dishwasher.

Ceramic Sinks. Clean your ceramic sink with a nonabrasive liquid or cream cleanser. Do not use bleach or abrasive cleaners. Remove stubborn stains and scuff marks, such as marks from aluminum saucepans, with a sponge soaked in — believe it or not — club soda.

Cast-Iron Sinks. Rinse thoroughly and use a soft cloth to dry after each use. To clean the sink, wet the surface, sprinkle with baking soda, and gently scrub with a nylon scrub sponge. Use abrasive cleaners only in an attempt to remove stubborn stains, and even then only sparingly. Do not leave in the sink dirty dishes, coffee grounds, tea bags, and other food items that could potentially stain the finish.

Faucets. Remove fingerprints, water spots, and germs from chrome faucets and fixtures with a cloth saturated with white vinegar or a disposable kitchen wipe.

Dishwashing by Hand

As often as we all do this, you'd think we already know how — and we probably do know the basics. But a few extra pointers won't hurt. You might learn a new trick or two.

1. Presoak heavily soiled pans and dishes. Put a few drops of liquid dishwashing detergent or sprinkle a little baking soda (except if you are washing aluminum pots and pans) in the dirty pans and dishes and fill with hot water. Let them soak until you are ready to wash dishes, or at least 30 minutes for heavily soiled items.

To clean badly burned-on food from a non-aluminum pot, fill the pot with 2 cups of water and 2 tablespoons of baking soda. Put it on the stovetop and bring the water to a boil. Remove the pot from the burner and add 1 tablespoon of dishwashing liquid. Allow the water to cool and then pour it out. If necessary, sprinkle the pan with baking soda and scrub with a nylon-mesh sponge. Rinse well.

Don't forget to clean the bottom of frying pans after each use. Use hot water and soap-filled steel-wool pads to remove stubborn grease.

2. The actual washing. Fill up a dishpan with hot water and a few squirts of liquid dish detergent. If dishwashing is a chore you dread, a little aromatherapy might help; try a dish detergent with the scent of lemon, apple, orange, or lavender. Some dish detergents even have ingredients that help soften your hands.

As a general rule, hand-wash items from least dirty to most dirty, which usually takes the following order:

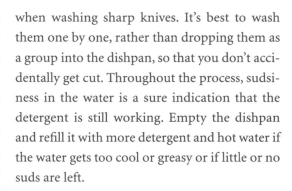

- Glasses
- Cups and mugs
- Flatware
- Sharp knives
- Lightly soiled dishes
- More heavily soiled dishes
- Pots and pans

Submerge items in the dishpan and use a dishcloth or sponge to wash them. Do be careful when washing sharp knives. It's best to wash them one by one, rather than dropping them as a group into the dishpan, so that you don't accidentally get cut. Throughout the process, sudsiness in the water is a sure indication that the detergent is still working. Empty the dishpan and refill it with more detergent and hot water if the water gets too cool or greasy or if little or no suds are left.

3. Rinse and dry. After washing them, rinse items one by one or stack them in a drainer with a drain board and rinse them all at once. If you have a double sink, rinse soapy dishes over the second sink. If you have a single sink, do your best to avoid getting rinse water in the dishpan, to avoid diluting the detergent. The hotter the rinse water, the faster dishes will air-dry. Air drying is actually more sanitary than towel drying. But towel drying is the best way to prevent spotting of glasses and allows you to buff flatware. Paper towels may be a better bet for drying pots and pans that could leave traces of grease on a cloth towel.

•EVERYDAY SOLUTION

Stained Plastic

Spray plastic food containers with nonstick cooking spray before pouring in tomato-based sauces, to prevent stains. To remove red sauce stains as well as onion and garlic odors from storage containers, use a plastic-cleaning booster in your dishwasher, along with your regular dishwasher detergent.

Automatic Dishwashing

Some people don't mind doing dishes by hand; others throw everything into the dishwasher. The nice thing about using a dishwasher is that it makes kitchen cleanup faster and easier. Another plus: newer dishwashers use about half as much water as washing by hand.

- **Loading.** There *is* a right way to load your particular dishwasher. Refer to your owner's manual for instructions on how to load properly. For best results, place the dirtier side of dishes so that they face the sprayer, and avoid overloading the dishwasher. Load dishwasher-safe plastic items in the top rack to avoid distortion due to heat. Place sharp knives pointed side down in the dishwasher utensil basket, or lay them flat on the top rack to prevent injury during the loading or unloading. Think twice before loading fragile items such as crystal, decorated glassware, and handpainted or antique china, which may become damaged by the force and temperature of the water. Other questionable items are those made of cast iron, wood, and aluminum. Check with the manufacturer to make sure that these items are dishwasher-safe. When in doubt, leave them out and hand-wash them.

- **Prerinsing.** With newer dishwashers, it's not necessary to prerinse dishes unless you plan to load them into the dishwasher but not run it for several days. Simply scrape off any excess food and let the dishwasher do the rest. If you do need to rinse dishes, you could load them without prerinsing and run the dishwasher on the "rinse only" cycle at the end of each day until you have a full load or are ready to start the wash cycle.

- **Washing.** Put dishwasher detergent in the main cup and the prerinse cup (or the main cup only, for detergent tablets). If you have soft water, fill both cups only halfway. If you have hard water, adding more detergent may yield better cleaning results. Use a rinse agent to help prevent spotting on flatware and glasses, especially if you have hard water. A rinse agent also helps dishes dry faster, because the water rinses off more completely. If you don't have a dispenser for the rinse agent, use a solid rinse agent, following the manufacturer's instructions. Most newer dishwashers have a heat booster; if yours does not, run hot water in the sink for a few minutes before starting the dishwasher, to ensure that the water filling the dishwasher is hot. If small particles of food or detergent are left on dishes after the wash cycle is complete, or if there's an odor in your dishwasher, the filter or air gap may need cleaning. Check your owner's manual for cleaning instructions.

- **Detergent.** Store all dishwasher detergent in a cool, dry place and close the package tightly to prevent it from becoming caked or lumpy. You might want to buy detergent in small quantities and aim to use up what you have within one to two months of purchase. If you tend to pile up dishes in the sink before putting them in the dishwasher, get in the habit of sprinkling them with baking soda. When you get ready to wash them in the dishwasher, you will be able to use less detergent. Always keep detergent in its original labeled container and store it out of reach of children and pets. Also be careful to not leave detergent in the dispenser cup, where it may be found and accidentally ingested by children. Use dishwasher detergent only as intended. It is formulated specifically for washing dishes in the dishwasher and could be damaging if used for any other purpose.

KNOW AND TELL

Some antibacterial dishwashing liquids contain ammonia. To avoid creating dangerous fumes, be careful not to combine these products with those containing bleach.

Washing Flatware

To hand-wash all types of flatware, use warm, sudsy water. Rinse well and dry immediately. You also can wash stainless-steel, sterling, and silver-plated flatware in the dishwasher. Following are some tips for doing so.

- To prevent damage to silver, do not mix stainless-steel and sterling-silver flatware in the same basket in the dishwasher.
- Avoid lemon-scented dishwasher detergents for loads containing stainless-steel flatware, as these detergents can damage stainless steel.

- Prerinse stainless-steel flatware immediately after use, before loading in the dishwasher.
- Position flatware with handles down, and avoid crowding in the basket. Try to mix spoons, forks, and knives in the basket to prevent like items from nesting.
- Do not spill dry detergent on wet flatware; it may cause dark spots. These can be removed with silver or stainless-steel polish. If possible, move the silverware basket away from the detergent dispenser cup.
- Use the gentle or energy-saver dry cycle to prevent heat spots from forming on your flatware.

Other tips for washing flatware, whether by hand or in the dishwasher, depend on what type of flatware you have.

- **Stainless steel.** Wash or rinse stainless flatware as soon as possible after use. Prolonged contact with acidic foods, milk, and salt can cause discoloration, corroding, or pitting. Never let flatware soak (even in plain water) or leave it unwashed overnight. Because knife blades are particularly sensitive to acidic foods, to soaking in water, and to air drying, it's a good idea to wash them promptly after each use and dry immediately. Do not store flatware in plastic or other wrappings that can trap moisture. Stainless does not require polishing, but you can bring back the original luster with a stainless steel cleaning agent. Never use any type of abrasive cleaner or coarse type of material to clean stainless steel. Wash and dry new stainless flatware by hand for the first few weeks to season it.

• **Sterling silver and silver plate.** Wash in warm water with a mild, phosphate-free detergent. Rinse well and buff dry immediately with a soft cloth for best results. If you choose to put silver flatware in the dishwasher, use a rinse agent in the wash so that water "sheets" off surfaces to prevent droplets from forming. All hollow-handled silverware should be hand-washed, as the handles may be loosened with exposure to heat and detergent in the dishwasher. Also do not allow hollow-handled silverware to soak in water. Avoid immersing silver-plated items for any length of time, as the base metal will corrode through the plating. Wash and dry new silverware by hand for the first few weeks or remove it from dishwasher after the last rinse cycle and hand-dry to enhance the patina.

Polishing Silver

Tarnished silver can be difficult to clean, especially if it has gone a long time between cleanings. Frequent light cleanings are simpler and less time-consuming than infrequent intensive cleanings. But the simplest way to keep silver untarnished is to prevent tarnishing by storing the silver properly.

Keep silver items in a cabinet or cupboard that closes securely enough to prevent contamination by air-borne sulfurs and chlorides. Do not store silver with plastic, wool, or felt, as these materials generate tarnishing. Use a dishcloth or cloth napkin to handle silver — except when using it to dine, of course! — because the body oils and salts on your fingers will also generate tarnish.

To remove tarnish, wash the silver first to remove any gritty or greasy dust and dirt, and

then dry it thoroughly. A silver polishing mitt may be all that is required to remove light tarnish, and you can use the mitt on a regular basis to maintain the silver's shine. For heavier tarnish, use a product specifically formulated for cleaning silver, and follow the instructions on the product label. If you choose to use a liquid silver dip, it is safer to swab the solution onto the silver and rinse thoroughly than it is to immerse the silver in the dip, particularly if the piece has hollow handles or feet, if it has wooden or ivory attachments, or if it silver plated. Don't make the mistake of trying to remove all the tarnish from decorative areas, where it actually enhances the appearance of the piece. Also, do not wear rubber gloves when washing or polishing silver, as the rubber emits sulfurs, which cause tarnishing. Instead, wear cloth gloves or hold the silver objects with cloths.

A quick way to remove tarnish from silver is to lay a sheet of aluminum foil in the bottom of a dishpan. Sprinkle the foil with salt and baking soda and fill the dishpan with warm water. Place the tarnished items in the pan and allow them to soak until the tarnish is gone. Then rinse, dry, and buff the silver to a shine with a soft cloth. *Please note:* This method is not advised for heirloom silver pieces, silver-plated items, or hollow-handled flatware.

Simple Kitchen Solutions

Some cleaning challenges are unique to the kitchen. Following are some of the most common cleaning challenges and their solutions, some of which are so simple you may wonder why you never thought of them!

CLOUDY GLASSWARE. To remove stubborn spots and hard-water film from glassware, load the dishwasher with the cloudy glassware. Do not add detergent. Start the dishwasher and allow it to run for 20 minutes, or until it is in the main wash cycle. Stop the dishwasher, open its door, and pour 2 cups of white vinegar into its bottom. Close the door and let the dishwasher complete the cycle. *Note:* If the glass still appears cloudy, it may be due to etching, which is a chemical reaction with the water or detergent. It's a tough way to find out that the glass was not dishwasher-safe, because the etching effect is permanent.

FLATWARE HEAT STAINS. To remove dishwasher heat stains from flatware, wipe the flatware with a soft cloth moistened with white vinegar or club soda.

FLATWARE RUST SPOTS. If rust spots appear on your flatware, you are probably using too much dishwasher detergent. To remove the rust spots, use a good all-purpose metal polish and rub vigorously.

BLACK OR GRAY MARKS ON DISHES. This is what happens when aluminum utensils rub against dishes in the dishwasher. Remove the marks by scrubbing them with a nylon scrub sponge and a little dishwashing liquid.

COOKING ODORS. The obvious approach to minimizing cooking odors is to open windows or turn on the exhaust fan when you are cooking. To remove particularly unpleasant cooking odors, pour a little vinegar in the offending pan or boil 1 tablespoon of white vinegar in 1 cup of water until the odor dissipates. You can also simply set out a bowl of vinegar to absorb strong food odors. Another option is to boil your favorite herbs or spices in water for a few minutes, until the heat causes them to release their odor. Pour the mixture into a bowl, add salt to it to discourage the growth of fungus, and let sit on a counter until the unpleasant odor is absorbed.

ALUMINUM POT TURNED BLACK. Remove dark stains in an aluminum vessel by cooking tomatoes or another acidic food in it.

CHAPTER SEVEN

BED, BATH, AND NURSERY

There's nothing quite like a clean bedroom and a freshly made bed to help you rest easier. All it takes is a few minutes a day and a minimum of effort each week to maintain a more healthful environment in your bedroom. The same can be said for the bathroom. A regular cleaning routine is the secret to having a sparkling-clean and fresh bathroom, especially with the range of revolutionary new cleaning products that practically do the cleaning for you.

Bedroom Cleaning Routine

Each morning, pick up and put away anything that does not belong in your bedroom, including glassware, dishes, and foodstuffs. Also, challenge yourself to make your bed in under 60 seconds. If it takes only a minute, you might as well do it, right? For a bed that practically makes itself, replace your top sheet and comforter or bedspread with a duvet and duvet cover. Just shake and fluff the duvet and your bed is made.

Before going to bed, invest the few moments it takes to hang up or put away clothes you will wear again, and put everything else in the hamper or in a bag that you will take to the dry cleaner. You may want to spray clothing that has been worn with a wrinkle-releasing product or fabric refresher to spruce it up for a second wearing. Wearing clothing an extra time or two saves the time, effort, and cost of doing laundry and helps prolong the life of fabrics.

My second-favorite household chore is ironing. My first being hitting my head on the top bunk bed until I faint.

— Erma Bombeck

At least once a week, throw open a window to freshen the air in each bedroom. Your weekly cleaning routine should include the following activities:

- Straighten the dresser top.
- Put away any clean clothes.
- Dust the wall hangings and other decorations.
- Polish any wood furniture.
- Dust the lightbulbs and lampshades.
- Change the sheets and pillowcases.
- Wipe down wall switches.
- Shake out any small area rugs.
- Vacuum the floors.

When cleaning the floors, don't forget to clean under the bed. Take a peek first to look for shoes or objects that may have rolled underneath. Use a dust mop on hard flooring to grab dust balls. At least once a month, give the baseboards a wipe with a damp cloth. Also, strip the beds and wash everything, including all washable pillows. *Helpful hint:* When changing linens, consider washing and then putting the same set of sheets back on the bed. It eliminates having to fold them, put them away, and get them out again later. For variety, switch to a different set when the seasons change.

Cleaning Closets and Drawers

Instead of waiting until that never-never day to come when you will have loads of time to clean out your closet and drawers, plan to spend 10 to 15 minutes each day until the job done. Tackle one task at a time. Make it your goal to let go of any clothing that doesn't fit, as well as clothes you haven't worn in a year or more and things that are just taking up valuable space when someone, somewhere, could really use them. See chapter 3 for tips on donating and selling clothing.

PLAIN & SIMPLE ORGANIZING TIPS

- Provide every bedroom with a laundry hamper and a wastebasket.
- Place a decorative bowl or basket on dresser tops to collect loose change and pocket items.
- Create storage space with closet shelving, freestanding drawer units, and underbed and over-the-door organizers.
- Install hooks in your closet or behind a door for airing worn clothes you will wear again before laundering.
- Keep the floor of your closet clear to enable you to vacuum it easily.
- Periodically take inventory of your closets and drawers; give away or sell anything you no longer love or wear.

1. One at a time, pull each of the four sewn corners of the fitted sheet over the four corners of the mattress. This is sometimes easier if you pull on the opposite corner, rather than the same-side corner, for the second.

2. Spread the flat sheet right-side down and over the fitted sheet, adjusting it so that the top lines up with the top of the mattress. (**Note:** The top of the sheet has a larger hem than the bottom.) Adjust the sheet until the same amount of fabric hangs over both sides of the bed and there is enough overhang at the bottom of the mattress to tuck it in.

3. Tuck the bottom end of the sheet tautly under the mattress.

4. Grab the hanging folded end at one corner of the sheet and pull it up even with the top of the mattress. Use your other hand to tuck the hanging edge under the mattress to create a new folded corner. Do the same with the other side.

5. Lay a blanket right side up over the flat sheet, lining up the top of the blanket about 6 inches below the top of the sheet. Tuck the bottom corners of the blanket under the mattress as you did with the flat sheet. Or try this timesaver: don't tuck the sheet (step 4) until the blanket is in place; then tuck and fold both at the same time.

6. Fold the top of sheet over the top of the blanket.

7. Insert the pillows into the pillowcases and lay them flat at the head of bed, with their open ends facing each other.

8. Cover the bed with a comforter or quilt, and top it with any other extra pillows (inserted into pillow shams) or decorative pillows you may have. Or, if you are using a bedspread or coverlet, place this over the top of the blankets and fold it down about 10 inches from the head of the bed. Lay the pillows on top of the fold and then pull the bedspread up over pillows to cover them, while keeping the fold tucked under the pillows.

Step 4

- **Start with your shoes.** Decide to give away or sell any shoes you no longer wear. Trash any shoes that are worn out. Put the rest away. Organize shoes by type (business, dress, casual) or by color. It helps to use a shoe rack, shoe cubbies, a shoe bag, or a set of shelves. Stackable, clear plastic shoe boxes keep shoes dust free and also make it easy for you to find a specific pair.

- **Take stock of accessories.** Gather all of your handbags, hats, belts, and scarves in one place. Put back only those things you enjoy wearing. Toss anything you no longer like or wear into your "Give Away" or "Sell" box (see chapter 3).

- **Remove out-of-season clothing.** If possible, store out-of-season clothing separately from in-season clothing. At the very least, move it to one end or the back of your closet.

- **Set aside clothes that need repair.** Schedule time to fix what you can fix or to take items to a tailor for repair. Discard the rest.

- **Try on what's left.** Take the time to try on everything in your closet. Choose to keep only those clothes that fit well and make you feel fabulous. Give away or sell the rest. If you can't bear to part with something, at least get it out of your everyday closet, where it's just in your way and taking up space. Instead, store it with your seasonal clothes. When the next season comes around and you see it again, maybe you will be ready to let it go.

- **Sort and hang similar clothing together.** For example, hang all your pants together, and do the same with jackets, skirts, blouses, and dresses. If you can, hang all your tops on the upper clothes rod and all the bottoms on the lower rod. (If you don't have a second rod, you can purchase one that hangs from the top rod.) You might also want to organize by color within each category of clothing.

- **Purge dresser drawers.** Use the same method as for your closet: Remove clothes that don't fit, things you don't like or don't wear, and out-of-season clothing. Try on what's left. Put back only the clothes that make you feel good.

- **Organize dresser drawers.** Store undergarments in top drawers and heavier items in lower drawers. Assign a specific type of clothing, such as T-shirts or workout clothes, to each drawer. If your drawers are overstuffed, consider getting a hanging garment bag with shelves to provide convenient storage for bulky sweaters and jeans.

- **Freshen closets and drawers.** Consider lining dresser drawers with scented drawer liners. You can also use sachets or unused fabric softener sheets under regular drawer liners and on closet shelves to keep your closets and drawers smelling fresh.

The Guest Room

Even if the guest room doesn't get much use, it still needs to be cleaned and freshened regularly. Once a month or so, remove the bedspread or comforter and toss it in the dryer for at least 10 minutes to remove dust and kill dust mites. Sweep away cobwebs; dust closet shelves, wall hangings, lampshades, and lightbulbs; polish the furniture; shake out any small rugs; and vacuum the floor.

A day or two before overnight visitors arrive, clean and refresh the room by opening a window. Clear space in the closet for guests to hang their clothing, and be sure to provide plenty of hangers. If guests will be sharing a bathroom, leave one set of towels for each guest on his or her bed to eliminate any guesswork about whose towels are whose. After visitors leave, strip the bed and wash all the bedding, including the mattress pad. Vacuum the mattress and, if desired, spray it with a fabric refresher. Allow the mattress to air out for a day, and then remake the bed.

Linens and Things

Once or twice a year, review what's in your linen closet. Donate usable sheets and towels that you no longer need to a charity. Thin, frayed towels can go to your local animal shelter. If you need to buy new sheets and towels, invest in the highest quality you can afford, for longer wear. With sheets, the higher the thread count, the better the quality. Better-quality towels absorb water better and are less likely to shed lint. In the next column are other suggestions for the care and cleaning of linens.

- Always launder brand-new towels and sheets before using them.
- Avoid using fabric softener in every load of towels, because fabric softener can decrease absorbency. If you wash towels every week, use fabric softener once a month.
- Dewrinkle sheets by putting them in the dryer for 10 minutes with a damp washcloth.
- Avoid using liquid chlorine bleach to whiten sheets, as it will eventually cause sheets to yellow.
- Consider storing a set of sheets between the mattress and the box spring, where they will be available for a quick change.
- Use a mattress pad to protect your mattress, to provide an extra layer of comfort, and to reduce the presence of dust mites (by allowing you to wash the pad regularly).
- Cover your pillows with zippered pillow protectors to protect them from dust and the oils shed by your skin and hair.
- Wash pillows as directed on the fabric-care label. In the absence of manufacturer instructions, wash them on the gentle cycle and run them through the rinse cycle twice to remove all traces of soap. Also run them through the spin cycle twice to facilitate drying.
- When drying feather pillows and down comforters, add two clean tennis balls to the dryer to help fluff up the down.
- Do not wash wool blankets unless you want smaller wool blankets; have them dry-cleaned instead.

The best defense against dust mites and other allergens is a good offense. Clean bedrooms and closets frequently and thoroughly. Vacuum and dust often to remove animal dander and surface dust. And keep dust mites under control with frequent washing and drying of bedding. Textiles that are infrequently cleaned are more inviting habitats for these creatures. Other ways to minimize allergens in the bedroom include the following:

- Encase your mattress, box spring, and pillows in dust-mite-proof covers.
- Wash linens weekly in hot water (at least 130°F, or 54°C) to kill dust mites. Drying on the regular or permanent-press cycle for 10 consecutive minutes also kills most dust mites.
- Put a hypoallergenic mattress pad on your bed, and wash it in hot water every week.
- Replace fuzzy wool blankets, feather- or wool-stuffed comforters, and feather pillows with synthetic or washable cotton blankets and antibacterial pillows.
- Wash pillows and blankets every month.
- Keep pets off the bed or out of the bedroom entirely.

For more tips on minimizing allergens in your home, see page 27 in chapter 2.

Bathroom Cleaning Routine

The bathroom has developed a reputation for being the nastiest, most dreaded room in the house when it comes to cleaning. But it doesn't have to be that way. Quick daily cleanups keep the bathroom clean and smelling fresh in between more thorough cleanings. The more often you clean, the less you have to clean. Nowhere in the home is this more true than in the bathroom. If you spend 5 minutes cleaning the bathroom three times a week, it takes only 15 minutes total. But if you wait to do it once a week, it can take up to twice as long to cut through the buildup of clutter, dirt, and scum.

There are some very simple things you can do every day to virtually stop dirt, bacteria, and mold and mildew in their tracks in less than 30 seconds.

- **Keep the shower clean.** Using a daily shower cleaner to prevent soap-scum buildup can make a big difference. (The kind you just spray on without having to wipe is easiest to use.) The key is to start with a clean shower and use the product as directed. Using a squeegee on shower doors and walls after each shower will help to discourage mold from growing.
- **Keep the sink clean.** Wipe the sink, faucets, and countertop after the final use every morning. Just spray some tub and tile cleaner on a paper towel and wipe. Or use a premoistened wipe — even kids can do that!

• **Keep the toilet clean.** Use a flush-release cleaning product in the toilet bowl. Or brush the bowl daily to keep it clean. Pour all-purpose cleaner in the toilet-brush holder to keep it fresh and ready for use. Spray and wipe the underside of the seat and other surfaces as needed with a disinfectant cleaner, or keep sanitizing wipes on hand for quick cleanups.

• **Hang towels.** Hang towels so they will dry as quickly as possible and stay fresher between launderings. Replace used towels every two or three days.

• **Get rid of moisture.** While showering, use an exhaust fan or open a window to vent the moist air. Be sure to close the shower curtain completely to prevent water from wetting the floor or nearby wall; wipe up any drips or puddles immediately. Pull the shower curtain to the closed position after use and gently shake it to remove excess water.

Once a week, give your bathroom a more thorough top-to-bottom cleaning. Open a window if possible to ventilate the room. Keep in mind that you are cleaning more than you can see — that is, germs as well as dirt, soap scum, and other grime. Use a diluted solution of all-purpose cleaner as directed on the product label or a commercial bathroom cleaner to clean sinks, counters, and shower stalls. Do not use abrasive cleaners such as scouring powders or any abrasive scouring pads on sinks and tubs. Do use separate sponges or cleaning cloths for cleaning the toilet area, which is likely to have the highest concentration of germs.

Make the job easier by letting cleaning products do their job while you do yours. Spray the

PLAIN & SIMPLE ORGANIZING TIPS

- Keep cleaning supplies handy for daily cleanups.
- Clear the countertop of as much clutter as possible.
- Put a wastebasket in the bathroom to collect paper litter.
- Install extra hooks or rods for hanging wet towels.
- Discard any bath or beauty products you no longer use. Also discard any products that have changed color or consistency or that smell funny.
- Keep medicines and other potentially harmful items out of reach of children.
- Make use of bathroom organizing products such as shower caddies and drawer organizers.

sinks, tub, shower door, walls, and floor with a scrub-free cleaner and let it work its magic on the soap scum while you wipe countertops and mirrors and clean the toilet. Shake out rugs and then vacuum and mop the floor. For quick and easy floor cleaning, a ready-to-use mop with a disposable mop head is indispensable. If you are using a regular mop, use ½ cup of all-purpose cleaner in 1 gallon of warm water or a squirt of dishwashing liquid in a bucket of water to mop the floor. *Helpful hint:* Save the mopping for last and mop your way out the door. Dip a sponge in the cleaning solution to clean the outside of the toilet and the floor area behind the toilet where your mop can't reach. And don't forget to empty wastebaskets. Make this chore easier by lining the basket with a small garbage-can liner or a plastic bag from the supermarket that can be easily removed and carried out to the trash.

If you prefer to do bathroom cleaning on a "catch as catch can" basis, try cleaning the toilet, sink, and mirror while supervising children in the bathtub. If you use a nontoxic product, you can clean the shower while you are in it. Scrub the walls and floor, then scrub yourself (but not with the shower cleaner!). Keep a container of cleaning wipes under the sink for cleaning on the fly.

Natural Cleaning Alternatives

If you're allergic to bathroom cleaning products, want to economize, or prefer to use nontoxic cleaning solutions, try one of these simple, all-natural solutions for cleaning everything in your bathroom.

- **Floors.** Mop tile and linoleum floors with a solution of 1 cup of white vinegar and 1 gallon of water.
- **Toilets.** Pour in 1 cup of white vinegar. Let stand for 5 minutes. Brush and flush. Or sprinkle baking soda around the inside of the toilet bowl and scrub with a toilet brush.
- **Sinks and countertops.** Wipe counters and sinks with a cloth saturated with white vinegar.

How To CLEAN A TOILET

1. Spray a disinfectant cleaner over the outside of the toilet tank and bowl as well as the toilet-bowl cover and seat (both the top and the underside). Allow it to sit for 10 minutes or as suggested by the manufacturer to kill germs.

2. Lower the waterline in the toilet bowl by pushing the toilet brush in and out of the trap until the water level drops. Spray disinfectant cleaner on the inside surfaces of the bowl, including under the rim, or pour about 1 cup of the disinfectant into the bowl and let it sit for a few minutes.

3. Brush the inside of the bowl and under the rim with a toilet brush. Flush, and rinse the brush in the clean flowing water.

4. Wipe the outside of the toilet with paper towels or a clean cloth.

Note: Do not allow pets to drink toilet-bowl water. Keep pets safe and healthy by getting in the habit of always closing the seat cover. It looks better when it's closed anyway.

Or wet the sink, sprinkle it lightly with baking soda, and use a moist cloth or sponge to gently scrub the sink. Rinse thoroughly to remove all the baking soda. On porcelain enamel sinks, you may be able to remove some stains (except rust) with 3 percent hydrogen peroxide diluted by half with water. Apply this solution with a sponge and then rinse immediately.

- **Faucets and fixtures.** Clean and shine faucets with a microfiber cloth dampened with water, a regular cloth saturated with white vinegar, or a sponge dampened with water and sprinkled with baking soda. Rinse the faucets and buff dry with a clean cloth.

- **Tubs and showers.** To remove soap scum or mildew, sprinkle baking soda on a damp sponge or soak a cloth with white vinegar. Use the cloth or sponge to wipe down the area, and then rinse. To remove a heavy buildup of soap and grime, wet the surface and then sprinkle baking soda on it. Let stand for 15 minutes before scrubbing. Rinse well. *Helpful hint:* Using a sponge mop to clean the shower and tub floor and walls makes the job easier.

- **Shower doors.** Saturate a cloth with vinegar and use it to remove soap scum and water marks from glass doors; dry with a clean cloth. To remove water spots from metal door frames, wipe them with a cloth dampened with a citrus-oil furniture polish; then wipe dry with a clean cloth.

Rising to the Challenge

Some bathroom cleaning tasks are more challenging than others. And, of course, it's always a challenge to clean a bathroom that has not been cleaned regularly. Following are some ideas to help you rise to the most daunting of bathroom cleaning challenges.

Toilet Bowl Ring. Erase stains in the toilet with a pumice stick, available at hardware stores. The stick will clean stains off any porcelain surface.

Mold and Mildew. Scrub the affected area with a mild detergent solution, such as a few drops of dishwashing liquid in warm water. Then scrub with a solution of ¼ cup of liquid chlorine bleach in 1 quart of water. Wait 20 minutes and repeat.

Straight vinegar is a natural alternative to liquid chlorine bleach, though it is not quite as effective at killing mold spores as bleach. To use, pour distilled white vinegar into a spray bottle and spray it directly onto the moldy area. Let the

make your own

Tub and Tile Cleaner

Formula #1. Mix 1⅔ cups of baking soda, ½ cup of dishwashing liquid, and ½ cup of water. Then add 2 tablespoons of white vinegar. Apply, scrub, and rinse.

Formula #2. Combine ¼ cup of borax and ¼ cup of baking soda. Add 1½ cups of hot water and stir until mixed. Apply, scrub, and rinse.

vinegar sit, without rinsing it off. But do not use vinegar on grout, as it may eat away at the grout. Other natural mold and mildew destroyers include grapefruit seed extract (GSE) and tea tree oil, which can be found at most health food stores (see the box on page 120 for GSE preparation instructions).

Odors. Keep a book of matches handy near the toilet; light a match and then snuff it out to quickly kill odors. If it's ammonia you smell, you need to clean the toilet bowl more often. To kill the musty odor caused by mold and mildew, you'll have to destroy the mold and mildew first, as discussed in the previous paragraph.

Shower Curtain Liner. Periodically wash plastic shower liners in the washing machine with hot water and detergent on the regular cycle. Throw in a bath towel to help "scrub" mildew and soap scum off the liner. Rehang the liner and allow it to air-dry. Or lay out the liner on your driveway or lawn, scrub it with an all-purpose cleaner, and rinse it before rehanging.

Showerhead. Erratic or weak water pressure from the showerhead usually indicates mineral buildup. To restore proper flow, unscrew the perforated faceplate, soak it overnight in white vinegar, and scrub it clean with a toothbrush before replacing it. Or soak it in a commercial formula for dissolving deposits. If you're having trouble removing the faceplate, you can try filling a plastic food-storage bag with white vinegar and securing the bag to the showerhead with rubber bands, making sure that the faceplate comes in contact with the vinegar. Allow to soak overnight, and scrub away the softened mineral deposits in the morning.

Faucet Aerators. If you notice that the flow of water through a faucet seems to be restricted, it may be due to a buildup of minerals and dirt on your faucet aerator. Cleaning the aerator may solve the problem. Before taking the aerator apart, close the stopper in the sink so that no loose parts accidentally go down the drain.

1. Unscrew the aerator from the spout, using a penetrating oil, such as WD-40, to loosen the connection if needed.
2. Disassemble the aerator, taking care to set the parts aside in order so that you can put them back together in order.
3. Clean the screen and disc with an old toothbrush and hot, soapy water. To remove stubborn mineral deposits, soak the parts overnight in white vinegar. If necessary, use a pin or toothpick to open any clogged holes in the disc.
4. Rinse all the parts with water and then put the aerator back together. If the screen and disc won't come clean, replace the aerator.

Cleaning the Medicine Cabinet

Every now and then, empty out your medicine cabinet. Clean all the shelves with an all-purpose cleaner or a solution of equal parts of vinegar and water. Discard all expired prescriptions. Check the dates on over-the-counter items and throw out anything that isn't current. If you're not sure what something is for, get rid of it. Seal these items in a plastic bag and toss it in an outdoor lidded trash can; leaving them in an open wastebasket poses a risk to children and pets.

Organize what's left into categories. Group together all first-aid supplies, including ointments and bandages. Other groupings may include cough and cold remedies, body lotions and sunscreens, dental supplies, and everyday toiletries such as deodorants and hair products. Two things you may want to consider storing

somewhere other than the bathroom are prescription medications and makeup. These should be stored in a cool, dry place, as they may be adversely affected by the humidity generally present in the bathroom.

To maximize storage space in your medicine cabinet, start by removing the shelves. Determine what you want to store on the bottom shelf, place those items there, and then insert a shelf just above them. Repeat for the next shelf. It helps to organize tall items together on one shelf, and short items on another. Purchase additional shelves, if needed, at a hardware store. If you still need more room for storing items, add freestanding shelving or a double-decker turntable in the cabinet under the sink. If bathroom storage space is at a premium, store extra bottles of shampoo, bars of soap, and other toiletries elsewhere, perhaps in a linen closet or bedroom closet.

EVERYDAY SOLUTION
No Storage Space

Use an over-the-door shoe bag to store all types of bathroom necessities: blow-dryers and curling irons, brushes and combs, hair accessories, bars of soap, extra bottles of shampoo, magazines, toilet-paper rolls, and even rolled-up washcloths and hand towels. *Note:* Before buying the shoe bag, check that your door has enough clearance to accommodate the metal hangers that need to sit on top of the door. If your door fits tightly to the doorjamb, the metal hangers may interfere with proper closing of the door.

A Healthy Nursery

Keeping the nursery clean is important for the health, safety, and emotional well-being of both children and parents. The most effective defense against the spread of illness is frequent hand washing, especially after use of the toilet or diapering of the baby, and before the preparation and consumption of food. Some germs, such as hepatitis A and rotavirus (a common cause of diarrhea), can survive for weeks on surfaces and objects. It's important to clean and disinfect surfaces that are likely to become contaminated, including toys that children put in their mouths, crib rails, the diaper-changing table, and the diaper pail.

Surfaces need to be cleaned first and then sanitized. Clean with a mild solution of water and dishwashing liquid, then follow up with an EPA-approved disinfectant. You can make your own disinfectant by combining 1 tablespoon of bleach and 16 ounces of cool water in a spray bottle. Spray the bleach solution over the entire surface. Allow it to stand for a few minutes, then wipe the surface dry with a clean paper towel. Label and store the bleach solution in a cool place out of direct sunlight and out of the reach of children. This solution loses its strength quickly. To ensure maximum effectiveness, mix up just a small daily batch.

Hydrogen peroxide is an alternative to bleach and other commercial disinfectants. Readily available at supermarkets and drugstores, 3 percent hydrogen peroxide is an inexpensive, natural germ killer. Buy it in the large-size bottles and pour it into a 4-ounce spray

For Safety's Sake

- After each use, clean and sterilize baby bottles and nipples.

- Keep the floors where your baby plays as clean as possible. Remove shoes to prevent tracking in dirt and pollutants. Mop wood and tile floors frequently. Use a vacuum with a HEPA filter to clean carpets and rugs.

- Keep the diaper pail locked to keep toddlers out.

- Always make sure you have good ventilation when cleaning around your baby. When disinfecting with bleach, do so when the baby is in another room, and open a window.

- As stated before (it's worth repeating!), keep all cleaning products out of the reach of toddlers. Ingestion could be lethal!

- When cleaning up body fluids, such as blood, vomit, or feces, you should wear rubber gloves and/or wash your hands afterward.

- Keep your fingernails short and wash your hands often to lessen the chance of spreading germs.

bottle for convenience. (Hydrogen peroxide is a clear liquid that looks like water, so be sure to label the bottle.) To disinfect surfaces, spray them, then wipe dry with a paper towel. Note: Hydrogen peroxide loses strength as it ages or if it is exposed to light. Check the expiration date before use and store it in the dark.

The quickest way to clean and disinfect is to use a product that does both. Look for something with an EPA number and the words "cleans and disinfects" on the label. Disinfectant wipes are probably the most convenient disinfectant cleaners, especially for spot-cleaning and disinfecting. However, do not use disinfectant wipes on your baby's bottom as they are designed for cleaning surfaces only. For diaper changes, use wipes specifically designed for use on skin.

- **Bottles and nipples.** Place the bottles upside down in the top rack of the dishwasher. Put the nipples in a small mesh bag, zip it up, and place the bag in the top rack also. *Note:* The temperature of the water coming into your dishwasher must reach at least 165°F (74°C) to properly disinfect the bottles and nipples. If you don't have a dishwasher, you can wash bottles and nipples with a bottle brush, dishwashing liquid, and water. Then place them all in a reusable sterilizing bag and put them into the microwave for 3 minutes to steam-clean and disinfect.

- **High chairs and booster chairs.** After each use, remove the high-chair tray and wash it in the sink or a dishpan with dishwashing liquid, warm water, and a scrub sponge. Rinse well and then dry it with a clean cloth or allow it to air-dry. Every few days, use a toothbrush to clean out crevices in the chair. Wash the seat, arms, legs, straps, and underneath areas with a cloth or sponge and hot, soapy water. Then spray or wipe surfaces with hydrogen peroxide and allow them to air-dry. If you choose to use an all-purpose disinfectant cleaner spray, allow the spray to sit for 30 seconds. Then wipe all surfaces with a wet cloth. Rinse the cloth and rewipe several times to remove all cleaner and food residue; then allow the chair to air-dry. Wash removable fabric covers every week or as needed.

- **Car seats.** It's important to keep a car seat clean. Dirt can collect in the recessed buckles (built into the seat, between a child's legs) and cause them to malfunction. Use a handheld vacuum or canned compressed air to clean crumbs from all crevices and recesses. Clean the body of the car seat with warm, soapy water; then wipe it dry with a cloth or towel. Use the same mixture to spot-clean the harness straps. Use a damp cloth or sponge to wipe the buckle clean. Consider purchasing a removable, machine-washable car-seat cover that you can wash and air-dry as needed.

- **Strollers.** Use a cloth or sponge and warm, soapy water to wash the frame, seat, and rain/sun cover. If it is removable, machine-wash the seat pad in cold water on the delicate cycle and let it air-dry. Spray the seat pad with fabric protector to prevent stains.

- **Portable play yards.** Periodically use a cloth or sponge and warm, soapy water to clean the play yard. Disinfect it, using hydrogen peroxide, an EPA-approved disinfectant, or a diluted solution of bleach (1 tablespoon of bleach in 16 ounces of water). Clean the play yard sheet immediately after illness or soiling with stool or urine.

- **Plastic toys and teething rings.** Unless the manufacturer's instructions say otherwise, wash plastic toys and teething rings in the top rack of your dishwasher. Place these and other small, lightweight pieces in a zipped mesh bag to keep them from falling into the bottom of the dishwasher. Or wash them by hand in hot, soapy water and allow them to air dry. Disinfect after illness or sharing with other children by wiping with hydrogen peroxide. Newborn pacifiers should be sterilized with bottles and nipples.

- **Soft toys.** Check the toys' labels. Launder washable items weekly or as needed. Use warm, soapy water to spot-clean toys that cannot be washed, then allow them to air dry. To reduce dust mites and other allergens, place toys in the freezer in a zippered plastic bag for four to five hours or overnight, once a week.

- **Changing table and crib.** If you are using a plastic pad on your changing table, swab it with

a disinfectant wipe after each diaper change, to kill any germs. If you use cloth pad covers, remove and wash them as often as needed. Wash crib sheets in hot water once a week. When you change the sheets, clean the mattress pad and crib rails with a cloth or sponge and hot, soapy water. It's a good idea to disinfect the changing table surface with a diluted bleach solution after soiling with stool, particularly if the soiling was the result of diarrhea or a stomach bug. Mix 1 tablespoon of bleach with water in a 16-ounce spray bottle. Spray the surface and allow the solution to sit for 10 minutes. Then scrub with a dampened sponge, rinse well, and dry with a paper towel.

- **Disposable diapers.** Empty solid waste into the toilet and flush. Then fold up the diaper, with the soiled side in the center, and toss it in the trash or a diaper pail. Sprinkle baking soda liberally into the trash can or diaper pail after each deposit, to prevent odors.

- **Cloth-diaper pail (dry method).** Shake solid waste into the toilet before putting the diaper in the pail. Sprinkle baking soda onto the diaper to help cut odor, or keep a deodorizer tablet in the pail. Each time the diapers are washed (see below), wash the empty pail in hot, soapy water. Rinse with clean, hot water. Sanitize with a liquid chlorine bleach solution (¾ cup of bleach

make your own

Natural Cleaner and Sanitizer

Grapefruit seed extract (GSE) offers a less toxic approach to preventing the spread of *E. coli*, *Salmonella*, *Staphylococcus*, *Streptococcus*, and many other dangerous bacteria, germs, and parasites.

To use: Mix 15 drops of grapefruit seed extract with 2 cups of warm water (or use 1 teaspoon per gallon of water). Pour the solution into a spray bottle. Double the amount of GSE (in the same amount of water) to create a super-strength disinfectant cleaner for more extreme jobs. Grapefruit seed extract also whitens sinks, tubs, and tile. Spray the area with the GSE solution and let sit for at least 15 seconds to air-dry. Wipe the area dry with a paper towel or clean cloth.

formula courtesy of Pure Liquid Gold

per gallon of water). Rinse and allow to air-dry. *Helpful hint:* If you use a cloth diaper-pail liner, have two of them, so you always have a clean one at the ready when the other is in the wash.

- **Cloth-diaper pail (wet method).** Fill a locking diaper pail half-full with cold water. Add ½ cup of baking soda or vinegar to help control odors and staining. Empty solid waste from each

diaper into the toilet before adding the diaper to the pail. Always keep the pail locked to keep out children and pets. When you have enough diapers for a load of wash, empty the diapers and the solution they've been soaking in into the washer and set it to spin to remove the water. Then wash as usual (see below). Wash the empty pail with hot, soapy water. Rinse and then sanitize with 1 tablespoon of liquid chlorine bleach per gallon of water. Rinse and allow to air-dry.

Washing Cloth Diapers. Prewash the diapers (and the cloth diaper-pail liner, if you're using one) with laundry detergent in cold water on the presoak cycle to remove soiling without setting stains. Then wash the load in hot water on the heavy soiling (longest) cycle with a cold-water rinse. Following are some washing options and cautions:

- Fragrance-free detergent is recommended, to avoid irritating the baby's sensitive skin.
- Add ½ cup of baking soda to the wash to help whiten and soften diapers; however, note that when you add baking soda to the wash, you don't need to use as much detergent.
- You can use bleach occasionally to sanitize and whiten the diapers, but regular use of bleach will cause premature breaking of the fibers.
- Fabric softener will reduce the diapers' absorbency, so use it only occasionally. An alternative to fabric softener is white vinegar; use ½ cup in the rinse cycle.

- Avoid using vinegar in a load that includes diaper covers, as vinegar will reduce the covers' waterproofing. Some diaper covers can be machine-washed and machine-dried; others need to be air-dried. Always follow the instructions on the care label.

Put the diapers in the dryer on the high heat setting for 60 minutes or until they're completely dry. Machine drying helps sterilize the diapers. You could also dry the diapers in direct sunlight, which also sterilizes them. When washing multiple loads of laundry, wash the diaper loads last. Then run an empty wash cycle with bleach to disinfect your washer before the next load. Otherwise, the next load of clothes could be contaminated with harmful bacteria from the dirty diapers.

Washing Infant Clothing. Baby clothes can be washed with other family clothing, using a fragrance-free detergent. Do not wash baby clothes with dirty diapers. Diapers should always be washed separately. Wash all new baby clothes and diapers before you use them, to remove chemical residues and ensure that they are clean and soft. To preserve fire-retardant qualities, launder baby clothing in detergent, not soap, and do not use fabric softener in the washer or dryer. Try adding ½ cup of vinegar or baking soda to the rinse cycle to soften the clothing.

Cleaning Kids' Rooms

Kids of all ages want their privacy. Let them know that if they keep their rooms cleaned up, you will not have to enter except for periodic, preannounced inspections. Establish a morning pickup routine that might include making beds, hanging up towels in the bathroom, and putting away pajamas. The evening pickup routine might include putting away toys and tossing dirty clothes in the hamper. Depending on their ages, children can also be expected to do some weekly cleaning of their bedrooms, which might include dusting or vacuuming. If you give children cleaning products to use, be sure to supervise them. See chapter 2 for more tips on getting children involved in the cleaning routine.

For the most part, "clean your room" is synonymous with "pick up your room," which is more about uncluttering. The more you can

---

ALLERGY ALERT

You can't avoid dust mites, but you can minimize the buildup of their population and waste products. While some exposure to dust mites may actually help strengthen a child's immune system, excessive exposure can cause asthma in children who have not previously exhibited asthma symptoms.

- Wash sheets, blankets, and bedcovers once a week in hot water.
- If your children have stuffed toys, make sure they are washable. Once a week, wash them in hot water and dry them in the dryer to kill dust mites. Minimize the number of stuffed toys on the bed at any one time.

keep things off the floor, the less cluttered a room looks and the easier it is to clean that room. The trick to getting kids to stay organized is to make it easy and fun.

- **Shoe bag storage.** A hanging shoe bag on the back of a door can be used to store small toys. Hang it low enough for children to easily reach into pockets to put away and retrieve their favorite toys. Store any collectibles and breakables in the upper pockets, out of reach.
- **Animal corrals.** Gather stuffed animals in a nylon hammock hung up in one corner of the room. Or hang a length of colored string or ribbon horizontally between two hooks at either end of a bare wall. Use clothespins to clip beanbag toys and small stuffed animals to the string. *Note:* You can use this same method to display artwork.
- **Shelves, not boxes.** Store toys and games on shelves with bins rather than in toy boxes. Finding what you want in a toy box generally makes a mess.
- **Lots of pegs.** Install wall pegs at kid heights for hanging book bags, pajamas and bathrobes, jackets, and clothes they will wear again.
- **Reachable clothes rods.** In the kids' closet, use higher rods for storing dressy and out-of-season clothes. Hang a second, lower rod to encourage them to hang up their everyday clothes. Home-supply stores sell rods that hang from an upper rod, as well as tension-mounted rods that can be fitted in the closet at any height.

Designate specific dresser drawers for specific items, such as socks, underwear, shorts, T-shirts, pants, and shirts. Use drawer organizers

to keep items in the same drawer, such as socks and underwear, separate from each other. You might also consider storing socks and underwear in a shoe bag with clear plastic pockets that you can hang in the closet or on the back of a closet door.

Increase the available drawer space by installing slide-out drawers under children's beds. Or put colorful stackable crates or a wire-bin system in the closet. These storage products are especially useful for younger children, who may have trouble opening heavy drawers or the top drawer of a standard dresser.

Getting Buy-In. It's important to get your kids involved in the process of uncluttering and organizing their rooms. Allowing them to have input into getting organized helps ensure that they will stay organized. Here are three basic organizing principles to keep in mind:

1. Make it easy to put things away. Provide containers for putting like items together so kids easily see what goes where.
2. Organize from the bottom up. Use lower shelves and drawers to keep frequently used items accessible, and store less frequently used items higher up.

3. Label everything. Label shelves, dresser drawers, and containers. For children who can't read, label with drawings, photographs, or pictures cut out of magazines or catalogs. As they learn to read, you can replace the pictures with words.

Weeding Out Kid Clutter. Reduce the amount of clutter by weeding out clothing and toys your children have outgrown. If you're planning to donate these items, explain to your children how they can help make a less fortunate child very happy by sharing those things they aren't using. If you have a garage sale, let the kids keep the money they get for selling their toys and clothes.

A good time to weed out toys is just before a birthday or other gift-giving holiday. Position the weeding out as making room for new things. With children who are reluctant to part with toys, it helps to focus their attention on what they want to keep rather than what they are willing to get rid of. Ask them to choose their favorites and set these aside. Then ask, "What else do you like playing with?" Put what's left in a box or bag for donation or a garage sale. Another idea is to pack up those things you know your child is no longer playing with and store the box in the attic or garage, where items can be retrieved if they are missed. If they aren't missed after six months, you can go ahead and donate the contents of the box.

A good time to pare down clothing is just before you go shopping for back-to-school clothes or at the start of a new season. Start by going through the current season's clothes and shoes. Pull out everything in the closet, and then

---

How To REMOVE URINE ODOR FROM A MATTRESS

1. Dampen the "accident" area with a clean, wet cloth.

2. Sprinkle the dampened area with borax detergent.

3. Use the wet cloth to thoroughly scrub the area.

4. Allow the area to dry, and then vacuum up the residue.

---

move on to the drawers. Discard worn-out and stained items as well as anything that's not worth fixing. Have children try on clothes and shoes for the upcoming season to see what fits and to find out what clothing they do and do not like. If they don't like it, it probably won't get worn. Make a shopping list for each child, using separate pages in a spiral notebook. Be sure to include sizes.

CHAPTER EIGHT

LAUNDRY AND STORAGE

Basements, attics, and garages tend to accumulate more than their fair share of junk. These rooms don't require frequent cleaning (thank goodness), but they should be cleared out and cleaned up periodically. The laundry room, on the other hand, should be one of your regular stops when you're cleaning the rest of your home. Good organization in all of these areas will go a long way toward making the job of cleaning quicker and easier.

The Laundry Room

Keeping the laundry room clean is pretty simple, once you get the piles of laundry picked up! After reading the following suggestions for cleaning and maintaining your laundry room, turn to chapter 10 for tips on creating a more efficient laundry workspace as well as everything you ever wanted to know, but did not know to ask, about doing laundry.

Housework can't kill you, but why take a chance?

— Phyllis Diller

Organizing the Laundry Room. Good organization makes the job of doing laundry and cleaning the laundry room more efficient and, thus, more enjoyable. Store laundry detergent and other cleaning supplies in an easily accessible place, out of the reach of children. Storage options range from installed cabinets and shelves to any number of freestanding carts and wire shelving units readily available through online retail organizing stores. If you have shelves, line them with a shelf liner that can be sponged down occasionally, as needed, to remove dust and grime.

Keep the tops of the washer and dryer clean and clear so you have some working space to fold laundry. If possible, set up a laundry pre-treatment area away from the washer and dryer, since many soil- and stain-removal products can damage the finish and control panels of these appliances. If you have to spray a product onto clothing, spray away from the washer and dryer, to avoid getting any on them.

Make it easier to clean the floor by keeping it clear. For example, hang the ironing board on a wall or the back of a door, and instead of a traditional clothes rack for air drying, consider a foldable wall unit. Put a wastebasket in the laundry room to collect used fabric softener sheets, lint, dustpan debris, and other trash.

How To | CLEAN YOUR IRON

Soleplate. Cleaning the soleplate, or the bottom of your iron, will remove the occasional buildup that can stain fabrics.

1. Turn the iron off and allow it to cool completely.
2. Wipe the soleplate with a sudsy cloth or nylon-mesh pad.
3. If the soleplate has a starchy buildup or corrosion, remove the contamination with a cloth saturated in white vinegar or a solution of equal parts of vinegar and salt, heated enough to dissolve the salt. (Never use abrasive cleansers or metal scouring pads.)

Reservoir. If mineral deposits that look like salt are coming through the holes in the soleplate, the reservoir of your iron needs cleaning.

1. Fill the water reservoir at least one-quarter full with white vinegar, and steam-iron a clean rag or towel until the reservoir is empty. The fumes will be somewhat obnoxious, so be sure to open a window, turn on a fan, or do both.

2. If deposits are still noticeable, refill the reservoir with water and steam-iron again.
3. Rinse the reservoir by filling it with distilled or purified water and then emptying it out. Repeat as necessary.

To prevent the buildup of minerals, use only distilled water in the reservoir, instead of water from the tap.

After every use. When you are finished using the iron, always empty the water from the reservoir while it is still hot so that the reservoir will dry out. Empty the water by slowly tilting the pointed end of iron down over a sink. Store the iron in an upright position.

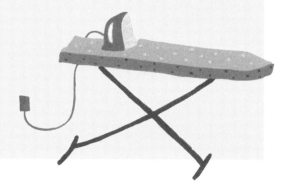

Cleaning the Laundry Room. Ironically, in the process of getting clothes clean, it's easy to make a mess. Quick cleanups will keep your laundry room in tip-top shape.

- Wipe up any spills on the floors, storage shelves, or appliances immediately.
- Keep a roll of paper towels handy, and use them to wipe down detergent bottles before putting them away, to keep your shelves cleaner.
- On a weekly basis, vacuum and mop the laundry-room floor, and use a soft, damp cloth or sponge to wipe down the outside of your washer and dryer to keep them looking like new.
- Clean the shelves periodically with a cloth dampened in a solution of equal parts of white vinegar and water, to cut through any grime created by spilled laundry detergent and other laundry aids.

Cleaning the Washer. If your washer drains into a sink, there should be a strainer in the sink drain; remove any lint that has collected in it before every load. Clean your washer tub of residual dirt or dyes, if needed, by pouring in 2 cups of white vinegar and running the washer through a complete hot-water cycle. About once a month or so:

- Clean under the lid and around the top of the washer tub to remove dust, dirt, lint, and soap scum. Use a cleaning cloth or sponge dampened with a solution of equal parts of white vinegar and water.

- Remove the liquid fabric softener and bleach dispensers and set them in a sink. Pour a little of the vinegar/water solution into them and scrub with an old toothbrush. Rinse with warm running water and replace in the washer.

Cleaning the Dryer. Clean the dryer lint trap after each dryer load. At least once a year, clean the dryer as follows:

- Remove the lint trap and use a lint brush or vacuum attachment to remove all the accumulated lint from under the lint trap and other accessible places.
- Pull the washer and dryer out from the wall and vacuum the backs of the machines and the floor underneath. You might as well mop the floor while you're at it.
- Inspect and clean the exhaust duct to prevent clogging. Even a partially clogged exhaust can lengthen the drying time, and lint buildup could cause a fire. To clean the exhaust duct, unplug the dryer. Disconnect the duct from the dryer. Then vacuum the duct with the hose attachment and reconnect the duct.
- Inspect the exhaust hood outside the house. Turn on the dryer inside the house, then head outside to check that the inside flaps of the hood move freely when the dryer is operating. If your hood points downward, making the flaps hard to see, hold a mirror under the hood to get a good look. Make sure that no birds or insects are nesting inside the duct or hood.

Every one to three years, depending upon usage, have the dryer thoroughly cleaned by a qualified service technician.

Clearing Out Storage Areas

Now we come to the clutter catchalls: the basement, the attic, closets, and the garage. Those things we don't want or need anymore but are not quite ready to part with for one reason or another tend to end up in storage. Ask yourself, "Could I get this again pretty easily and inexpensively if I ever needed it?" If the answer is yes, let it go. Recognize that when you go through years of accumulation, many items are going to bring back memories and emotions. Give yourself some time to reminisce with these "old friends" before parting. If you truly can't decide whether to keep or toss something, put it in a box marked "Undecided," write the date on the box, and put it in storage. Make a note in your calendar to take another look at the contents six months later, and see whether you are then able a decision.

The hardest part of uncluttering and organizing a basement, an attic, or a garage is getting started. Start by scheduling a family cleanup day or a progressive cleaning party (see sidebar). Or, if you decide to go it alone, set aside 30 to 60 minutes each week for your storage organizing project. Sort things into categories:

- *Donations* — things that are in good condition that someone else might use
- *For-Sale Items* — things you can sell at a yard sale or through a newspaper ad, a consignment shop, or an online auction
- *Trash* — anything broken and not worth fixing, worn-out, or otherwise unusable
- *Keepers* — anything you have used in the past month or two and things you truly love and cherish

See chapter 3 for ideas on where to donate what and how to sell unwanted belongings. Put the trash items out with your regular garbage pickup, unless they fall into the category of household hazardous waste. In addition to the cleaning supplies mentioned on page 11, other hazardous waste items include:

- Paint and paint thinner
- Motor oil and gasoline
- Antifreeze
- Brake and transmission fluids
- Car batteries

Check with your local household hazardous waste collection program to find out how to properly dispose of these items. Some communities offer an annual collection service.

Sort "keepers" into subcategories such as holiday decorations, sports equipment, tools, gardening supplies, household supplies, memorabilia, and clothing. Set up a designated storage area and move all the "keepers" there, keeping them organized by category. Store seasonal or seldom-used items in lidded plastic boxes. Storing boxes on shelves is preferable to stacking them, because it's easier to get at the boxes you need when you need them. Store heavier boxes on bottom shelves and lighter boxes on top shelves.

PLAIN & SIMPLE ORGANIZING TIPS

- Base decisions about what to store where on the level of accessibility required.

- Limit attic storage to things you need to access only occasionally, such as holiday decorations and tax records.

- Declutter storage areas at least once a year.

- Sort and then store like items together.

- For easy stacking, buy tubs that are all the same size, and label each one with its contents.

- Consider using lidded plastic storage tubs rather than cardboard boxes, to keep pests, dust, and moisture out.

- In the basement, keep storage boxes high and dry on sturdy shelves or pallets.

- Create designated spaces for storing categories of things in your basement, attic, or garage.

Cleaning Basements and Attics

Good lighting is essential to a thorough cleaning. Bring in temporary lighting if it's needed, or improve existing lighting so you can see what you are doing. While a finished basement should be cleaned on the same schedule as any other common living area (see chapter 5), an unfinished basement can be cleaned as seldom as once or twice a year. The same goes for the attic. The annual or semiannual cleaning of these storage areas should include the following:

- Vacuum the stairs.
- With a vacuum or broom, remove spiderwebs from ceiling corners and beams, in stairwells, above doors, and around windows.
- Vacuum and, if possible, mop the floor.
- Remove and shake (preferably outdoors) any dustcovers you've placed over stored items.
- Declutter and reorganize the storage areas as needed.
- Clean lightbulbs and light fixtures.
- Wash any windows.
- Vacuum the smoke detectors.
- Wipe down the exterior of the furnace and hot-water heater with a sponge or cloth dipped in warm, sudsy water or a solution of equal parts of vinegar and water.
- Drain the tank of your hot-water heater (see chapter 14).

The area around your furnace and hot-water heater should be kept clean and free of clutter and flammable materials. Cover large items in storage with sheets or tarpaulins to keep off the dust. Do not store antiques and heirloom items in the basement, attic, or garage if these areas are not conditioned (heated and cooled like the rest of your home); extreme temperatures and high humidity can cause permanent damage.

Cleaning and Preventing Mold

Dark, dank basements are the ideal breeding ground for mold. A common cause of allergies, mold can make it hard for some people to breathe and hard for your body to fight off infections, and can even cause serious illness. If your basement smells musty, you probably have mold (see Control Moisture on page 28). Mold generally appears as black or white stains or smudges. To find out whether a stain or smudge is mold, carefully dab at it with a drop of household liquid chlorine bleach. If the spot's color changes or disappears, it is probably mold. Get in the habit of inspecting your basement regularly for moldy odors, leaky pipes, and foundation leaks, which could contribute to the growth of mold.

Once you've found it, you'll want to clean up mold immediately to prevent it from spreading throughout your home. To clean areas larger than 10 square feet, or if the mold damage was caused by sewage or other contaminated water, you should hire an experienced contractor. If you do the cleanup yourself, wear long rubber gloves, safety goggles, an N95 respirator (available at many hardware stores), and a shirt with long sleeves. Shower immediately afterward to remove mold spores. Following are some pointers for cleaning mold off different types of surfaces:

- **Hard surfaces.** To clean furniture and other washable surfaces, scrub them with hot, soapy water. Rinse by sponging them with a clean, wet rag, and dry thoroughly. Set up fans to speed the drying.
- **Concrete surfaces.** To clean large areas, prepare a solution of ¾ cup of liquid chlorine bleach to 1 gallon of water. Open the windows in the area for ventilation. Apply the bleach solution to the floors and walls with a mop, and allow it to sit for 5 minutes. Then rinse and mop up the excess water. To remove small growths of mold, spray the affected areas with straight vinegar and allow them to dry without rinsing. The smell will dissipate in a few hours.
- **Drywall.** Clean the surface with a damp rag. Use soapy water or baking soda as a scrubbing agent. Don't let the drywall get too wet.
- **Rugs, upholstery, and mattresses.** Take the items outdoors, brush off loose mold, and then vacuum the surfaces. Afterward, wash the brush and dispose of the vacuum bag to prevent

recontaminating your home with mold spores. Leave the items outdoors and allow the sun and air to dry them, which should stop the mold growth. If mold is still noticeably present by sight or smell, make a very sudsy solution with water and soap, detergent, or carpet shampoo. Sponge the thick suds onto the rug or fabric, but be careful not to get the item too wet. (You can also spot-treat upholstery with a mixture of equal parts of rubbing alcohol and water.) Wipe off the suds with a damp cloth and let the cleaned items dry thoroughly before using them again.

- **Other soft surfaces.** When clothing, pillows, blankets, or stuffed animals become moldy, you can sometimes salvage them by laundering them in hot water. Get rid of wet, badly damaged, or musty-smelling materials that cannot be washed.

Absorb any lingering musty odors in the basement by placing a lump of dry charcoal in an open metal container, or set out a few small bowls of vinegar.

Once you've cleaned up the mold, what can you do to keep it from coming back? Keeping the basement tidy will allow air to move around more easily. In general, the less clutter you have, the better, because a cluttered basement is more likely to retain moisture that could lead to mold

Cleaning a Flooded Basement

One of the most challenging cleanups in any home is restoring a flooded basement. The first step in the cleanup process is to remove standing water. You may need to buy or rent a sump pump or wet/dry shop vacuum. Start drying the basement as quickly as possible to minimize wood decay and mold growth. Open doors and windows to allow moisture to escape. Once the standing water has evaporated, it is safe to use fans to speed up the drying process. Place fans so that they blow air out of the space, rather than in, to avoid spreading mold. If you decide to use a dehumidifier, close the doors and windows to the space it's being used in. Once the basement is dry, you can begin mold cleanup as described above.

If your heating system was flooded, clean it out thoroughly before using it again; this may be a job to leave for a professional. The system might work, but dirt-clogged chimneys and smoke boxes could cause the furnace to explode. Your homeowner's policy may cover the cost of professional cleanup, so check your policy.

and mildew problems. Here are a few simple things you can do:

- Clothing, paper, and furniture are the three biggest moisture magnets. Keep only what you really need, and donate the rest.
- Mold needs moisture to grow. Running a dehumidifier will remove moisture from the air. Make sure you empty the reservoir and clean it frequently.
- In the summer months, open basement windows to air out the space; or, in a finished basement, keep the windows closed and use a dehumidifier or an air conditioner.
- Avoid air-drying wet clothes in an already damp basement.
- Store firewood in a shed or garage, not in the house.
- Avoid having carpets on the basement floor.

If mold growth in your house is extensive or persists after cleanup efforts, seek the services of a professional mold remediation company.

Cleaning the Garage

Keeping the garage floor clean helps reduce the amount of dirt and debris that gets tracked into the house. Once a month or so, clean the garage floor, using a workshop vacuum or push broom. Also vacuum both sides of the garage doormat. If there is a floor drain or water trough at the entrance, check to make sure it is clear.

At least twice a year, clean dirt and cobwebs from the walls, ceilings, corners, and window-

For Safety's Sake

Be aware that pets are attracted to the smell and taste of antifreeze, which can kill an animal unless it receives immediate treatment. To prevent accidental poisoning, clean up drips and spills immediately. You might also consider using antifreeze made with propylene glycol, a less toxic substance.

sills with a broom or shop vacuum attachments. Then wash the windows inside and out. While you're at it, check for any termites or ants, or signs of other rodent or insect habitation. Refer to chapter 15 for advice on how to get rid of these and other pests that may have found their way into your home.

Periodically, you may want to pressure-wash the floor with cleaning agents to cut through dirt, salt, and oil. If you rent or buy a gas-powered pressure washer, be sure to place the engine outside the garage to prevent the buildup of deadly carbon monoxide gas. Then proceed as follows:

1. Remove everything from the garage floor. You may also want to remove anything hanging from the walls, as the spray from the pressure washer will likely splash the walls.
2. Starting from the back of the garage, use the water stream from the pressure washer to push the dirt on the floor outside. It's

OIL STAINS ON CONCRETE

One Challenge . . .

There are commercial products designed to clean and degrease concrete floors, many of which contain acid. But in less than the time it takes to go out and buy one of these products, you may be able to remove or lighten oil stains by using less toxic solutions. If your stain proves especially persistent, see "Driveways and Sidewalks" (page 149) for more possible solutions.

Three Solutions

1 Lightly wet the area and sprinkle baking soda or dishwasher detergent over it. Allow to sit for several minutes. Bring a pot of water to a boil and pour it on the stained area. Scrub with a stiff-bristled brush. Rinse and repeat as necessary.

2 Spray the oil spot with WD-40 and then immediately wipe up the greasy residue with an old rag that can be tossed out.

3 Sprinkle a fresh spill with cat litter and let it sit overnight to absorb the oil. Then sweep up litter, which will carry the oil away with it. Cat litter will also absorb antifreeze spills.

best to use the fan sprayer attachment for this close-up job, rather than the spear tip, which is designed to reach up-and-away places such as the roofline on your siding.

3. Leave the garage door open to allow the floor to air-dry, or use a squeegee to remove the water.

Because greasy stains can be difficult to remove, it makes sense to prevent them. To catch drips from your vehicle's engine and other gas-powered machinery, such as your lawn mower, purchase special absorbent mats to place under them. Or simply tear up a large cardboard box and position it as you would a mat. Replace the cardboard occasionally, before the oil soaks

through to the floor. Sealing your concrete floor or coating it with epoxy paint will also help prevent stains from penetrating the surface, thereby making them easier to clean up.

Organizing your garage will make it easier to find things and put them away. Sort and store items by category: lawn and garden, sports equipment, work tools, automotive, and storage.

Plan your space to make tools and other things accessible. Make it your goal to get things off the floor. Make use of freestanding shelves, or install shelving if possible. There are also a growing number of garage-organizing products available, ranging from simple wall and ceiling hooks and holders to cleverly designed storage systems.

CHAPTER NINE

OUTDOOR LIVING AREAS

It's not just the interior of your home that needs regular cleaning; the exterior of your home, yard furnishings, and other outdoor property need attention, too. Spring and fall typically mark the time when most outdoor cleanup jobs are scheduled, but there are some jobs that demand attention all season or even all year long. Outdoor cleanup not only makes your home look better but also adds to your enjoyment of relax-and-play space around your home.

PLAIN & SIMPLE ORGANIZING TIPS

- Use a hose reel to store garden hoses.
- Have designated storage areas for frequently used sporting gear and toys.
- Pick up toys and other lawn clutter before mowing.
- Clean items before putting them in summer or winter storage.
- Collect all the owner's manuals for your outdoor equipment and put them in a binder; store the binder with your equipment.

Home Exterior

Cleaning the exterior of your home is a job well worth the time and energy it takes. Clean shingles not only look better, they last longer. Clean windows and screens let the sunshine in while improving the view from inside. Clean siding can make your house look like new. Clean gutters help prevent stained siding and rotting roof edges, while also directing rainwater and snowmelt away from your foundation, where it could seep into your basement.

Plan to give your home's exterior a good cleaning once a year. Some tasks, such as cleaning windows and gutters, may need to be done twice a year. Pick a cool, cloudy day to do the job. As a general plan, start with the roof (if it needs cleaning), and then move to the gutters, followed by the siding, the screens, the windows, and exterior doors and lighting.

Roofs. If you live in a warm, humid climate where mildew grows rampant or in a heavily forested area under shade, you probably need to clean your roof once a year. Otherwise, you run

the risk of having the mildew destroy your asphalt shingles or cedar shakes. Roof cleaning also removes stains caused by algae, pine pollen, berries falling from overhead trees, and dirt. For safety reasons, most people opt to hire a professional roof cleaner. A warning to do-it-yourselfers: Be very careful not to stand on the roof immediately after cleaning it, as wet shingles can be very slippery.

Once your shingles are clean, consider installing roof protector strips, which inhibit the growth of mold, moss, and algae.

Gutters and Downspouts. Gutters and downspouts should be cleaned at least twice a year, generally in late fall and late spring, and more often if needed. While you may be tempted to just blast the gutters clean with a garden hose or pressure washer, don't. You'll end up with mud, leaves, and other debris all over your siding and yard. Instead, clean the gutters out by hand.

1. Put on a pair of work gloves to protect your hands from sharp metal parts.
2. Starting at a drain, use a garden trowel or a scoop made from a plastic milk jug to shovel leaves and other large debris out of the gutters.
   Helpful hint: Minimize ground cleanup by scooping material directly into a large plastic garbage bag, which you can simply drop to the ground when it's full. Or place an S-hook on a ladder rung and hang a pail from it; when it's full, you can empty the pail into your compost pile.

For Safety's Sake

If you are using a ladder, make sure it is sturdy and well secured. Never stand on the top two rungs, lean to one side or the other, or climb a ladder without another person present. If you are at all uncomfortable about working on a ladder, consider hiring a professional to clean your roof, gutters, siding, and windows.

3. Once you remove the large debris, flush the gutter in the direction of the drain, using a garden hose and sprayer attachment.

4. If the downspout is clogged, insert a garden hose into the lower end of the downspout and spray water upward. If that doesn't force out the clog, run the hose from the top of the downspout. If the clog still won't come loose or you determine that it's in a bend of the downspout, guide a plumber's auger or snake up the downspout and draw out the debris.

5. Inspect your gutters for leaks or sagginess. If you find any, now is a good time to make the necessary repairs.

There are a variety of protectors designed to deflect leaves and other debris from gutters to keep them cleaner. If you decide to install one, be sure it can be easily removed and reinstalled,

SMART PURCHASE

With a pressure washer, you can wash just about everything under the sun, from siding and screens to driveways, vehicles, and tools. If you want a machine that can do it all, look for one with a pressure rating of up to 3,000 pounds per square inch (psi) and an injection port for drawing in liquid detergent. Pressure washers are also readily available from tool-rental companies.

as it — and your gutters — will likely require occasional cleaning. Beware of strainers or screens; leaves can pile up on top of them and prevent water from flowing into the gutters.

Siding. If you live on a dusty road or in a dry climate, you may need to wash your siding up to two times a year. To remove dust and cobwebs, all you need is a garden hose with a sprayer attachment. To remove heavier dirt, mud, and grime, look for an all-purpose house wash in a container that attaches to your garden hose. Or use a long-handled, soft scrub brush along with house-wash detergent or a slightly sudsy solution of dishwashing liquid and water. Wash from the bottom up, and rinse from the top to the bottom. If you decide to rent or buy a pressure washer, be sure to adjust the pressure to no more than 300 to 500 pounds per square inch, and always hold the sprayer wand several feet away from the house to avoid damaging the wood siding.

If mildew (black or gray spots) is present on your wood siding, ask your paint dealer to recommend an appropriate house wash that includes a mildewcide. After washing, allow the house to dry for at least two to three days in dry weather before repainting.

Screens. At least once a year, give window screens a good scrubbing. If you take screens out in the fall, clean them before putting them into winter storage, and cover them to keep off the dust. Before reinstalling the screens, clean the windows and their frames. A stiff bristle brush will clean metal window tracks very nicely.

- To clean screens that are only a bit dusty or dirty, simply spray the screens with a garden hose and sprayer attachment and allow them to air-dry.
- To clean very dirty screens, lay them flat on a clean picnic table, deck, patio, or driveway. Put a squirt or two of dishwashing liquid in a bucket of water so it's just a little sudsy. Dip a soft nylon brush into the solution and gently scrub first one side and then the other side of each screen. Spray them with a garden hose to rinse, and allow them to air-dry thoroughly.

Windows. To wash exterior windows quickly and without a ladder, attach a bottle of window cleaner designed to fit a standard garden hose, and spray away. With this method, windows can be washed at the rate of one per minute, and the special for-

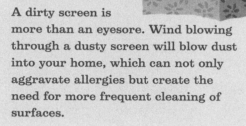

mula allows them to dry without spots or streaks. Look for this type of product in your supermarket. Refer to chapter 4, page 70, for more tips on washing windows.

Doors and Lighting. Sweep away cobwebs in the entrance. Wash the front door. Clean and shine the brass knocker if you have one. Clean any outdoor light fixtures and lightbulbs.

How To CLEAN A BIRDBATH

Birds are not likely to splash around in a dirty birdbath. Frequent cleaning not only attracts more bird visitors but also helps prevent algae growth, disease transmission between birds, and mosquitoes, which are likely to breed in standing water. For best results, clean the bath and change the water at least once a week.

1. Empty the bath completely by tipping it to one side.
2. Scrub the bath with a small scrub brush or pot scrubber. If the bath is very dirty, scrub it with a slightly sudsy solution of dishwashing liquid and water or a specialized birdbath-cleaning product.
3. Rinse the bath thoroughly; if you used soap, be sure to remove all traces of the detergent.
4. Refill the bath with fresh water.

Helpful hint: Tossing three or four copper pennies or a piece of copper pipe into a birdbath seems to help prevent algae from growing in it. It doesn't hurt to try.

*I am a marvelous housekeeper.
Every time I leave a man,
I keep his house.*

— Zsa Zsa Gabor

Decks

A clean deck not only looks better but also lasts longer. Leaves and debris that become trapped between the boards in turn trap moisture, which leads to the growth of mildew or the rotting of the wood. A deck situated in a humid environment is particularly susceptible to developing mildew. And a shaded deck is the perfect environment for green algae, which can be slippery when wet, increasing the likelihood of injury due to a slip or fall. So keep that deck clean.

Once a year, thoroughly clean and reseal your wood deck. Cleaning removes dirt, algae, moss, and other organic matter. Resealing slows the return of organic buildup and involves applying a clear or semiclear liquid sealant to all exposed surfaces. Many professional firms offer this service. If you decide to do it yourself, avoid cleaning a deck on a hot, windy, or sunny day, as the cleaning solution and preservative may evaporate too quickly. Here's what to do:

1. Clear the deck of furniture and toys, and cover any fragile plants in the ground near the deck.
2. Sweep the deck free of large debris, and use a garden hose and sprayer attachment to rinse mud and soil from the surface. To remove trapped leaves and debris from between boards, set the sprayer nozzle on your garden hose to the most powerful setting. Working your way from one end of the deck to the other, direct the spray between the boards to jettison the debris. If necessary, use a paint-stirring stick or other tool to manually remove stubborn debris. If you use a pressure washer, use the sprayer fan and be very careful to keep the nozzle at least a few feet from the deck to avoid gouging the wood.
3. Wash the deck with a commercial deck-cleaning product or a sudsy mixture of laundry detergent and water. Apply the cleaning solution to the deck and scrub with a push broom or long-handled stiff brush. Then spray the decking with the garden hose to rinse.
4. To remove algae (green) or mildew (black) buildup, mix a solution of one part bleach to four parts water and pour it over the deck, taking care not to get any of the bleach solution on nearby plants. Use a push broom to scrub off algae and mildew. Note that while liquid chlorine bleach will kill mold, mildew, and algae, it also can change the color of the wood. If you have any concerns about that, use an oxygen bleach cleaner instead. If your deck has heavy algae or mildew buildup, allow whatever cleaning solution you use to sit on the wood for 10 to 15 minutes while you scrub with a stiff bristle brush. You may need to let the surface dry and repeat the process to clean very discolored areas.
5. Rinse the decking thoroughly and allow it to dry for a few days.

6. Coat the deck with a penetrating preservative, such as a linseed-oil-based stain, which will be soaked up by the wood. In addition to offering protection from damaging ultraviolet rays, some wood preservatives actually waterproof the deck; others contain mildewcide.

Outdoor Furniture

Keeping outdoor furniture looking like new is not difficult. In fact, it's possible to double the life of some patio and pool furniture with proper cleaning and maintenance. Even vinyl straps and fabrics that are permanently stained can be refinished for far less than it costs to buy new furniture.

The quickest, easiest way to clean vinyl, plastic, and metal furniture is with a garden hose and a sprayer attachment. Furniture with waterproof fabric can also be hosed down. Remove the cushions and spray the furniture to get it wet; then wash with soapy water and spray again to rinse. Or use a cleaning product that attaches to a standard garden hose to speed-clean patio furniture and play sets. Avoid using abrasive cleaners or cleaning tools. If you use a pressure washer, use it only on the lowest pressure setting with the sprayer fan, to avoid blowing lighter furniture around.

Do not throw furniture in the swimming pool to clean it, as prolonged exposure to pool chlorine will severely damage the finish of the furniture and cause corrosion of the aluminum inside the tubing. Besides, you'll just make the pool dirty!

To clean specific types of furniture, it's best to follow the manufacturer's cleaning instructions. If the instructions aren't available, use the following tips.

Outdoor Fabrics. As a general rule, it's a good idea to clean the fabric on outdoor furniture weekly or biweekly as follows:

1. Vacuum or use a soft brush on the fabric to remove dirt and debris.

2. Wipe down the furniture with a damp cloth.

3. To spot-clean stains on acrylic, polyester, canvas, and cotton fabrics, sponge the area with soapy, lukewarm water. If necessary, mix ¼ cup of liquid all-fabric (oxygen) bleach in 1 gallon of warm water and sponge the mixture over the fabric. Always test the bleach on an inconspicuous area of the fabric first to ensure it won't damage the fabric. Rinse by sponging with plain water.

4. Air-dry. Turn cushions on their sides, with the zipper or seam side down, for faster drying. Doing this on a windy day will also speed the process.

Vinyl-Strapped Furniture. Clean vinyl outdoor furniture with a soft brush, using a sudsy mixture of mild laundry detergent and very warm water. If that doesn't remove stains, try scrubbing with a specialty vinyl cleaner or a solution of a capful or two of household liquid chlorine bleach in 1 gallon of water. Apply vinyl protectant to the straps when you're done cleaning. If the vinyl is so worn that you can't get it clean, it's time to replace the vinyl straps.

KNOW AND TELL

Suntan oil and pool chlorine can stain and eventually eat away the finish of vinyl and other fabrics. Extend the life of pool furniture by spreading towels on chairs before you sit down in them.

Acrylic and Vinyl-Coated Polyester Weaves. It is usually sufficient to wash this kind of fabric with a solution of 1 fluid ounce of dishwashing liquid in 1 gallon of lukewarm water. Rinse thoroughly with water and air-dry. *Note:* Using cleaners on waterproof fabrics will remove some of the waterproofing. It's a good idea to reapply waterproofing at the start of each season. Clean the fabric first; then spray with a fabric waterproofer.

● **Suntan lotion stains.** For stubborn stains or blotches caused by suntan lotion, use fabric spot remover, following the directions on the container. Rinse thoroughly. You can also try using a nonabrasive household cleaner or rubbing alcohol on a sponge.

● **Heavy soiling or mildew.** For allover cleaning of very dirty or mildewed acrylic fabric, prepare a solution of 1 cup of liquid chlorine bleach and 1 cup of mild dishwashing liquid in 3 gallons of water. Spray or sponge the solution onto the fabric and allow it to soak in. Scrub with a soft brush and rinse thoroughly with clean water. Allow to air-dry. (Don't use this solution, or any type of bleach solution, on acrylic prints, as they are likely to fade.)

Olefin and Polyester. Periodically sponge down furniture with these fabrics with a mild solution of detergent and water, and then rinse, to keep the fabric looking fresh and new and to prevent mildew. To remove a stain, sponge it with warm water as soon after its occurrence as possible. If necessary, apply a laundry prewash and leave it on the stain for 10 minutes; then wash it with warm water and a detergent solution and rinse thoroughly.

Aluminum Frames. Clean the frames with warm, soapy water, and rinse thoroughly. Do not use abrasive cleaners. Twice a year, wax the frames — the arms, legs, and other nonstrapped areas — with a nonabrasive car wax. Do not use compound wax, and be sure to wipe off any wax that gets on the vinyl straps.

Molded Resin. Clean lightly soiled resin furniture with 1 tablespoon of laundry detergent in 1 gallon of water. For more heavily soiled or stained furniture, use a commercial all-purpose spray cleaner. Avoid using abrasive powders, chlorine bleaches, and silicone cleaners.

CLEAN MILDEWED CUSHIONS

Mildew has a tendency to grow on damp, soiled fabrics and cushions. To clean these items, try the following.

1. Mix 1 gallon of water, 1 cup of chlorine bleach, and a squirt of dishwashing liquid. (*Important:* Check the label of the dishwashing liquid to make sure it does not contain ammonia, which should not be mixed with bleach.) Before cleaning the entire cushion, test the solution on a small, inconspicuous area and let it dry, to make sure the solution won't fade the color. Chlorine bleach may not be suitable for all prints.

2. Saturate a rag or soft brush with the solution and begin scrubbing the cushions, one small area at a time.

3. Rinse well with water. Let the cushions dry completely before returning them to the furniture they belong with.

Acrylic Tabletops. Wash periodically with warm, soapy water. Do not use window cleaners or products containing ammonia or solvents, as these may damage the finish. At the beginning of each season, apply an automotive paste wax to keep your acrylic table looking like new. Never put plastic covers over acrylic tabletops because the resulting heat buildup may cause the acrylic to bow.

Glass and Fiberglass Tabletops. Use a glass cleaner with ammonia to remove dirt and grime. You can remove mineral deposits with a product formulated for that purpose. To remove mildew on a table with a rim-locked glass top, spray it with a solution of ¼ cup of liquid chlorine bleach in 16 ounces of water. Be sure to clean both the top and the bottom of the tabletop. Let the solution stand for a few minutes, and then rinse with a garden hose and sprayer attachment.

Plastic Tabletops. Clean the tabletop with warm, soapy water or, if needed, a diluted bleach solution (1 ounce of liquid chlorine bleach in 16 ounces of water). To restore its luster, apply a coat of automotive paste wax. Do not use solvents, scouring powder, or undiluted liquid chlorine bleach.

Stone and Faux Stone Tabletops. When necessary, clean these surfaces with warm, soapy water. If necessary, use a mild abrasive cleaner to release embedded dirt. Rinse thoroughly with clean water.

Teak. Teak does not require any special maintenance apart from occasional cleaning. If the furniture is left outside to age naturally — exposed to light, air, and rain — the surface of the teak will gradually change to a soft silver-gray as the pigments in the surface layer of the wood start to fade away. This is normal.

- To clean without altering the silver-gray color, once a year scrub gently with a slightly sudsy solution of soap flakes (not detergent) in warm water to remove dirt, grease, and stains.
- To maintain the original color, use a teak cleaner and follow the instructions on the product label.
- To restore teak that has become badly weathered (gray-black in color) or extremely dirty, use a teak cleaner and brightener.
- Do not use any type of oil on teak furniture that is used outside. This may cause mildew and irregular coloring.

Wood. Follow the manufacturer's recommended cleaning procedures for wood furniture. If the wood has been exposed to moisture and dirt, spotting and mildew may occur. To restore the luster of finished wood, sand with a fine-grade sandpaper, clean with a wood cleaner, and then reapply oil to the surface. To clean unfinished wood, use a soft-bristled brush to apply a solution of 1 cup of ammonia, ½ cup of white vinegar, and 1 gallon of water. Rinse well and wipe dry.

Wrought Iron or Steel. Wash your furniture with a mild liquid soap such as car wash soap.

Q & A : Outdoor Cleaning

Q *How do you clean algae off a slate patio?*

A Use a garden hose to wet the stone slabs. Put a squirt or two of dishwashing liquid in a bucket of water so it's just a little sudsy. Dip a stiff broom into the bucket and use to clean the slate and grouting in between the slabs. Rinse thoroughly.

Q *What's the best way to clean bird droppings off furniture and other outdoor items?*

A Leave bird droppings alone until they dry. Brush off what you can, and then wipe the spot clean with a damp, sudsy sponge or cloth.

Q *How should I clean trash cans?*

A Pour ¼ cup of liquid laundry detergent and ¼ cup of liquid chlorine bleach in a 5-gallon bucket filled with hot water. Wearing waterproof gloves, dip a cloth or long-handled brush into the bucket and use it to scrub the outside of the trash can. Next, pour the sudsy mixture into the trash can and scrub the inside with a mop or long-handled brush. Rinse the can with water from a garden hose. Turn the can upside down to drain and dry. Wash trash cans every couple of weeks to prevent sticky buildup and to discourage animals from getting into your garbage. Place all trash in sealed bags to keep your cans cleaner longer.

Scuff marks on wrought iron can be removed with a light abrasive. Twice a year, wax the frames with a nonabrasive automotive wax. Do not use compound wax. To remove excessive rust, apply a rust remover, following the instructions on the product label, and wipe clean.

Wicker. Furniture made of wicker has a tendency to dry out, so keep it out of the sun.

- For light cleaning on an as-needed basis, vacuum the furniture with a brush attachment or brush off dirt and debris. Then wipe it down with a soft, damp cloth.
- You can also hose down wicker furniture to rinse off dust and grime. Turn the piece on its side so that the water can run off rather than lodge in the weave, which could cause the strands to warp and dry out of shape.
- To clean very dirty wicker, mix ½ cup of wood oil soap in 1 gallon of warm water. Wet a cloth with this mixture and gently wipe one small section of the wicker at a time. Use a toothbrush or paintbrush to clean the tight spaces between the weave. Rinse with a hose, wipe with a dry cloth, and allow 24 to 48 hours to dry completely.

Hammocks. Remove the hammock from its stand. Lay it flat on a smooth surface, such as a clean patio or picnic table. Use a soft-bristled brush and a sudsy mixture of dishwashing liquid and water to clean one side. Rinse well, and then repeat on the other side.

Umbrellas. Some umbrellas allow you to remove the fabric from the frame and wash it in a washing machine (check the label). To clean a fabric umbrella on its frame:

1. Remove the extension pole (so the umbrella will be easier to reach) and open the umbrella. Or remove the umbrella from the table, open it, and lay it on its side.
2. Apply a slightly sudsy mixture of dishwashing liquid and water to the fabric with a sponge. Lightly scrub with a soft-bristled brush if needed.
3. Use a garden hose to rinse off the umbrella. Wipe the hardware dry and allow the fabric to dry thoroughly before closing the umbrella, to prevent mildew.
4. If the pole is unpainted aluminum, wipe it down with WD-40 to remove any light rust that might interfere with the working of the umbrella. If the pole is painted metal, apply a coat of automotive wax.

Cleaning Your Barbecue Grill

There's more to cleaning your grill than just scraping the grate with a brush or scraper. And contrary to popular belief, simply heating the grill on high does not clean the grate.

According to grillmaster Steven Raichlen, author of the award-winning *Barbecue Bible!*, *How to Grill*, and *BBQ USA*, the secret to successful grilling is "Keep it hot. Keep it clean. Keep it lubricated." He recommends cleaning and lubricating the grilling grate every time you fire up the grill. Preheat the grill to high, and brush the grill with a brass-bristled brush. Then take a paper towel, fold it into a small, tight pad, dip it into a bowl of vegetable oil, and rub it across the bars of the hot grate, using a pair of long-handled tongs. Repeat as often as necessary, replacing the paper towel as needed. The grill grate should have a bright sheen of oil and the pad should come away clean when you're finished rubbing.

For Safety's Sake

At the start of the grilling season, or at least twice a year if you use your gas grill year-round, perform the following quick check to make sure it is safe to use:

1. Remove the grates and metal baffles or ceramic or lava stones.

2. Visually inspect the manifolds and burner tubes for spiders, dead leaves, or other blockages, and remove them with a long bamboo skewer or a knitting needle.

3. Check the tiny holes in the burner tubes. If any are blocked, open them with a pin or needle.

4. Make sure the burner controls turn freely. If they're stuck or frozen, lubricate them with a little oil or WD-40.

5. Hook up the propane, and with the burner controls in the "off" position, open the tank valve. Do you smell gas? If you do, close the tank valve and make up a mixture of equal parts of dish soap and water. Open the valve again and brush the solution over the valve and the hoses leading into the grill. If there is a leak in the system, you'll see a large bubble. In that case, call your grill manufacturer and order replacement parts.

6. If there are no leaks, turn on the burner valves and push the igniter button. Always have the lid open when you light your grill. Make sure all the burners light and the burner controls work.

Of course, the grilling grate is not the only part of your grill that needs regular cleaning. You also need to clean out ashes regularly. Do this when the grill is cold. Raichlen recommends using a garden trowel to scrape any burned-on ash or crud out of the firebox or, if you have a kettle grill, the metal bowl. While you're at it, scrape out the ash catcher or ash pan, if your grill has one, and empty the grease catcher or drip pan.

Clean the interior and exterior of your grill with a nylon scrub sponge or brush and a sudsy mixture of dishwashing liquid and water, or spray on a citrus-oil-based all-purpose cleaner and wipe clean with a sponge. Cover your grill when it is not in use, to keep it clean and rust-free. And be sure to clean your grill before putting it away for the season.

A Sparkling-Clean Pool

Keeping your pool clean and clear is simple with a little know-how. A regular maintenance routine will keep debris and other undesirables out of the water and regulate the balance of the chemicals in the water. For tips on opening and closing a pool, see page 258, in chapter 16.

- **Circulate water.** A stagnant pool will quickly develop algae. Run your pool pump 1 hour daily for every 10°F of the highest average daytime temperature; for example, on an 80°F (27°C) day, you would run the pump for 8 hours. Most pumps come with a timer so you can run them automatically every night. If your pool does not look clean in the morning, check that the pump is running.

For Safety's Sake

Standing water creates the perfect breeding ground for mosquitoes, which can carry West Nile virus. This can be a serious health hazard for your family and neighbors. Store wheelbarrows, buckets, and other open containers upside down to keep rain from collecting in them.

- **Skim the pool daily.** Every day, remove debris from the skimmer basket and use a skimming net to remove floating debris. Check the pump skimmer baskets once a week and clean them out as needed.

- **Keep your filter clean.** Some filters need to be backwashed periodically. All filters need to be cleaned once or twice a year. Follow your pool manufacturer's instructions for cleaning, or hire someone to do the job.

- **Brush pool walls and floors weekly.** Brushing helps prevent algae and bacteria from taking hold. Pay special attention to the tops and sides of steps, where these nasties like to grow.

- **Test, test, test.** Testing is the best way to prevent problems. Purchase and use an inexpensive testing kit or strips to test chlorine and pH levels twice weekly, and adjust them as needed. Once a month, take a sample of your pool water to your local pool chemical retailer, where it can be tested for total alkalinity and calcium hardness. When either of these chemicals is out of whack, it becomes difficult to maintain the proper balance of pH and chlorine. Once each season, you should test your pool water to make sure it has adequate chlorine stabilizer, which protects chlorine from being broken down by the sun's ultraviolet rays, and makes it last longer.

- **Shock your pool regularly.** Shocking, or superchlorinating, removes sunblock residue, perspiration, makeup, body oil, urine, and other contaminants from pool water. Shocking should be done after dust or rainstorms blow debris into the pool, after a large number of bathers have been in the pool during exceptionally hot weather (which can deplete chlorine), and whenever the pool water looks cloudy.

- **Prevent algae.** Regular maintenance as described above should prevent algae, but you can eliminate any algae that does form with algicide products designed specifically for pools. Check the label for precautions around children.

Q & A : Pool Problems

Q *We have a white line on our tile at the water level. What causes it, and how do we get rid of it?*

A The stain is the result of calcium and magnesium deposits, which naturally occur in hard water. Run your hand along the edge of the pool at the water line; you often can feel the deposits even before you can see them. To prevent the line from forming, use a nonabrasive scouring pad to clean the calcium film from around the perimeter. Do this every couple of weeks. Once you can see the stain, it's harder to get off. You can try scrubbing with a pumice tool, but you may have to have the tile cleaned professionally.

Q *How do we get rid of algae that started on the surface of the pool and is now clinging to the sides?*

A You're probably dealing with black algae or spot algae, which can "pit" plaster surfaces. Adjust the pH to 7.4. Then vigorously brush the spots and treat the water with an algae-destroying product. Repeat the treatment as necessary.

Q *Our pool water is cloudy. What should we do?*

A Cloudy water is most often an indicator of poor water filtration. Run the pump for 10 hours or until the water is clear. If it doesn't clear up overnight, shock your pool with a superchlorinating product as directed on the label.

Chemistry Basics

Balanced chemistry helps keep the water clear and also makes swimming more comfortable by preventing eye and skin irritation. The four issues of concern are free chlorine, pH, total alkalinity, and calcium hardness.

CHLORINE. Chlorine sanitizes water and also kills bacteria. Measuring the amount of free chlorine tells you how much chlorine is available to do this work; the ideal range is one to three parts per million. Add chlorine tablets or sticks to increase the free chlorine level.

pH. This is the most important factor in balancing your water. The ideal pH range is between 7.2 and 7.6. If the pH is too high, add muriatic acid or another pH decreaser. If it is too low, add pH increaser.

TOTAL ALKALINITY. Total alkalinity is the total concentration of several chemicals that help stabilize pH. Total alkalinity should be between 125 and 150 parts per million.

CALCIUM HARDNESS. Hardness refers to the amount of calcium dissolved in the water. The desired range for is between 200 and 250 parts per million for plaster pools and between 175 and 225 parts per million for vinyl, fiberglass, and painted pools. If calcium hardness is over 500 parts per million, drain some water from the pool and replace it with fresh water. The higher the calcium hardness level, the more chemicals are required to maintain the proper balance.

Sports and Recreational Gear

If your lifestyle revolves around sports, you need to know how to clean up your gear. Fortunately, it's pretty simple, so you can get back out there and play!

Sleeping Bags. Follow the directions for care on the sleeping-bag label. It may be fine to run the bag through the rinse and spin cycles of your washing machine, on the gentle or delicate setting in cool water. If in doubt, however, wash your sleeping bag by hand in the bathtub with a nondetergent soap — pure soap, vegetable soap, or soap flakes — or a mild fabric wash for hand-washables.

1. Work the suds in gently. Do not twist or wring.
2. Rinse thoroughly until all the suds are gone.
3. Repeat the washing and rinsing until the suds stay white, which should be two or three times at the most.
4. Rinse very thoroughly the last time to remove all traces of soap.
5. Press the bag firmly but gently to remove as much water as possible.
6. Let your bag air-dry; warm, windy days provide the best drying conditions. It might be safe to tumble it dry on a gentle cycle in a large commercial dryer on low heat. Toss in a clean tennis ball to help prevent the down from clumping. Remove the bag promptly once it's dry, and lay it flat until it's cool.

Tents. Do not machine-wash or machine-dry your tent. Instead, on an as-needed basis, simply vacuum it to remove loose dirt and dust, and spot-clean with a sponge and warm water.

If the entire tent needs to be cleaned, proceed as follows:

1. Hose down the tent with clear water, or immerse it in a bathtub with cold water and a nondetergent soap — pure soap, vegetable soap, soap flakes, or a specially formulated tent cleaner.
2. Using a soft-bristled brush, scrub the tent gently to lift off dirt.
3. Rinse the tent thoroughly several times to remove all traces of soap residue.
4. Dry your tent by pitching it in the shade or hanging it on a clothesline out of direct sunlight for a period of several days.
5. After cleaning, apply a coat of water repellent.
6. Pack up and store the tent. But to prevent mildew, be sure the tent is completely dry before you do so.

Bicycles. Whether you commute with pedal power or ride for pleasure, periodic cleaning of your bicycle will keep it at peak performance. Even if you aren't riding on muddy trails, your bicycle picks up grease and grime over time.

1. Use a garden hose to gently spray off any dirt and grime. (Do not use a pressure washer, as this will blow out the grease that keeps your bicycle running smoothly.)

For Safety's Sake

The Home Safety Council recommends following these storage tips to create a safer backyard:

- **Practice poison prevention.** Store pesticides, herbicides, and lawn-treatment chemicals in their original containers, on high shelves or inside locked cabinets, out of the reach of children.
- **Put away tools when they're not in use.** Garden tools such as rakes, spades, forks, pruning clippers, files, and metal plant stakes should not be left lying around. Store these with their sharp points aiming down.

2. Apply a cleaner/degreaser formulated for bikes to the frame, rims, and drivetrain and anywhere you have dirt or grime.
3. Rinse off the cleaner and dry the bicycle with a soft cloth.
4. Apply a bicycle-specific lubricant to your chain to prevent rust, shed dirt, and promote smoother and faster shifting.

Golf Clubs. Serious players will clean their clubs after each swing to keep the grooves clean and the flight of the ball more pure. Whether you do this after every swing or after your game, use a special wire brush (available at

golf pro shops) or the tip of a golf tee to clean out the grooves on the club.

To remove caked-on dirt, immerse the club in just enough water to cover the head of the club. After soaking it a few minutes, use a special wire brush to clean the face and grooves of the head. Dry it thoroughly with a clean cloth.

You'll also want to clean the grip on a regular basis. Again, serious players do this after every swing, but you may feel less ambitious about this. Just rub a wet towel vigorously back and forth over the grip until you see grime on the towel.

Driveways and Sidewalks

To remove leaves and other debris from your driveways and sidewalks, start with a broom, rather than a hose, to conserve water. To remove lighter stains, such as those left by leaves or tires, wet the surface with a slightly sudsy mixture of dishwashing liquid and water and then brush the driveway or sidewalk with a push broom. Or use a pressure washer to blast stains off.

Oil stains on concrete and asphalt driveways can be difficult to remove; they're even more difficult to remove than oil stains on garage floors, since garage floors tend to have a smoother, more sealed surface. It's easier to remove fresh oil stains, so you should clean them up as soon as possible after you notice them. Older oil stains may take several treatments to clean. Some stains may never come out, and some may reappear as the oil that has penetrated the driveway rises to the surface. Commercial driveway cleaner/degreasers are available, but none work exceptionally well all the time. You can also have your driveway professionally cleaned. After cleaning, consider sealing your driveway to help prevent stains from setting.

To remove an oil stain, try any of the following possible solutions.

- A surprisingly effective solution for fresh stains is to blot up the oil with paper toweling. Then sprinkle the stain with regular cat litter (not the clumping kind) or cement mix. Leave it overnight and then just sweep it up in the morning.
- Wet a fresh stain thoroughly with a citrus-based all-purpose cleaner spray and cover it with several layers of paper toweling with a brick or another heavy object on top. Wait several hours; then rinse.
- Use an old paintbrush to apply paint thinner to older stains. Then cover with an absorbent material such as cat litter or cement mix. Leave it overnight and then sweep it up. Repeat if needed.
- Wet an older stain, apply dishwasher detergent or powdered laundry detergent, wet the powder slightly, and leave it on overnight. Rinse it off in the morning.

Washing Vehicles

How often you wash your car is entirely up to you. You may think, "Why bother? It will just be dirty again tomorrow." But regular washing and waxing keeps your car looking its best, which can help it hold its value. And in snow country, regular washing and waxing keeps road salt from corroding your finish. Industry experts recommend washing your car once a week. The easiest way to get a car clean is to take it to a car wash. Or if you want it to look like new again, have it thoroughly cleaned, or "detailed," inside and out by a professional service. If you do it yourself, the more often you do it, the easier it is.

What You Need

- ❏ Source of water
- ❏ Garden hose
- ❏ Bucket
- ❏ Soap formulated for use on cars
- ❏ Large, soft sponge
- ❏ Soft cloths
- ❏ Wheel cleaner (optional)
- ❏ Tire protectant (optional)
- ❏ Vacuum cleaner
- ❏ Glass cleaner
- ❏ Paper towels

Having all your car-washing supplies and equipment handy makes the job go quicker and easier. Organize and store all automotive cleaning products and supplies together on a shelf or in a bucket that you can simply grab when you need it. Following are some general tips for washing your vehicle:

- Remove dead bugs, bird droppings, and tree sap as soon as you notice them.
- Use a soap that is specifically meant for washing cars, to avoid stripping your vehicle's wax finish.
- Wash your car in the shade and dry it with clean, soft towels to prevent the spotting and streaking that result when moisture on the exterior evaporates quickly.
- Start by giving your car a thorough rinse to remove all the surface dirt and debris; that way, you won't be pushing around all those particles as you sponge, which could potentially scratch the car's finish.
- Wash and rinse one section at a time, starting at the top and working down.
- Use horizontal strokes rather than circular motions to clean.
- Wash and rinse cloths or sponges often in a bucket of clean water.
- When rinsing, spray from the top to the bottom.

Some vehicle parts are more challenging to clean than others. Wheels and tires, for example, are generally the dirtiest parts of your car. It's advisable to use separate cloths to clean the tires and wheels to avoid transferring the debris on them to the body of the car, where it could scratch the paint.

- **Wheels.** Remove brake dust with a wheel-cleaning product designed for your type of wheels (for example, alloy or steel). Spray or brush on the product and then it rinse off in the time specified on the product label; it's generally 30 to 60 seconds.

- **Tires.** Use a whitewall cleaner on tires to remove brake dust. After washing, spray on a tire protectant for a glossy, just-washed appearance.
- **Chrome.** Shine chrome with a soft cloth dampened with distilled white vinegar. As needed, use a chrome polish to really bring out the shine.
- **Windshield wipers.** Dip a cloth in white vinegar and use it to clean road grime from windshield wipers.

Auto manufacturers recommend that you wax your car at least twice a year and as often as every three months. Waxing helps protect the finish from dirt and UV rays. It can also lessen the appearance of or even eliminate minor scratches. And it makes it easier to keep your vehicle clean in between washes. *Helpful hint:* To quickly and easily remove wax residue from black trim, spray tire protectant on a cloth and use it to wipe off the white marks.

There are some simple things you can do to keep your car cleaner between washes.

- Keep cleaning supplies, such as a microfiber cloth or premoistened glass-cleaning wipes, in your glove compartment for quick touch-ups as necessary.
- Keep a trash bag in your car and get in the habit of emptying it as needed.
- Treat your windshield, windows, mirrors, and lights with a product that not only repels water but also resists the adhesion of dirt and grime.
- Dust your car regularly with a car dust brush, available in auto parts stores. You can use this brush to dust the dashboard, too.

REMOVING WINDOW DECALS

One Challenge:

Window stickers and decals can be very difficult to remove. Following are three tricks that work every time.

Three Solutions . . .

1 Wet the sticker with white vinegar and allow it to soak in. Then scrape off the sticker with a putty knife.

2 Spray the sticker with WD-40; then wipe it off with a clean cloth. The sticker should come up. WD-40 will also remove tar from your car without damaging the paint.

3 Spray the sticker with a commercial adhesive remover designed for cars, usually found at an auto parts store. Wipe it off with a clean cloth. The sticker should come up.

- Spray and wipe the body with a quick detailing product designed to remove surface dust and enhance the shine.
- Remove fuzz from a soft top with a tape roller or adhesive tape wrapped around your hand, sticky side out.

Cleaning the interior of your car at the same time as you clean the exterior will keep it from getting overly dirty.

- Remove all trash.
- Shake out the floor mats. Vacuum the mats and then the car floor. Vinyl mats can be hosed down and dried.
- If the floor carpeting is dirty, prepare a solution of water and carpet-cleaning product, as directed on the product label, and use it to scrub the carpeting with a stiff-bristled brush. Be careful not to soak the carpets. Allow the carpeting to dry thoroughly, keeping the car doors or windows open for better ventilation.
- Vacuum the seats with the upholstery attachment.

- Wipe down the seats, doors, dashboard, steering wheel, and console with a damp cloth or, if necessary, an automotive interior cleaning solution.
- Clean the windows with a glass cleaner that does not contain ammonia, as ammonia can damage window-tint film.
- If your car has leather seats, several times a year clean and condition them with leather treatment products. Spot-clean fabric seats as needed with a foaming spray cleaner for upholstery.

KNOW AND TELL

When choosing where to wash your car, consider the fact that at a self-serve car wash, all the rinse water and contaminants are sent to a sewage treatment plant. If you wash your car at home and the rinse water is allowed to run down the street into storm drains, it will be dumped into rivers and other bodies of water, without treatment.

Part 3

Everyday Challenges

Have you ever made it through a day when you did *not* come into contact with something that needed to be cleaned? Probably not. Every day we face the challenges of dirty shoes, dirty clothes, and dirty dogs. In many households, laundry is the biggest challenge, which is why it's the biggest chapter in this section. It covers everything from a bit of history to the latest in laundry products — and how *do* you get cranberry sauce out of your tablecloth?

Once you learned more than you ever wanted to know about laundry, you'll be ready for a rundown of the many joys of pet ownership, including the challenge of cleaning up after cats, dogs, birds, hamsters, fish, and other common pets. And finally, this section answers questions about how to clean all your personal items, from hairbrushes to eyeglasses to jewelry and more.

CHAPTER TEN

CLEAN CLOTHES

Getting clothes clean is easier than ever today, thanks to innovations in laundry products and fabric care. With a little know-how and the right products, your clothes will not only look good after being washed but also last longer. And you'll suffer fewer costly and emotional disasters in the laundry room.

Then and Now

If you dislike doing laundry, imagine what it was like before the modern washing machine was invented. Back then, you had to haul enough water to fill a washing tub, heat it over a fire, add soap, scrub each item against the washboard, and then bring the water to a boil as you stirred the wash with a stick. After boiling, you had to remove the clothes and rinse them in another tub. Finally, you had to wring out the clothes, hang them on the line to dry, and repeat the whole process for the next load.

It may be far easier to do laundry today, but it's still work. According to a 2003 Whirlpool survey, the typical U.S. family does eight to ten loads of wash each week. That's 40 to 70 pounds of laundry a week! An earlier survey by Procter & Gamble found that the average person generates well over a quarter of a ton of dirty clothes per year. Have you ever added up how much time you spend washing and drying clothes? Depending on your lifestyle, your schedule, and the amount of clothing you own, it could be hundreds of hours each year.

One thing is certain: laundry is less of a chore when you do it more often. If you frequently run out of clean clothes to wear or regularly face piles of dirty laundry, make a decision now to start a wash whenever you have a full load or to do two or three loads every Monday night or Saturday morning. Pick a day that works for you, and stick to it. Then you'll always have clean clothes when you want them.

Many homemakers in the nineteenth and early twentieth centuries, even those of limited means, sent out at least some of their washing to professional laundry services. In fact, as commercial laundries gained in popularity, it appeared that laundry might be permanently deleted from the household to-do list. Then along came the electric washing machine, which, to the woe of homemakers, brought the task of doing laundry back into the home and eventually put commercial laundries out of business.

Streamlining the Process

Laundry is one of those household chores that can seem endless, especially in large households. No sooner do you finish a load of wash than you have another to do. There's probably not much you can do about that, short of rewearing clothes and buying more socks and underwear. But you can take steps to make the whole process more efficient — and enjoy better results with less effort.

Collecting Dirty Laundry. The closer a hamper is to where household members get undressed, the more likely it is that dirty clothes will end up in it. Place a hamper in each bedroom, and if necessary, put one in each bathroom. For the dual purpose of collecting and transporting laundry, a lightweight plastic basket with handles or a hamper with a removable liner is a good choice.

Items that need to be dry-cleaned or hand-washed should be collected separately from other clothes. Consider hanging in your closet or on the back of the bedroom door a small mesh bag for hand-washable items and a larger bag for items that need to be taken to the dry cleaner.

Transporting Laundry. Invest in a set of laundry baskets for transporting laundry to and from the laundry room. Assign one basket to each family member. Write each person's name on a piece of masking tape and affix it to the appropriate basket. Have each individual use his or her basket to bring dirty laundry to the laundry and also to return clean clothes to his or her room. Now, some family members may never get around to putting their clothes away, choosing instead to live out of the basket of clean clothes until they run out. But the basket method may increase the likelihood that clothes will get put away, simply because the basket will be needed for transporting dirty clothes. It's worth a try.

Q & A : Laundry List

Q. *If a fabric care label says "hand wash," can I wash the item in the washing machine on the delicate cycle?*

A. It is not advisable. You may be able to get away with it by putting the item in a mesh bag to minimize agitation. But your safest bet is to follow the care label instructions. Dry cleaning may also be an option.

Q. *I swear I lose socks in the wash. Could it be possible?*

A. Yes, sometimes lightweight objects like socks and underwear get sucked under the agitator and down the drain with the dirty water. To help prevent this from happen-ing, load heavier items such as towels and jeans first and then top off the load with lighter items. Or put socks, especially baby socks, in a zippered mesh bag.

Q. *What causes static in clothes?*

A. Static cling is caused by the buildup of electric charge, which is usually caused by one surface being rubbed against another. Overdrying clothes, particularly nylon and other synthetic fabrics, and drying at too high a setting can cause static cling. Using fabric softener sheets in the dryer can help prevent static cling. There are also products you can spray on your clothes to prevent them from holding an electrical charge.

Sorting Dirty Laundry. It's quicker and easier to do laundry when dirty clothes are presorted into the three major types of wash loads: whites, lights, and darks. The simplest way to do this in the laundry room is using a triple-sorter laundry cart with three large fabric bags that hang from a sturdy metal frame. If you are using the basket method described in the previous paragraph, have family members sort their laundry into the appropriate bag and then stack their empty baskets on top of the dryer, on a shelf, or in a corner of the laundry room. Alternatively, you can remove bags from the cart to collect laundry from various locations around the house, or you can wheel the entire cart from room to room if you live on one floor.

Washing and Drying. Keep your detergent and laundry aids handy — store them on shelves or in a cabinet near your washing machine. If storage space is limited, look for shelves that attach to the washer or dryer. Rolling caddies are also available. The washer and dryer tops are a great place to fold laundry — if you keep them free of clutter. Some rolling laundry carts include a hinged top that can be used for folding clothing and a rod for hanging items as they come out of the dryer. Another option is to install a single rod or set of rods that fold back to the wall when they are not in use. Or keep a tension rod on hand that you can mount in the doorway when you need it and take down when you're done. (Such a rod is also very useful for hanging guests' coats when you have a party.)

Sharing the Load

Since everyone in your home wears clothes, it makes sense that laundry should be a shared responsibility. Three-year-olds can help match clean socks. At the age of six, children can be expected to put away their own clean clothes. Nine-year-olds are quite capable of sorting laundry. And all family members over the age of twelve can learn to do laundry. Write how-to instructions for each type of wash load, and tape them to the washer or pin them to the sorting bags for easy reference.

For ease in returning laundry to its proper owner, you might consider color-coding children's clothing. Assign a different color to each child, and use a set of laundry markers to dot clothing tags and the toes of white and light-colored socks in the appropriate color for each child. Post a key to the color-coding system on your dryer so that whoever is doing the folding knows whose clothes are whose.

Laundry Basics

According to a 2004 survey released by GE Harmony, 85 percent of women claim to be primarily responsible for doing the laundry in households across the United States. Further questioning revealed that almost 75 percent choose to do the laundry because they just don't trust anyone else with their clothes.

The key to avoiding laundry disasters is not trial and error but knowledge. Do you know what's supposed to get washed with what? Or what's the best temperature for washing clothes? You can learn a lot about doing laundry by reading fabric care labels. It's also a good idea to look for care labels *before* you buy a new article of clothing, especially if you prefer to live a simple, carefree life. Do you really have the time to hand-wash items? Are you willing to pay for dry cleaning? Or are those special-care items destined to end up on the floor of your closet, never to be seen or worn again?

Whether you're doing laundry for the first time or teaching someone how to do laundry, refer to the following step-by-step guide for achieving the best results wash after wash.

STEP 1: Sort the Laundry. Sort first by color: whites, lights, and darks. The most common laundry mistake is mixing colored clothing with whites. You should never wash light and dark fabrics together, because the dyes from the dark clothes may bleed into the lighter-colored fabrics, especially in warm or hot water. One red sock can turn an entire load of white clothing into pink clothing. Even in cold water, washing

GUIDE TO FABRIC CARE SYMBOLS

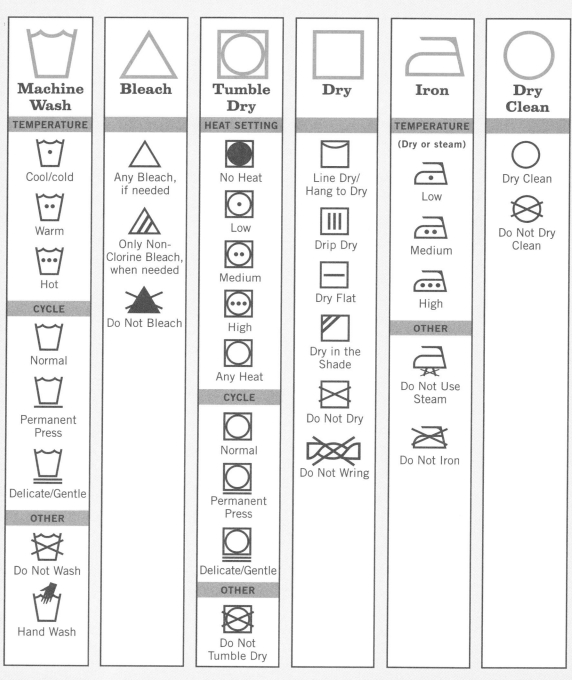

Machine Wash

TEMPERATURE
- Cool/cold
- Warm
- Hot

CYCLE
- Normal
- Permanent Press
- Delicate/Gentle

OTHER
- Do Not Wash
- Hand Wash

Bleach
- Any Bleach, if needed
- Only Non-Clorine Bleach, when needed
- Do Not Bleach

Tumble Dry

HEAT SETTING
- No Heat
- Low
- Medium
- High
- Any Heat

CYCLE
- Normal
- Permanent Press
- Delicate/Gentle

OTHER
- Do Not Tumble Dry

Dry
- Line Dry/Hang to Dry
- Drip Dry
- Dry Flat
- Dry in the Shade
- Do Not Dry
- Do Not Wring

Iron

TEMPERATURE
(Dry or steam)
- Low
- Medium
- High

OTHER
- Do Not Use Steam
- Do Not Iron

Dry Clean
- Dry Clean
- Do Not Dry Clean

courtesy of the Soap and Detergent Association

brightly colored fabrics with whites results in less-than-white clothing over time. Generally, keep the following in mind as you sort clothing to be washed:

- Whites include white and light-colored sheets, towels, and plain white clothing, such as T-shirts, underwear, and socks that can withstand a hot-water wash without shrinking. Read those fabric care labels!
- Lights include colorfast pastels as well as white or light-colored fabrics with prints.
- Darks may include medium-colored and bright colorfast fabrics as well as dark-colored clothes.

A colorfast fabric is one that does not bleed dye in water. To determine whether an item is colorfast, place it in a sink full of water and let it sit for 10 to 15 minutes, or wash it separately in the washer. Dye in the water is a sure sign that the fabric is not colorfast. Continue to wash the item separately until the color no longer bleeds in the water. If an item's fabric care label says "Wash separately," it is probably not colorfast. Fluorescent colors are generally much less colorfast than other colored fabrics; wash these separately or test for colorfastness first.

After sorting laundry loads by color, sort by fabric type and degree of soil. Separate more delicate items, such as woven knits and sheer fabrics. Wash the delicate items separately, using the delicate setting on your washer, hand-washing them in the sink and hanging them to dry, or having them dry-cleaned. Also, do not wash towels and fuzzy fabrics like fleece with corduroys and permanent-press garments, such as those

made of nylon, that attract lint. Wash heavily soiled items such as gardening or work clothes separately from everyday items that are lightly soiled. Because soils are deposited in the wash water, washing heavily soiled items with lightly soiled items can make the latter even dirtier!

STEP 2: Select Wash Temperature. The choice of water temperature depends on the amount of soil, the fabric type, and the colorfastness of fabrics in the wash load.

- **Hot water.** A water temperature of around 130°F (54°C) is recommended for keeping whites white. You should also use a hot-water wash for diapers and for heavily soiled clothes such as gardening clothes. Do be careful not to wash a freshly stained item in hot water without first attempting to remove the stain. Hot water can set a fresh stain, especially if it is blood, wine, or coffee.

- **Warm water.** Use water in the range of 90° (32°C) to 110°F (43°C) to wash light-colored fabrics, noncolorfast fabrics, permanent press fabrics, and moderately soiled fabrics.

- **Cold water.** Use water at a temperature of about 80°F (27°C) or colder to wash lightly soiled loads, dark or bright colors that might fade or bleed, and delicate items, including washable woolens, that may shrink in warm temperatures.

When in doubt about what temperature to use for a particular article of clothing, read and follow the laundering instructions on the fabric care label. For best results, it's generally recommended that you select the hottest temperature the load of fabrics can withstand. However, warm and cold water are more economical and energy-efficient choices than hot water, as most of the energy used by the washing machine is for heating the water. Choosing to rinse in cold water saves energy while also protecting colors and reducing wrinkling of permanent-press fabrics.

STEP 3: Select Washing Action. This setting controls the agitation level of the washer. Choose the gentle cycle or hand-wash cycle for delicate fabrics and the permanent-press setting to reduce wrinkling of man-made fabrics. Use normal or regular agitation for all other wash loads. Also, adjust the wash cycle time as needed: longer wash times for heavier, more soiled clothing and shorter wash times for lighter, less soiled clothing.

STEP 4: Add Detergent to the Washer. Begin to fill the washer tub with water, and then add detergent (and any laundry aids; see page 168). Adding detergent to the water before adding clothes allows it to disperse properly and prevents detergent residue in clothing (a potential problem if you are using powdered detergent).

STEP 5: Prepare Clothes for Washing. Before adding each item to the washer, check to make sure it is wash-ready.

- Pretreat stains and heavily soiled spots.
- Zip zippers and fasten hooks to prevent them from snagging other items of clothing.
- Tie strings and sashes loosely to avoid tangling.
- Check all pockets and remove anything in them, including lint.
- Remove all unwashable trimmings, including belts, pins, and buckles.
- Turn down shirt sleeves.
- Turn clothing right side out. Exception: turn prints and dark clothing inside out to preserve their color.
- Mend fallen hems and rips prior to washing.

STEP 6: Load the Washer. Add laundry before the water fills the tub completely. Do not overload the washer. This is one of the most common laundry mistakes. Clothes need room to move around for effective cleaning. So don't pack them in. Shake and drop items loosely into the tub and fill it no more than three-quarters full with clothing.

It's best if you can mix large items such as sheets and towels with smaller items such as pillowcases and washcloths to balance the load. Don't wind large items around the tub, because they may become tangled in the agitator and be damaged. If you have only an apartment-size or regular-capacity washer, take your bedspreads, quilts, and comforters to the laundromat or have them professionally cleaned for best results.

● **For Best Results**

When you take clothes out of the washing machine, closely examine any items that were stained before washing. Because you may not be able to see stain residue on wet material, you should air-dry these items. If the stain is still there, treat it again and rewash the garment. Never put a stained item into the dryer, as the heat of the dryer is likely to permanently set the stain in the fabric.

Adjust the water level to the size of the load: small, medium, large, or extra large.

Check the water level once the washer starts washing. If the clothes are not completely covered by water, increase the water level and add a little more detergent.

KNOW AND TELL

According to an article with the imposing title "Application of Quantitative Risk Assessment for Formulating Hygiene Policy in the Domestic Setting," by C. P. Gerba (*Journal of Infection*, 2001), researchers have proven that simply washing clothes does not kill germs.

E. coli, *Salmonella*, and other bacteria remain on clothing and in the washing tub — and even show up in subsequent loads. Machine drying kills almost all *E. coli*, but not *Salmonella* or *Mycobacterium fortuitium*, a common bacterium that causes skin infections.

It is recommended that you use liquid chlorine bleach and hot water in wash loads containing underwear (and other clothing contaminated by fecal matter) as well as dish towels, dishrags and sponges, dirty handkerchiefs, and other items that may be contaminated with bacteria. If this is not possible, you should launder these items last and then run an empty load with cool water and 1 cup of bleach to sanitize the tub before the next load. You should also wash your hands after sorting laundry and after transferring wet laundry to the dryer.

STEP 7: Dry Clothes. Check the lint filter to make sure it is clean. The lint filter is usually located in the dryer door opening or on top of the dryer. Clean lint from the screen before putting clothes in the dryer, or get in the habit of removing lint when you remove dry clothes. If you don't want to use your fingers, you can swipe up the accumulation of lint with a used fabric softener sheet.

Check fabric labels for drying recommendations. Set aside items that need to be line-dried or dried flat. Then select the appropriate dryer temperature for the load. Use the normal or regular setting for drying cottons and heavier items such as jeans, sweatshirts, and towels. Select the permanent-press or medium temperature setting for drying lighter-weight or synthetic fabrics. The permanent-press cycle has a special cooling-down period. The low setting is for drying delicate items. The air-fluff setting is not intended for drying but is useful for shaking dust from curtains and linens or for refreshing or softening fabrics.

Avoid overloading the dryer. If clothes have room to circulate, they will dry faster and have fewer wrinkles. On the other hand, if you have two very small wash loads, it is more energy-effi-

For Safety's Sake

Never leave a dryer running while sleeping or when you leave the house, because lint buildup in the outside vent or a faulty dryer can lead to a fire.

cient to combine them in one dryer load. Shake out clothes before putting them in the dryer so that they won't ball up and will dry faster. Loosely fold larger items before drying them, to help prevent tangling and minimize wrinkling.

If you have an automatic timer, use the setting for "Less Dry." Otherwise, set the timer for the number of minutes you think it will take to dry the load. Always err on the side of under-drying. Besides wasting energy, overdrying can cause shrinkage and wrinkling. If you are uncertain about how long to dry a load, set the timer for 30 minutes and then check to see whether clothes are dry or nearly dry. Heavier items such as jeans and towels will require a longer drying time. Separate lightweight and heavyweight items for faster, more uniform drying. To reduce drying time, try adding fabric softener to your rinse cycle when washing; according to the U.K. Textile Services Association, clothes rinsed in fabric softener have been found to contain about 10 percent less water at the end of the wash cycle.

Of course, hanging clothes on the line is the most economical method of drying, and it has other benefits as well. You may be able to cut back on bleach and stain remover, especially for any white underwear and socks, as the sun will naturally bleach them. For fewer wrinkles, add fabric softener to the rinse cycle and hang clothes to dry on a breezy day. Even when the fabric care label says it's okay to machine-dry, line drying is the safest bet for new or snug-fitting clothing. Hang big items first — sheets, towels, trousers — and then smaller items. Hang pants by their legs, shirts by their tails, and socks by their toes in pairs.

STEP 8: Fold, Hang, and/or Iron. Remove clothes as soon as the dryer stops, to minimize wrinkling. Taking clothes out of the dryer while they are still ever so slightly damp also reduces the need for ironing. Hang or fold the clothes, smoothing out any wrinkles. Here's another reason to use fabric softener in the wash: it makes clothes less prone to creasing, and according to the U.K. Textile Services Association Limited, its lubricating effect has been shown to reduce the frictional resistance between the iron and the fabric, reducing the average ironing time by 10 percent.

Need to dewrinkle a load of clothes left too long in the dryer? Toss a damp, lint-free towel into the dryer and run it on the low setting for 10 to 15 minutes. Alternatively, use one of the wrinkle-releasing products that can be sprayed onto clothing to eliminate the need for ironing. If you don't like to iron, these products do the job nicely. Spray in a sweeping motion until the garment is slightly damp. Tug and smooth away wrinkles as directed on the product label. Hang to dry. *Helpful Hint:* Pack a wrinkle-releasing spray in your suitcase.

If you have clothes that must be ironed, these tips may be useful:

- Sort garments according to the amount of heat required for the fabric type. Start with those items that require a low heat setting, such as silk and synthetics, and finish with items that require higher heat, such as cottons and linens.
- Steam makes it easier to press clothing. Use distilled water, and pour it into your iron before turning it on. This will avoid having water rather than steam drip through the vent holes.
- Iron smaller areas, such as collars and cuffs, first and larger areas last to minimize wrinkling of the areas you've already ironed.
- Spray-on starch makes it easier to iron heavier fabrics such as cottons and cotton blends and provides a crisp finish.
- Never iron an article of clothing that is stained, as the heat of the iron can permanently set the stain.

Same-Day Service

If you have to do laundry daily to keep up with demand, establish a family rule that all dirty laundry must be in the laundry room by 8 A.M. and clean laundry may be picked up after 8 P.M., or whatever hours work best for you.

I will clean house when Sears comes out with a riding vacuum cleaner.

— Roseanne Barr

How To

FOLD A FITTED SHEET

1. Holding the sheet so that the top side faces you, slide your left and right fists into the two top corners.

2. Bring the right corner over to the left corner and use your right fist to tuck it in, lining up the seams as you do so. Then run the thumb and forefinger of your right hand down the open ends of the sheet all the way to the end. Pick up the bottom two corners, bring them up to the top two corners, and use your fist to tuck them in.

3. Lay the sheet on a flat surface. Straighten and line up the corners and edges. Turn in the two "rough" edges to make a rectangular shape.

4. Fold the sheet in half lengthwise and then in half again.

5. Fold both long ends in (once or twice, depending on the final size desired) so that you have square shape.

Choosing and Using Detergent

The primary job of every detergent is to loosen and remove soils and stains. The kind of detergent you choose is largely a matter of preference and needs. You might prefer a particular detergent for its scent or for its price, or because it's the detergent your mother always used. If you have allergies or sensitive skin, you'd choose a mild detergent that is free of fragrance and dyes. If convenience is a priority, you might prefer a two-in-one laundry detergent with bleach, fabric softener, or a stain-fighting agent. Some detergents are formulated for specific purposes. For example, if you tend to wash clothes after every wear, as with children's clothing, you might want to look for a detergent that helps prevent colors from fading. And if you have a high-efficiency, tumble-action washer, you need to use a special, low-sudsing detergent.

Most detergents, even the new detergent/bleach combinations, work well in any temperature but are best in temperatures over 65°F (18°C). If you prefer to wash in cold water, a detergent that is formulated for cold-water washing will be most effective. Detergents are generally categorized as light duty or general purpose. Light-duty detergents, the mildest type, are available in liquid or powdered form for washing delicate and hand-washable items. General-purpose detergents come in three forms: liquid, dry, and tablet.

- **Liquid detergent** is formulated to work well in cold water. But it also works well in warmer water, and its dissolvability makes it the best choice for hard-water washing. Liquid detergents are more effective than dry detergents for removing food and other greasy, oily stains. And the liquid form is easy to use for pretreating grease spots and stains just prior to laundering. *Note:* Do not allow this pretreatment to sit on clothing, as it may discolor fabric; wash the garment immediately or rinse it out completely after treating the stain.

- **Dry or powdered detergent** can be used for cold-water washes but will dissolve better if it is mixed with a little hot water. Let the washer agitate the detergent for a few minutes before adding clothes, to help it dissolve. If there's a powdery residue on your clothes after they're washed, the detergent was not dissolved properly. Dry detergent is the preferred choice for removing mud, clay, and ground-in dirt on children's play clothes and other heavily soiled garments. To use dry detergent as a prewash stain or soil remover, mix it with a little water to form a paste. Apply to the stain and then wash the garment immediately or rinse it out completely.

- **Tablet detergent** has been proven to dissolve well in all temperatures. While tablets cost slightly more than other types of detergent, they eliminate the need to measure out your detergent. The portability and convenience of tablets make them a great choice for those who do their laundry at self-serve laundromats. Like powdered detergent, tablets should be added to the wash water before the clothes are added. Allow the detergent to agitate in the washer to dissolve properly.

How Detergent Works

The most important ingredient in detergent is the surfactant, or surface active agent. Surfactants are organic compounds consisting of two parts: a water-loving portion and a water-hating portion. The water-hating ends attach themselves to the soil particles present in or on the fabrics being washed, while the water-loving ends are attracted to the water. The surfactant molecules surround the soil particles, break them up, force them away from the surface of the fabric, and suspend them in the wash water so that they can be rinsed away.

courtesy of the Soap and Detergent Association

The amount of detergent needed for the best cleaning varies depending on the size of the load, the degree of soiling, and water conditions. An average wash load consists of the following:

- A 5- to 7-pound load
- Moderate soiling on the clothing
- Moderately hard water: 3.6 to 7.0 grains per gallon (61 to 120 parts per million)
- About 17 gallons of water for a top-loading washer or 8 gallons for a front-loading washer

Use an appropriate amount of detergent for each wash. Read the detergent label to learn what amount is recommended for an average wash load. Adjust that measurement as necessary: Use more than the recommended amount for larger loads, heavily soiled clothes, or harder water. Use slightly less than the recommended amount for smaller loads, lighter soiling, or softer water.

How do you know whether you are using the right amount of detergent? More is not always better. Excess suds can reduce cleaning effectiveness and are hard to rinse out. A sure sign that you are using too much detergent is having suds left in the tub after the wash cycle is complete. However, little or no sudsing does not necessarily mean that you are not using enough detergent, since it may be just that you have hard water, which naturally decreases sudsiness. Indications that you might be using too little detergent include clothes that have become grayed or yellowed over time and clothes that aren't coming out clean.

Read & Follow Detergent Labels

All detergents are not alike. More concentrated detergents, also known as ultra detergents, require that you use less of them for washing. For best results and most economical use, always read the label on the box or bottle.

Hand Washing

Delicate items such as bras and lingerie or any item with a fabric care label that recommends hand washing should not be machine-washed. Place these items in a sink basin filled with cool water. As with regular machine wash loads, take care not to mix fabric colors.

Add a capful of dishwashing liquid or a light-duty detergent designed for hand washing. Or swish a bar of laundry soap (not regular bath soap) in the water. Gently squeeze the suds through the fabric and then let the items soak for 10 minutes. Rinse them with cool water. Do not wring the water from the items. Instead, lay them flat on a white towel, then roll up the towel and squeeze dry. Unroll the towel and hang the items or lay them flat to dry (as recommended on the fabric care label).

Laundry Helpers

A variety of laundry aids can be used to enhance wash results. These include bleaches, stain removers, detergent boosters, fabric softeners, and water softeners. Some detergents now come with built-in fabric softeners, color-safe bleach, or a bleach alternative. Following are some of the options.

Liquid Chlorine Bleach. Liquid chlorine or household bleach (sodium hypochlorite) is the product most commonly used to whiten whites in the wash, remove stubborn stains from colorfast materials, and disinfect and deodorize fabrics. Through the process of oxidation, chlorine bleach converts soil into colorless particles that can be removed by detergent and carried away in the wash water.

How to use: Measure out the amount recommended on the label. Carefully pour the chlorine bleach into the washer's bleach dispenser prior to filling the washer. Do not exceed the fill line on the dispenser. If there is no dispenser, dilute the recommended amount of chlorine bleach with 1 quart of water, and add the bleach solution to the wash water 5 minutes after the wash cycle begins. If you add chlorine bleach at the same time as the detergent, the effectiveness of both products will be reduced. Be careful not to splash or drip chlorine bleach on clothing, as it can permanently remove color from the fabric. Be aware that frequent use of chlorine bleach may wear down and shorten the life of fabrics. Do not use chlorine bleach on wool, silk, or mohair fabrics or on fabrics with spandex.

All-Fabric (Oxygen) Bleach. This kind of bleach is an alternative to liquid chlorine bleach for maintaining whiteness and brightness on most fabrics. The oxidizing agent, hydrogen peroxide, provides a gentler bleaching action than chlorine, making it safe for most washable colored fabrics unless otherwise directed by a fabric care label. Most effective when used regularly, this color-safe bleach is available in liquid or powder forms.

How to use: You can combine powdered color-safe oxygen bleach with a powdered detergent in the detergent dispenser if it's large enough. But do not combine liquid color-safe oxygen bleach with detergent in the dispenser.

Reduce Packaging Waste

- Look for refillable detergent and laundry-aid products.
- Buy in economy sizes.
- Opt for concentrated formulas.
- Recycle paper and plastic packaging.

Mixing liquid oxygen bleach with a powdered detergent will cause caking in the dispenser; mixing it with a liquid detergent can decrease the effectiveness of both products. The best practice is to add liquid or powdered color-safe oxygen bleach, along with the detergent, to the empty washer tub before filling it with water. Oxygen bleaches work best in warm to hot water.

Bluings. Bluings are designed to counteract the natural yellowing of fabrics. They contain a blue dye that is taken up by fabrics in the wash or rinse.

How to use: Measure out the appropriate amount of bluing for the size of your load of wash, following the instructions on the label. However, don't pour it on full strength. Dilute the recommended amount of bluing with water, and add the solution to the washer at the start of the wash or in the final rinse cycle.

Detergent Boosters. Available in powdered or liquid form, detergent boosters are especially effective in hard water for enhancing the cleaning power of the detergent. Liquid boosters can also be used for pretreating stains. Baking soda is a natural detergent booster.

How to use: Add the booster to the wash water along with the recommended amount of detergent for your wash load. If you are using baking soda, add ½ cup to the wash water.

Enzyme Presoak Stain Removers. Enzyme presoaks come in powdered form and are very effective in removing protein stains like baby formula, blood, bodily fluids, dairy products, and eggs. That's because enzymes are proteins, and the general rule of stain removal is that "like dissolves like." Enzymes break down the stains so that they can be more easily lifted out of the fabric with the aid of the detergent.

How to use: Before washing, presoak any stained laundry in the washer tub, a sink, or a pail. Follow the instructions on the enzyme presoak product label. You can also add enzyme presoak to the wash water to boost the cleaning power of your detergent. Note that some detergents include enzymes; check the product label.

Prewash Soil and Stain Removers. These products come in a variety of forms and are effective at removing heavy soiling and stains, especially on polyester fibers. They penetrate the fiber of the fabric and help break up the stain, allowing it to disperse in the wash water. Liquids, sprays, aerosols, gels, foams, sticks, and wipes are very effective at removing oil-based stains such

as animal fats, bodily soils, cooking oils, cosmetics, and motor oils. Most of these products are detergent based. Aerosol sprays are solvent based, making them slightly more effective on set versus fresh oil stains. Laundry soap bars work best on fabric softener, perspiration, and tobacco stains. *Note:* Don't confuse laundry soap bars with bar soap; laundry soap bars are specifically designed for laundry, while bar soap is designed for cleaning the human body.

How to use: Use liquid, gel, foam, or spray prewash products just before washing the garment. If the stain remains after the garment has been washed, apply a second treatment, rubbing directly into the stain. Stick stain removers and wipes are designed to be used as soon as possible on a fresh stain. Once it has been treated, you can let the garment sit for up to one week before washing it. *Caution:* Do not use prewash soil and stain removers on neon and fluorescent colors, as they may cause the colors to run or fade.

Color Removers. Color removers can help remove rust spots from clothes washed in water that contains iron and manganese. They can also help remove dye stains that were transferred from colored items to the whites they were washed with.

How to use: Read and follow the package directions.

Fabric Softeners. Fabric softeners are designed to make clothes feel softer and smell fresher. They also reduce static cling, reduce drying time, minimize wrinkling, and make ironing easier. There are several types of fabric softeners: liquid rinse-added products, dryer sheets, and packet-type softeners, which attach to the fin of the dryer drum. All are designed to lightly lubricate the fibers of fabrics, adding fluffiness to textured fabrics such as towels and imparting a smooth feel to flat finishes.

- **Rinse-added fabric softeners** come in concentrated and diluted form. Be sure you know which type you are using, and follow the instructions for use.

How to use: Measure, dilute (if necessary), and pour the fabric softener into the washer's fabric softener dispenser at the start of the wash or into the wash water during the rinse cycle. Never pour fabric softener directly onto fabric, as it can cause staining or spotting. Do not use laundry aids such as bluing or water softener in the rinse cycle when you are using fabric softener.

- **Dryer sheets** are a simple, convenient way to soften and freshen clothes. Fabric-softening agents and fragrance are embedded in a nonwoven sheet of synthetic fabric or polyurethane foam. The heat and tumbling action of the dryer help transfer the softener to the clothes.

How to use: Place a single sheet on top of the wet clothes, close the dryer door, and start the dryer. If you're drying two wash loads in an extra-large-capacity dryer, use two sheets.

- **Dryer packet softeners** are another convenience product, but unlike dryer sheets, they are designed to be used multiple times. The softener is activated by the heat of the dryer and released by the tumbling action onto clothing items as they are dried.

How to use: Affix the packet to one of the dryer fins as directed on the package label.

For Safety's Sake

Fabric softener may reduce the effectiveness of flame retardancy in children's sleepwear. As a safer alternative, instead of fabric softener, add ½ cup of white vinegar to the rinse cycle to help soften clothes and keep colors bright. However, note that vinegar can cause some fading of darker clothes.

Warning: Do not use liquid chlorine bleach in the wash if you plan to use vinegar in the rinse; use all-fabric oxygen bleach instead. The combination of chlorine and vinegar, even in diluted forms, can create obnoxious fumes, particularly in the confines of a small laundry room.

Water Softeners. Hard water has a high concentration of calcium and magnesium. These minerals tend to reduce the effectiveness of laundry detergents and may also leave behind a residue that causes fabrics to feel stiff and harsh. Water-softening products work by deactivating these minerals. Choose from powdered or liquid water softeners.

How to use: Add powders to the wash or rinse water. Add liquids to the rinse water only. Follow the manufacturer's recommendations for the amount to use.

Removing Stains

If at all possible, it's best to treat spills and stains on washable garments immediately — while the stains are fresh and before they dry. The more quickly you treat a stain, the less likely it is to set. (However, if the garment is labeled "dry clean only," do not attempt to remove the stain; take it to a dry cleaner for best results.) Blot liquid stains with a clean white, lint-free cloth or paper towel. Gently scrape or brush off excess solids, if there are any. Avoid excessive rubbing, as it may spread the stain or damage delicate fabrics.

There are four basic types of stains: protein, tannin, oil based, and dye. There is no one stain-removal product or technique that removes all types of stains. Following is a quick guide to the simplest methods of stain removal for each of the four types.

Protein Stains. These include baby food and formula, milk and dairy products, egg, gelatin and pudding, bodily products (perspiration, blood, mucus, urine, feces, and vomit), mud, white glue, and school paste.

How to remove: Soak the stain in cold water while it is still fresh. Agitating the fabric by hand or in the washing machine helps breaks the stain free of the fabric fibers. Next, wash the garment in warm — not hot — water. Inspect it before machine-drying. If the stain remains, resoak the garment for at least 30 minutes and then rewash. Colored stains may require bleach for removal. For the removal of old or dried stains, scrape off any crusted matter and then soak the stain in cold water with a detergent or an enzyme presoak product. You can also try applying a paste of baking soda and water to the stain, allowing it to remain on the fabric until the stain disappears.

Common Stain-Removal Remedies to Avoid

DISHWASHER DETERGENT. Although sometimes suggested for use on food stains, dishwasher detergents are intended for use in closed dishwashers, with very hot water. They are so highly alkaline that they can irritate your skin if you use them in stain removal. They also may fade colors or damage wool, silk, or nylon fibers.

HAIR SPRAY ON BALLPOINT INK. Certain hair sprays are effective on ink stains from ballpoint pens, but they may deposit a gummy residue and perfume that then have to be removed along with the ink. Hair spray also may affect color in some fabrics.

IRONING CANDLE WAX. If you happen to get candle wax on your clothing, ironing the spot between sheets of blotting paper will only drive the stain deeper into the fabric. This process is widely used, but it's not recommended, because it will make any color from the dye of the candle more permanently set and the wax harder for the detergent or solvent to reach to carry the stain away.

MILK ON WASHABLE INK. Milk does not remove the ink, and applying milk gives you an additional protein stain.

SALT TO MAKE DYES COLORFAST. This old remedy does not work with today's dyes. If the bleeding of a particular dye in cotton, rayon, or ramie fabric is decreased with a saltwater soak, the effect will not be permanent. When the fabric is wet again, unless there is salt in the solution, the dye will be free to leave the fabric. Salt cannot affect colorfastness of synthetic-fiber fabrics or their blends, because they are colored with dyes that have chemical structures not affected by salt.

SHAMPOO. Clear gel-like shampoos are sometimes suggested for stain removal. While shampoos are usually not harmful to fabrics and may work on light oil stains, laundry detergents are just as effective and less expensive to use. Additionally, colored, opaque, or milky-looking shampoos may contain ingredients that will stain fabrics or foam so much that they will be difficult to rinse out.

WHITE VINEGAR. Vinegar (acetic acid) may weaken cotton, rayon, acetate, triacetate, or silk fibers and may cause color change. If you're using vinegar as a stain-removal agent, test for colorfastness by applying it first on a hidden seam allowance. Vinegar will not help remove or set creases in today's synthetic or permanent-press fabrics.

from Quick 'n' Easy Stain Removal, *Iowa State University Cooperative Extension*

Tannin Stains. These include coffee and tea, alcoholic beverages, soft drinks, berries, fruit and vegetable juices, cologne, felt-tip watercolor pen, and washable ink.

How to remove: Rinse the fresh stain with cold water, or if the fabric will withstand hot water, secure the fabric tightly with a rubber-band over a bowl or mug and carefully pour boiling water through the spot from about 2 feet above. Then wash the garment with detergent in the hottest water allowed according to the fabric care label. Removing older stains may require liquid chlorine or all-fabric bleach or the application of a baking soda paste as described above for removing old protein stains.

Oil-Based Stains. Here we have automotive oil, car-door grease, hair oil, bacon fat and lard, butter and margarine, cooking fats and oils, mayonnaise and salad dressing, hand lotion and facial creams, and suntan lotion and oil.

How to remove: First, test the garment for colorfastness (see page 161). If the garment is

colorfast, pretreat the stain with a heavy-duty liquid detergent and a prewash spray or powdered detergent mixed with enough water to make a runny paste. Work the pretreatment into the fabric. Then wash the garment, using the hottest water allowed according to the fabric care label. Inspect the garment before machine-drying, and repeat if necessary.

Dye Stains. These include dyes bled into the wash water by other garments, seepage of color from one part of the garment to another, felt-tip pen and India ink, tempera paint, Kool-Aid, cherry and blueberry juices, mustard, and grass.

How to remove: If the dye was transferred from the garment's bright-colored trim to its main fabric during the wash, rewash with a heavy-duty detergent in warm or hot water. For removal of other dye stains, pretreat with a heavy-duty liquid detergent. Rinse. If the garment is white or colorfast (see page 161), soak the stain in a diluted solution of powdered all-fabric oxygen bleach or liquid chlorine bleach as directed on the product label.

Mystery Stains. If you don't know what the stain is, consider its location on the garment: stains on the front of clothes are often food or beverage stains (protein or tannin); collars and underarms are prone to perspiration stains (protein); and black stains on pant legs at knee level may be grease or dirt stains (oil based) from getting in and out of the car.

Always start with the gentlest stain-removal method. Rinse or soak the garment in cold water for at least 30 minutes, or for several hours if it is an older stain. If that doesn't remove the stain, soak again with one of the following (after testing it for colorfastness):

- A prewash stain-removal product
- Liquid detergent and lukewarm or hot water
- A paste made from powdered laundry detergent and a little water

Launder the item as usual and let air-dry. If the stain persists, it may be a combination protein/oil stain. Retreat the stain with a prewash spray and then wash it with detergent and, if the garment is white or colorfast, all-fabric oxygen

Cleaning your house while your kids are still growing is like shoveling the walk before it stops snowing.

— Phyllis Diller

bleach or liquid chlorine bleach. Dry cleaning fluid can be used to remove oily/waxy combination stains such as lipstick, crayon, candle wax, shoe polish, and tar, provided these products are used with care. The safest method for you and your clothing is to entrust the stain removal to the expertise of a professional dry cleaner.

Laundromat Tips

Lugging laundry back and forth to the laundromat can be a real drag. Here's how to get the best results while minimizing the effort required and maximizing use of your time:

- Do your sorting at home so you know in advance how many washing machines you will need.

- Premeasure dry laundry detergent into plastic zippered bags, or use laundry tablets.

- Opt for fabric softener sheets over liquid fabric softener, for convenience.

- Wipe out washer tubs with a disposable disinfectant wipe before loading your clothes into them. Or, if appropriate, use liquid chlorine bleach in the wash to kill any germs left over from previous wash.

- Bring your own change. ***Helpful hint:*** Empty film canisters make great quarter containers; each canister holds 20 quarters.

- Clean the dryer lint filter before using the dryer.

- Do not leave your laundry unattended.

- Bring plenty of hangers.

- Plan to use laundry time to catch up on reading, writing, sewing, or other projects. Consider designating a tote bag for carrying books and other items you want to bring along with laundry aids.

Professional Dry Cleaning

If a garment's fabric care label says "dry clean only," do not attempt to wash it. Clothing made of rayon, silk, and wool blends may shrink, change colors, or lose their shape if washed in water. Even when a label gives you the choice between "hand-wash" and "dry-clean," seriously consider dry cleaning. You can save money washing by hand, but dry cleaning will keep the garment looking like new with no more effort than it takes to drop it off and pick it up.

Convenience is one of the main reasons why people choose to use a professional dry cleaner for all of their best garments. Stain removal is the other big benefit. With their special solvents and experience, dry cleaners can remove some of the most disastrous-looking stains. For best results, never store clothing with spills or stains. Exposure to light, air, and warmth can permanently set the stain. Instead, blot up the excess stain with a white cloth or paper toweling and take the item to the cleaner as soon as possible (within 24 to 48 hours). You may wish to mark and identify any stained areas with little pieces of masking tape.

Always remove freshly dry-cleaned garments from their plastic bags and allow them to air out before wearing them or hanging them in a closet. In this way, you avoid breathing perchloroethylene, the chemical used in dry cleaning. If the clothing has a strong chemical smell, it's because either the item is still not dry or the dry cleaner is not removing enough of the solvent. Let it air out for at least a day before hanging it in your closet. If this happens frequently, consider using a different dry cleaner. Removing the bag also allows the fabric to breathe. The plastic bag traps air, causing a moisture buildup that can ruin fabric. For long-term storage of garments, hang them in a zippered garment bag.

Prices can vary greatly from one dry cleaner to the next. There are discount cleaners, traditionally priced cleaners, and high-end cleaners. In addition to price, also consider customer service. Most dry cleaners will repair loose buttons and sew on new ones, if necessary. Many offer tailoring, seasonal storage, drive-through service, and perks for loyal customers. The best way to find a good cleaner is to ask around.

Dry Cleaning: How It Works

Dry cleaning involves no water, but it isn't actually "dry." The process involves a liquid solution that contains optical brighteners, soil suspenders, and other additives. During the dry-cleaning process, clothes are placed in a machine that repeatedly flushes soil from clothes with the solvent. Heavily stained garments may go through a stain-removal process prior to being cleaned. After the cleaning, the solvent is drained, and excess solvent is extracted from the clothes. A drying process vaporizes any solvent left in the clothes, which are then pressed to perfection.

Home Dry Cleaning

Home dry-cleaning kits offer some of the benefits of professional dry cleaning at a fraction of the cost. These kits are best used for freshening garments, dewrinkling, and removing water-based stains such as those from cola, wine, or soup. They are also effective in removing such odors as those caused by perspiration, smoke, or mothballs. And they are useful in a pinch or for extending the time between visits to the dry cleaner. They are not effective at removing large stains, heavy or ground-in soil, lint, or pet hair.

Most kits include a stain remover or stain-absorbing pads, a heat-activated cloth, and a reusable dryer bag. Use the stain-removal device to pretreat any visible soils or stains. Then do up all the fastenings (buttons or zippers) on the garments you wish to clean, and put the garments in the special dryer bag, along with the heat-activated cloth. Seal the bag and toss it in the dryer. If the kit does not include a bag, toss the garments and the heat-activated cloth in the dryer as directed by the kit instructions. Set the timer for the recommended heat and time. As it is heated, the cloth creates steam, which serves to dewrinkle garments, and a fragrance, which freshens them. When the cycle is done, immediately remove the garments, shake them out to remove any remaining moisture and wrinkles, and hang them to dry. Iron or steam-press as needed.

For Best Results

Follow these plain and simple tips to keep all of your garments looking their best in between cleanings:

- Place clothes on hangers immediately after taking them off.

- Allow garments to air out before rehanging them in your closet.

- Check for spills and stains on clothing after each wearing. Treat stains immediately, or take the stained garment to the dry cleaner.

- Use a clothes brush regularly to remove surface dust and lint from your clothing.

CHAPTER ELEVEN

PET CLEANUP

We love our pets, but the cleanup that goes along with them is something most of us could do without. As with other cleaning activities, there are simple things you can do to minimize the time and effort it takes to clean up after our companion animals. The benefit, of course, is that simplifying the work can add to the enjoyment of our pets.

KNOW AND TELL

The U.S. Environmental Protection Agency reports that pet allergens can still be detected in a home several months after a pet has been removed, even when that home has been thoroughly cleaned. If animal dander triggers asthma for you or a family member, the most effective method to control exposure is to keep your home pet free. For some people, however, it suffices to keep pets out of the bedroom and away from fabric-covered furniture, carpets, and stuffed toys and to vacuum carpets, rugs, and furniture two or more times per week.

The Daily Routine

Primary care of your pet begins with feeding and watering. Whatever type of pet you have, it's important to clean the food and water bowls daily to prevent the buildup of dirt and bacteria. Wash pet bowls in hot, soapy water and rinse thoroughly. Discard scratched and chipped dishes, which can easily harbor bacteria. For convenience, keep a second set of bowls to use while the first set is being cleaned. A good choice is heavy bowls that are less likely to be tipped over. A spill-proof design will reduce unnecessary cleanup of food and water. Place pet bowls on a washable mat or tray to protect your flooring against spills and drips. Wash the mat or tray with hot, soapy water at least once a week or as needed. You may also want to disinfect the mat or tray periodically.

Daily care of your dog or cat also includes waste removal to protect the health of your family, your pets, and the environment. If you can't do daily yard cleanup yourself, consider hiring a pet-waste-removal service. Check the yellow pages under "Pet Services." Indoors, scoop cat litter daily. Cats are very particular about where they deposit their waste and may choose to relieve themselves outside the litter box if it is smelly or dirty. Or they may wait to use the box until it is clean, which can result in constipation or increase the risk of urinary tract infection.

Pet Waste and Your Health

It is your responsibility as a pet owner to clean up after your pet — on your own property as well as in public places. Pet waste can carry viruses, bacteria, and parasites that are extremely harmful to humans and animals. Some of the diseases that can be spread from pet waste include:

- *Salmonellosis:* the most common bacterial infection transmitted from animals to humans; symptoms include headache, fever, muscle aches, vomiting, and diarrhea

- *Campylobacteriosis:* a bacterial infection that causes diarrhea in humans

- *Toxocarisis:* an infection of roundworms transmitted from dogs to humans; symptoms include fever, rash, vision loss, and cough

Wash Your Hands!

Always use disposable gloves, a plastic bag, or a scoop when handling pet feces, and wash your hands thoroughly afterward. Also wash your hands after playing or working in areas where pets are allowed to relieve themselves and after cleaning the litter box.

Another common germ that can be transmitted to people through animal feces is *E. coli*, the effects of which can range from minor flu-like symptoms to more severe stomach cramps, vomiting, fever, and even kidney failure. Children run the greatest risk of infection, because they're prone to playing in the dirt and then putting their hands in their mouths or rubbing their eyes with their hands. If your yard has feces in it, just playing ball outside can lead to infection by harmful germs — from the ground to the ball to your hands.

Picking up after your pet reduces the risk of disease and keeps the areas where you walk clean. Keep in mind, too, that feces attract flies that may enter your home and spread disease everywhere they land. Leaving pet waste is also an invitation for your dog to clean up feces in a most unsavory way known as coprophagy. Prompt cleanup will discourage dogs from developing this bad habit. For ease of cleanup, consider the possibility of confining waste to a

QUIZ: What Do You Do with Pet Poo?

Which of the following are proper ways to dispose of pet waste?

A Flush it down the toilet.

B Bury it away from gardens, wells, ditches, or areas where children play.

C Wrap it and put it in the garbage for disposal.

D Collect it in an in-ground pet-waste digester.

E Leave it to decompose on the grass or soil or in an animal pen.

F Leave it on paved surfaces, or dump it down a storm drain or into a ditch.

Answers: The correct answers are A, B, C, and D. However, if local regulations prohibit flushing pet waste, burying it, or sending it to the landfill, answer D would be the only acceptable method of disposal. Answer A is not advisable if your household is on a septic system, because the additional waste may clog up your septic tank, especially if you are flushing feces with bits of clay litter.

---

specific area. This is easiest to accomplish during puppy training or if your dog is always leashed in the yard.

Proper disposal of pet waste reduces the level of contaminants in stormwater runoff that degrade the water quality of our lakes and streams. Animal droppings contain the bacterium *E. coli*. Its presence in water indicates fecal contamination and the potential for waterborne disease. Pollution from *E. coli* bacteria is a common cause of beach closings. Additionally, the decay of pet waste in our waterways uses a high level of oxygen from the water. This can kill fish and plant life by reducing the amount of dis-

solved oxygen available to them. Pet waste decay in warm, still waters promotes the growth of algae, which also can kill aquatic life.

You might wonder how your pet waste can contaminate water if you don't live near water. If animal waste is allowed to accumulate in yards and animal pens or if it is left on sidewalks, streets, or drainage ditches, rain or snowmelt will carry it along to nearby storm sewer systems that eventually channel it — untreated — into local bodies of water. The U.S. Environmental Protection Agency has determined that pollution from stormwater runoff is the largest cause of water-quality problems in the United States. Pet waste is a significant part of this pollution.

Disposing of Pet Waste

Always clean up after your pet. When walking your dog, get in the habit of bringing along a bag in which you can collect feces. Check pet stores and catalogs for handy little bag dispensers that attach neatly to your dog's leash or your belt. Or tie a plastic grocery bag to the handle of the leash.

If you're going to put the pet waste in the trash, double-bag it. Force out all excess air from the bag to prevent bursting action at the landfill when the trash is compacted. Then tie the bag shut tightly.

Trash goes to a lined landfill, which is designed to prevent pollution from leaking into waterways. It does, however, use up valuable landfill space. An alternative to sending pet waste to the landfill is to flush it down the toilet. The water from your toilet goes either to a septic system or to a wastewater treatment facility, both of which are designed to remove pollutants before the water reaches a lake or stream.

Another landfill alternative is to bury pet waste. Microorganisms in the soil will help break down the waste. Just dig a hole at least 5 inches deep, toss in the feces, and fill the hole with dirt. This is a good strategy if you are hiking in the woods, provided you carry a trowel or other digging tool with you. But don't bury pet waste close to a lake, a waterway of any kind, or your vegetable garden. A more convenient method for burying is the in-ground pet-waste digester. A digester uses enzymes to break down feces and

allows the residue to sink harmlessly into the surrounding soil. It's like a mini septic tank for pet waste. Simply bury the covered canister in a corner of your yard, leaving only the handled lid exposed. It's a simple, affordable, and ecologically sound method for disposing of pet waste.

Pet Waste No-No's

- Do not dispose of or leave pet waste in a ditch, storm drain, street, sidewalk, or trail. Not only is it illegal in many areas, it contributes to the pollution of nearby streams and lakes.

- Do not bury waste from dogs, cats, ferrets, raccoons, pigs, and other carnivorous (meat-eating) pets in food-growing areas or near water (to prevent possible contamination).

- Do not add carnivorous pet waste to the compost pile. The pile will not get hot enough to kill parasites and other disease-causing organisms. It may also attract all sorts of vermin, particularly rats. (It is okay to compost the waste of vegetarian animals, such as sheep, chickens, gerbils, rabbits, horses, cows, and goats.)

- Do not hose pet waste into the ground. Scoop and remove it.

- Do not put out any type of pet waste for collection with yard debris.

The Lowdown on Cat Litter

A good rule of thumb is to have one litter box per cat or no more than two cats sharing one litter box. Keep in mind, though, that if two cats share a box, it will need more frequent cleaning. Cats with infectious diseases such as feline leukemia or worms should not share a litter box with healthy cats.

The ideal litter is the one that appeals to you as well as your cat. If your cat likes the litter you are currently buying, changing types or even brands may result in litter-behavior problems. Absorbent clay-based litters account for the majority of litter purchases. These include sand-like (clumping) litters and gravel-type (nonclumping) litters.

- **Clumping litter.** Clumping litter reduces much of the work of cleaning the cat litter box. When dampened, it forms solid clumps that can be removed with a slotted scoop. The drawback is that the finer particles tend to stick to a cat's paws. Keep a broom handy to prevent it from getting tracked through the house.

To Flush or Not to Flush

If you flush cat feces, make sure only the feces, not the litter, goes down the toilet. Clay-based litter can clog up the toilet and your septic tank. Dispose of used clay litter in the trash.

- **Nonclumping litter.** This type of litter tracks less than clumping litter, but it requires more work to clean up. Solid matter should be scooped daily, of course, but in addition, the entire box of litter needs to be emptied and replaced at least once a week. One way to make this process easier is to use a litter-pan liner that can be lifted out, tied off, and thrown away. The box itself also requires regular cleaning.

- **Flushable alternatives.** Several litter alternatives are available. They include litter beads or granules, which capture and evaporate urine and are designed to last several weeks, though scooping of solid waste is still required. The downside is that beaded litter has a tendency to track and scatter due to its shape, making it difficult to sweep up. Wheat litters are another viable alternative in terms of feline acceptance, clumpability, and odor control. Wheat litter has the added advantage of being flushable, even into septic systems. The drawback is that the lightweight nature of the product gives it a high propensity to scatter and track.

Whatever type of litter you choose, fill the box to a height of no more than two inches. Too much litter underfoot is not pleasant for cats.

Other considerations for litter-box management are as follows:

The Best Box. While a simple pan is all you really need, a covered litter box will help reduce unpleasant odors and minimize messy "fallout" from digging and burying action. Another advantage of the lidded box is that it forces a single entry/exit point. You can further minimize

the tracking of litter by placing a specially designed litter mat in front of the door to the box. Some lidded boxes have a swinging door; be aware, though, the door can sometimes stick, shutting cats out. The most sophisticated litter box, the self-cleaning litter box, takes the daily work out of cleaning the litter by automatically sifting solid waste out of the litter when the contents of the box reach a certain weight.

Location, Location, Location. Cats like their privacy, so it makes sense to put the litter box in an out-of-the-way place. This will also minimize odor and the tracking of litter into the main living area of your home. Just remember the old adage "Out of sight, out of mind." Locate the litter box in a place where you won't forget about it. Also think about efficiency. A good location is one that allows storage of extra litter and easy disposal of waste.

Odor Control. The best way to control litter-box odor is to clean the box frequently. Scoop daily, if not more often. If you notice an odor, it's time to scoop; if the odor lingers, it's time to change the litter and clean the box. Scented litters may mask unpleasant scents, but keep in mind that what smells good to you may not smell good to

your cat. Do not place a room deodorizer or air freshener near the litter box, for this reason. Also, do not use strong-smelling chemicals or cleaning products when washing the box. Washing with soap and water is sufficient. If you choose to disinfect the box, be sure to it rinse thoroughly to remove the scent of the disinfectant.

Multiple-cat litter formulas are designed to minimize odor with a larger concentration of deodorizer. Baking soda is a natural, unscented way to neutralize odor between litter changes. Sprinkle the bottom of the pan with a thin layer of baking soda and then fill it with litter. Carbon crystals sprinkled on top of the litter will also absorb odor naturally.

For Safety's Sake

The feces of cats that eat mice or other raw meat can contain parasites that cause toxoplasmosis. Handling cat feces or failing to wash your hands after cleaning the litter box puts you at risk of catching this disease, which can be fatal to children under two and can cause serious health problems for unborn babies and anyone with a suppressed immune syndrome. So wash your hands thoroughly after scooping or cleaning the litter box. And if your kids have a sandbox, keep it covered when it's not in use, to prevent cats from using it as a litter box.

Pet Stains and Odors

When you have pets, they are bound to have "accidents." The sooner you can clean up stains and odors, the better your chances of removing them completely. That's important, not just so that your home looks and smells nice, but because complete removal will discourage possible repeat offenses. Try to figure out why the accident happened. Is your pet also drinking more water? Diabetes may be the cause. Could your pet have a urinary tract infection? Or is your cat trying to tell you that its litter box needs cleaning? Consult with your veterinarian to rule out the possibility of illness.

Fresh Urine Stains. The Carpet and Rug Institute recommends following these five simple steps to remove pet stains and odors from carpeting and upholstery:

1. Use a white towel or white paper toweling to blot the damp area as soon as you discover the accident.
2. Prepare a solution of ¼ teaspoon of liquid dishwashing detergent and 1 cup of lukewarm water. Use a clean white towel to apply the solution to the damp spot. Avoid overwetting the spot, as the water will carry urine along with it down into the padding.
3. Absorb the moisture with paper toweling, rinse with warm water, and repeat the application of detergent. Continue rinsing and blotting with the detergent solution and water as long as there is a transfer to the toweling or an improvement in the spot.
4. Follow the detergent application with a solution of 1 cup of white vinegar and 2 cups of water. Apply with a towel as described in step 2, and blot dry. If the stain is on a rug or carpet, stand on the toweling to help it absorb the moisture.
5. Apply a ½-inch layer of paper towels to the area, and weight them down with a flat, heavy object. When they are thoroughly wetted, replace them with fresh paper towels. Continue to change paper towels until they no longer absorb any moisture from below.

For noncarpeted floors, all you need is toweling to wipe up the liquid and a solution of equal parts of white vinegar and water to clean, sanitize, and eliminate the odor.

Older Urine Stains. Some stains simply cannot be removed once they've set. But it's always worth a try. Start with the procedure outlined above for fresh stains. If the stain persists, try using an all-natural enzyme-based cleaning product (see the sidebar below for an explanation of how and why these products work).

For removal of stains that have set in your carpet, your best bet is to call a certified carpet cleaner. Or, if you prefer the do-it-yourself approach, try the hydrogen peroxide solution

Enzyme-based Cleaners

Enzyme-based cleaners are the most effective do-it-yourself stain- and odor-removal products on the market; they're commonly sold in pet stores and through pet-supply catalogs. The rule for stain removal is "like dissolves like," which is why organic enzymes work so well on organic stains and odors. The enzymes actually digest the stain- and odor-causing proteins. However, if you have previously used cleaners or chemicals on the affected area, enzyme-based cleaners will not be effective unless you have completely rinsed away all traces of the old cleaner.

described in chapter 4, or rent an extractor or a wet-vac machine (not a steam cleaner) that forces clean water through your carpet and dirty water out. Once the stain has been removed, use a carpet odor neutralizer.

Urine Odors. A number of deodorizing products only mask the odor with perfume. To really remove the urine odor, you have to completely remove the urine. If the odor still lingers, try using an enzyme-based cleaner. Or, to remove urine odor from your carpet, call a certified carpet cleaner. If the urine soaked through into the carpet padding, you will probably need to replace that portion of the carpet and padding.

Do not use ammonia or other cleaning chemicals with strong odors on the stained spot, as they do not effectively cover the urine odor and may encourage your pet to reinforce its urine scent mark. To discourage a pet from resoiling a previously soiled area, lay a sheet of foil on the spot for a week or two, or cover the area with a plastic outdoor tablecloth or other material that will be unappealing for your pet to step on. You can even buy mats designed to keep pets away; stepping on the mats sets off an alarm.

Vomit and Feces Stains. Start by scraping up the solid material. If it has dried, vacuum up any remaining bits. Use a damp white cloth to blot up as much of the stain as you can; if the stain's on your flooring, such as a carpet or rug, stepping on the cloth will help. You should see at least some transfer of the stain to the cloth before proceeding to the next step. Spray or pour 3 percent hydrogen peroxide liberally over the entire stain (without soaking it) and cover immediately with a dry white towel. Covering the hydrogen peroxide is important; if sunlight hits it, it just turns to water. Let the towel sit on the stain for 8 hours. Repeat if necessary. If the stain still remains, try using an enzyme-based cleaning product.

Note: Do not use the kind of hydrogen peroxide used for bleaching hair. That would also bleach your carpet. The 3 percent formula available at pharmacies is safe (and cheap).

Cleaning Washable Items. Machine-wash towels or other stained or smelly washable goods with detergent plus the contents of a 1-pound box of baking soda. Afterward, air-dry it all. If the stain or odor remains, wash the load again, using a enzyme-based laundry aid. Do not put the item into the dryer until the stain or odor is completely removed, to avoid setting it permanently.

Now You See It

If you can smell a urine stain but can't find it, try using a black light, available at hardware stores. Turn off the overhead lights and turn on the black light. The formerly invisible urine stains should stand out. Mark the boundaries of each stain with masking tape. Refer to the advice in this chapter (page 185) on how to remove the stains.

Hairy Problem

To reduce the occurrence of hairballs vomited up on your furniture and floors, try grooming your cat regularly. There are also cat foods specially formulated to reduce this unpleasant aspect of cat ownership. Pet expert Arden Moore suggests putting a dab of petroleum jelly on your cat's nose; the cat will lick it off and ingest it, which helps move the hairball buildup out of the stomach.

Pet Hair and Furnishings

If you are like most pet owners, you love your pet but hate having pet hair here, there, and everywhere. A little prevention goes a long way. Start with regular grooming. The more you brush your dog or cat, the less pet hair you will have to clean from carpets, rugs, and furniture. Long-haired animals should be brushed daily, and short-haired animals once a week. Brush your pet outside or on a hard floor for easier cleanup afterward.

Regular grooming is easiest when you get your pet accustomed to brushing from an early age. You can do this in one of two ways: either use brushing as a therapeutic tool or make it a game. Either way, grooming becomes an opportunity to bond with your pet as well as a simple way to keep your home from being overrun with pet hair. It's also a good time to check for fleas and ticks.

If you choose to make brushing a game, your goal is to get your pet excited about being brushed so that eventually just seeing the brush will bring your pet running to you. Start with short sessions. With brush in hand, ask in a happy voice, "Do you want to get brushed?" Stroke your pet with the brush and then say, "Good boy (or good girl)." Repeat the stroking a few times and use the word "brush" to help your pet associate it with the activity. Gradually lengthen the sessions.

Alternatively, you might opt to use brushing as a therapeutic tool, particularly if your pet is not used to regular grooming. Wait until your pet is in a comfortable, relaxed state and then alternate stroking with your hand and stroking with the brush. Speak in calm, soothing tones to reassure the animal. If your pet gets agitated, stop brushing, revert to stroking with your hand, and try again another day.

When choosing a dog or cat, keep in mind that animals with long or silky coats will require regular daily grooming. Some dogs, such as poodles, bichons frises, and Bedlington terriers, do not shed at all, but do need to be clipped on a regular basis. Smooth-coated cats and dogs are the easiest to groom: all you need is a comb or a grooming mitt.

Before brushing, run your hands through your pet's coat from back to front to massage the

For Best Results

- Bathe and groom pets regularly.
- Keep an old towel handy for wiping off paws when your pets are coming in from outside.
- In areas where your pets spend a lot of time, vacuum at least twice a week, to help keep pet hair and dirt from becoming embedded in your carpets.

skin and loosen dead hairs. This massage will help to stimulate and distribute natural oils in the skin, which gives a healthy shine to the coat. Then use the type of grooming that is best suited to your pet — a brush, comb, or mitt — to brush your pet from head to tail. Don't forget to brush the underbelly. Also don't forget to brush or comb hair between toes and pads, which can collect small stones, chewing gum, and other debris.

If you can't — or choose not to — keep your pets off beds and other furniture, at least save yourself some time and effort by covering your pet's favorite resting spots with a washable blanket or sheet. Slipcovers and bedspreads are good alternatives if you're concerned with appear-

How To BRUSH A LONG-HAIRED CAT

Start by combing your cat's belly and legs with a wide-toothed comb, untangling any knots you might find. Then brush its body fur all over in an upward motion from scalp to sky. Make a part down the middle of your cat's tail and brush out the fur on either side.

ances. If you're buying furniture, take into consideration that leather does not attract hair anywhere near as much as fabric upholstery.

The easiest, most effective and inexpensive way to remove pet hair from carpets and upholstery is to "lay rubber." Rubber has a way of picking up embedded hair that most vacuum cleaners can't. Use a rubber-bristled push broom or long-handled squeegee to push pet hair into rolls that can be picked up. There are also smaller versions of the squeegee blade that are perfect for removing hair from upholstered furniture and are easy to clean and keep clean.

Here are a few more proven tips and tools for ridding upholstered furniture and clothing of pet hair:

- **Rubber glove.** Wear a clean rubber dishwashing glove or a gardening glove with nubby rubber palms. Wet the glove, shake off excess water, and wipe the fabric surface with your hand in a rolling motion (from palm to back) to swipe away pet hair. Rinse the glove and repeat as needed.
- **Damp sponge.** Use a clean white, barely dampened sponge to "stroke" pet hair from the fabric surface. Rinse the sponge as needed and after use to remove hair. A white sponge will prevent transfer of dye to fabric.
- **Fabric softener sheet.** Swiping a used fabric softener sheet over furniture is also quite effective for picking up pet hair.
- **Lint remover.** If you have a clothing brush or roller that you think works great, consider yourself lucky. Otherwise, make your own hair and lint remover with a wide strip of sticky tape

wrapped around the palm of your hand, with the sticky side facing out. Press and pat down your furniture upholstery or curtains, using your palm. When that portion of the tape is filled with hair and lint, pull the tape around your hand so that you have a clean sticky spot. Repeat as necessary. This works great on clothing, too.

Helpful hint: Spray a static-removal product on upholstered furniture, drapes, carpets, or clothing to make it easier to remove hair. Or make your own pet-hair-lifting solution with one part liquid fabric softener and three parts

Tips for Vacuuming Pet Hair

- Spray a static-removal product lightly over your carpet or furniture. Wait a few minutes, then vacuum as usual.

- If your pets have fleas, throw out or empty the vacuum bag outdoors after each vacuuming.

- Throw out or empty your vacuum bag when it is half-full, to prevent the vacuum from getting clogged with pet hair.

- If you are in the market for a new vacuum cleaner, ask other pet owners for recommendations. Be sure to look at cleaners that come with a turbo tool specifically designed to pick up animal hair.

water in a spray bottle; mist furnishings ever so slightly prior to attempting your choice of hair removal. Test this solution on an inconspicuous area of your upholstery to make sure the water does not stain the fabric.

Pet beds also need to be cleaned regularly. Remove and shake out blankets and pillows at least once a week. For easy care, choose bedding with a removable cover, or cover it with something that can be thrown in the washer and dryer, such as an old sheet, blanket, towel, or T-shirt. Prevent fleas and ticks from becoming a problem in your home by getting your animal on a preventive program; consult with your veterinarian. For tips on how to get rid of fleas and ticks, see chapter 15.

Bathing Your Dog

A monthly bath is more than sufficient for most dogs, and some dogs need bathing far less often. How often to bathe your dog depends on the type of dog (short or long hair), whether or not your dog is primarily an indoor or outdoor pet, and any conditions that may be present, such as dandruff or itchy skin due to allergies. In general, if your dog is dirty or smelly, it's time for a bath.

For minimal mess, it's best to bathe your dog outdoors, provided it is warm enough that your dog will not catch a chill. Always use warm water to bathe your dog. If the water from your garden hose is cold, you will need a couple of buckets of warm water to pour over your dog — and a helper to fetch a few more buckets of warm water for rinsing. Use only specially formulated dog shampoo, as the pH of human shampoo (even baby shampoo) is too harsh for a dog's skin and coat.

If you bathe your dog indoors, be sure to put a nonskid bath mat in the tub to keep your dog from slipping or scratching the tub. A sprayer attachment that hooks up to the faucet is also very helpful. *Helpful hint:* Pour or spray water gently over your dog to avoid panicking him. To prevent your dog from shaking off water — and soaking you in the process — gently grab and lift the scruff or back of its neck.

- Always brush your dog before bathing to remove loose hair, tangles, and mats.
- Place cotton balls in your dog's ears to keep them dry; remove them before or after drying.
- Working from head to tail, soak your dog's fur all over with warm water.
- Lather the shampoo around the neck of your dog and use your fingertips (not your fingernails), a washcloth, or a sponge to massage the shampoo into its fur and skin.
- Wash the neck and back first and work toward the tail and bottom. Lift and wash the legs and feet one by one.
- Use a washcloth to gently wash your dog's face. Take care to avoid getting soap in its eyes.
- Rinse your dog thoroughly from head to tail to remove all traces of shampoo.
- Gently squeeze excess moisture from your dog's fur, then towel dry.
- Use a blow dryer on the lowest setting to finish drying, or brush the dog's coat until completely dry.
- Reward your dog afterward with words of praise or a favorite treat.

Small-Animal Cages

It's important that your rabbit, hamster, or other furry friend have a clean, dry cage. A dirty cage causes stress and illness. For easy cleaning, look for a cage with a solid-surface floor and a large door or a lid that lifts off; this will also make it easier to take your pet out of its cage. Deluxe hard plastic structures with prefabri-cated tunnels and chambers may look appealing but can be very difficult to clean. A water bottle is preferable to a bowl, as bedding frequently gets kicked into an open bowl. If you choose to use a water bottle, look for one that can be easily cleaned with a bottle brush.

Locate the cage where it is easily accessible for daily care. Use only soap and water or animal-safe cleaning products for cleaning your pet's cage, nest box, bowls, and toys. To keep the cage cleaner, clip any vegetables you feed to your pet to the wire frame of the cage. Always wear gloves when cleaning up after your pet, and do not allow young children to clean cages.

Daily. Refill the water bottle, or wash out the water bowl and refill it with clean water. Clean up any droppings with a wet paper towel; the dampness will keep dry droppings from turning to dust that you might inhale. Remove any fruits or vegetables that your pet has not eaten.

For Best Results

- Have two or more sets of food and water bowls or water bottles so that you always have clean ones at the ready.
- Keep all your cage-cleaning supplies handy in an easy-to-carry plastic tote.
- When you get ready to start cleaning, place a garbage can next to the cage for easy removal of food and pet waste.
- Use nontoxic cage wipes to clean and deodorize your pet's cage in a single step.

Every Other Day. Clean the corner where your pet urinates. Remove dirty litter, replacing it with fresh litter.

Weekly. Clean the whole cage and everything in it. Completely empty the cage, and wash and rinse the bottom of the cage with mild detergent. Dry thoroughly before refilling the cage with fresh bedding.

Weekly cleanings are very important to prevent the growth of mold in the soiled shavings, which may make your pet sick. The best time to clean your pet's cage is when it is awake, not when it is snoozing. If you put your furry little friend in an exercise ball while you clean its cage, close the door of the room it's in for safety. If you allow a rabbit to roam freely, be sure to keep it away from electrical cords so that it won't be tempted to chew on them.

Bird Cages

Birds are not the neatest of pets, and cleaning up after your feathered friend is one of those never-ending jobs you love to hate. Daily quick cleanups make the thorough weekly or monthly cleanings less of a chore.

Daily. Establishing an everyday cleaning routine will not only reduce your work in the long run but also provide you with an opportunity to keep an eye out for any signs of illness that may develop in your bird.

- Use hot water and a scouring sponge to wipe food and feces off the cage, perch, and toys.
- Change the paper lining the bottom of the cage.
- Wash the food and water bowls at least once daily with hot, soapy water and rinse thoroughly. You may use a disinfectant provided that it bird-safe. Be sure that the food bowl is completely dry before adding seeds or pellets, to prevent moldiness.
- Keep a handheld vacuum or a broom handy to clean up debris that has fallen from the cage to the floor.
- You can minimize "fallout" with a cage apron. For easier cleanup on carpeted floors, place an office chair mat under the cage.

Do not use the self-clean feature of your oven around a bird; it can be deadly. The same is true of heavy cooking fumes. Do not use scented candles, room fresheners, or strong cleaners such as carpet cleaners in the presence of birds.

Weekly/Monthly. Whether you need to do a thorough cleaning weekly or monthly will depend on the size of your bird or the number of birds you have. Make it easier on yourself and your birds by relocating them to another cage while you are cleaning the primary cage.

1. Remove the cage bottom or turn the cage upside down to shake out seeds and loose droppings.

2. Place the cage in the shower and run hot water over it. Scrub the cage with hot water, dish detergent, and a scouring sponge or brush. Do the same with toys and accessories. Use sandpaper to remove dried-on matter if necessary. You can also use white vinegar or a nontoxic enzyme-based cleaner to soften droppings. If necessary, allow the tough spots to soak for 30 minutes.

3. Once it's clean, rinse the cage thoroughly to remove all soap residue. Then spray the cage, toys, and accessories with a nontoxic disinfectant. Rinse thoroughly to remove all traces of disinfectant. Allow the cage to dry completely. *Helpful hint:* Have a second set of clean, disinfected toys and accessories ready for immediate return to the clean, dry cage. Discard any items that do not come clean or need replacing.

4. Empty and wash the cage apron, and then wash and disinfect the floor below the cage and nearby walls if necessary. Line the cage with fresh paper. *Helpful hint:* Use several layers of paper lining that can be removed daily, one at a time, as they get dirty.

5. Finally, refill the food and water bowls and return your bird to its clean home.

A self-cleaning bird cage makes this process much simpler and easier while creating a healthier environment for your bird. A revolutionary concept in bird care, the self-cleaning bird cage uses water to carry waste and allergens into a collection device that can be emptied daily with no muss or fuss. Look for this type of product in pet stores, or do an Internet search for the keywords "self-cleaning birdcage."

Reptile Cages

A safe, healthy home for your reptile begins with a meticulously clean cage. Washing alone is not enough; the cage and everything in it must be disinfected to eliminate bacteria that can cause skin infections on your pet. Regular disinfecting will also prevent infection from *Salmonella*, a bacterium often found in the feces of snakes, iguanas, and other reptiles.

Daily. Remove spills, uneaten food, shed skin, urate (a chalky white substance eliminated along with urine), and feces. Clean and disinfect the food and water dishes. Use this cleaning time as an opportunity to assess your reptile's health. For example, note whether or not the normal amount of food has been eaten and whether the urate and feces appear normal.

Weekly. Start by relocating your reptile to a backup cage away from the cleaning process. Then don a pair of rubber or latex gloves and begin the following cleaning sequence:

1. Remove all equipment, toys, rocks, sticks, and so on from the cage.
2. Sift the sand to remove feces and other debris from the disposable substrate material. Bag and dispose of the waste.
3. Use a clean sponge to wash all cage surfaces, decorations, and other furnishings with a mixture of hot, soapy water. Use a putty knife, toothbrush, and special terrarium cleaner to remove dried waste and liquids.
4. Rinse the cage and accessories, using a second clean sponge.
5. Disinfect the cage and all accessories in a bleach solution of 1 cup of liquid chlorine bleach per gallon of water. Sponge the bleach solution onto the components and allow to stand for 5 to 10 minutes.
6. Use a third clean sponge to rinse everything thoroughly, removing all traces of bleach.
7. Dry the cage with paper towels, and make sure that all the accessories are completely dry before returning them to the cage, to prevent the growth of mold.

As Needed. Before introducing natural items to the cage, clean them. Boil rocks in water for 30 minutes. Rinse branches and sand thoroughly, and sanitize them by placing them in an oven at 200 to 250°F (93 to 121°C) for 30 minutes.

For Safety's Sake

- Wear household cleaning gloves when you are cleaning your reptile's cage.
- If possible, avoid cleaning your reptile's cage and accessories in sinks or tubs that are used for human bathing or food preparation.
- After cleaning your reptile's cage, clean and disinfect all the sponges, brushes, gloves, buckets, and sinks you used in the cleaning process.
- Always wash your hands in hot, soapy water after handling your reptile.

The gift of the family novelist is to turn the cleaning of a closet into an inventory of love and loss — to scan a poem from a shopping list.

— Marilyn Gardner

Fish Tanks

Fish are not the easiest pets to care for. However, the more meticulous you are about cleaning your tank, the healthier your fish will be, and the easier your tank will be to care for in the future. As a preventive measure, position your aquarium away from windows, as sunlight can contribute to the growth of algae in your fish tank.

Contrary to what you may have heard, algae-eating fish do not eliminate the need to clean your tank. That's your job! Think of algae-eating fish as helpers.

Never use soap or other chemicals to clean anything that goes in your aquarium. Regular required maintenance includes the following.

Daily. Check to make sure that all of your fish are present and healthy. If you find a dead fish, scoop it out with a net immediately and bury or flush it. Remove all the food that is not eaten within 10 minutes of feeding. It's a good idea to stir the gravel with your net to help particles in the gravel get into the filter. Also make sure that all equipment is plugged in, turned on, and operating properly.

Controlling Algae

Add light and nutrients to water and you've got a proven formula for algae growth, which not only is unsightly but can also be detrimental to aquarium life. Here are some pointers for minimizing the problem:

- Keep the fish tank out of direct sunlight.
- Leave lighting on for no more than 10 to 12 hours a day.

- Siphon and add fresh water weekly.
- Scrape the glass regularly with an algae scraper.
- Consider adding algae-eating fish such as mollies in a freshwater tank or snails in a saltwater tank.
- Avoid overfeeding the fish, to minimize excess organic material.

Weekly. The weekly cleaning is a bit more intensive, but you do not need to remove the fish to do it.

1. Scrape algae off the inside of the glass walls with a special algae scrubber or nonabrasive mitt. Scrub any rocks or decorations that have algae on them; you do not need to remove them to do this.
2. If you have live plants in the tank, trim off excess growth and dead leaves.
3. Siphon off 15 to 20 percent of the water and replace it with clean tap water that's been allowed to sit in an aquarium-use-only bucket for 24 hours to eliminate chlorine.
4. Clean the gravel with a specially designed gravel cleaner that vacuums up decaying organic matter. This prevents organic matter from blocking passages between the pebbles, which restricts water flow.

For Safety's Sake

Do not clean your fish tank with your bare hands. A bacterium that can be carried by aquarium fish can cause open sores that are slow to heal. Wearing household cleaning gloves will protect you against this germ.

As Needed. Be sure to change the filter as often as recommended by the manufacturer. Once a month or so, remove any decorations that are very scummy. Clean them, using an algae scrubber, rinse them well, and return them to the tank. Disconnect the filter tubing and clean it with a filter brush. Periodically clean the outside glass by spraying glass cleaner on a paper towel. Also, use a damp cloth to dust external aquarium features.

CHAPTER TWELVE

PERSONAL ITEMS

Anything that gets regular use requires regular cleaning. This chapter outlines plain and simple cleaning methods for personal items — everything from brushes to handbags and shoes to jewelry. Ever wondered how to remove mildew from leather, grass stains from athletic shoes, or that gunk on your curling iron? You'll find answers to these dilemmas and more in the following pages.

Cosmetic Brushes and Tools

Do you know what's on your makeup brushes? Dust, old makeup, and oil from your skin get trapped in the bristles. Bacteria from unclean brushes can cause breakouts and also contaminate makeup. Frequent cleaning helps prevent the buildup of dirt and bacteria, ensures even application of makeup, and extends the life of your brushes. Regular washing is especially important for brushes used to apply foundation and concealer, as these products tend to adhere to and build up more quickly on bristles.

What You Need
- ❏ Running water
- ❏ Mild shampoo
- ❏ Hair conditioner

Make regular cleaning of your brushes a part of your makeup routine. Spritz bristles weekly with a quick-drying, antimicrobial brush cleanser and wipe them down with a tissue to prevent makeup and bacterial buildup. Or wash the brushes at least once a month, even if you have not used them, as dust has a way of settling into the bristles. But don't just soak the brushes in the sink; soaking may cause the entire brush section to come unglued from the handle. Instead, follow this washing routine:

1. Wash your hands.
2. Wet the bristles under warm running water.
3. Gently wipe a tiny amount of mild shampoo on the

brush, rub gently to form a lather, and squeeze the lather through the bristles.

4. Rinse well under cool running water.

5. Repeat steps 2 and 3 if there is visible makeup residue in the rinse water. When all the visible residue is gone, squeeze the excess water from the brush head.

6. If your brush is made of natural hair, work in a thin layer of hair conditioner to coat the bristles, and then rinse with cool water. (You can skip this step for synthetic brushes.)

7. Shake excess water from the brush and reshape the head.

8. Air-dry the brush by laying it flat with the bristles hanging over the edge of a sink basin or counter. Do not lay brushes on a towel. Do not blow-dry.

Any cosmetic tools that come in daily contact with your skin can become a breeding ground for bacteria. Following are some simple guidelines for keeping all of these tools and your skin clean.

• **Reusable cosmetic sponge.** Wash this type of sponge at least once a week with a mild shampoo. Gently wipe a tiny amount of mild shampoo onto the sponge and squeeze gently to form a lather. Rinse well. Allow the sponge to air-dry on a paper towel. A more hygienic approach is to use a fresh disposable sponge every day.

• **Eyeshadow applicators.** Wash these every week, in the same way you clean a cosmetic sponge (above), and replace them as needed with a clean disposable applicator.

• **Compact sponge and powder puff.** Wash these every week, as you would a cosmetic sponge (above). Store the sponge or powder puff on top of the plastic sheet provided with the compact or upside down in the compact. This prevents the oils from your skin from collecting on the surface of the powder.

• **Eyelash curler.** Clean the metal pieces with a cotton ball dipped in eye-makeup remover. Swipe the pads with the same remover, and replace them every few months or as needed.

• **Shower puff.** Once a week, toss any synthetic shower puffs into the washing machine and wash them in hot water.

• **Loofah sponge.** Rinse your loofah under hot water after every use to flush away dead skin cells and prevent bacteria from growing. Shake it to remove excess water, and hang it to dry outside the shower to avoid mildewing. To clean your loofah, rinse it in clean water; then soak it in a solution of 1 teaspoon of liquid chlorine bleach and 1 quart of warm water. If possible, let it dry in the sun. Loofah sponges will last a long time if washed and allowed to dry completely after each use. An alternative to the loofah sponge is an ayate washcloth. Made from the agave plant, mildew-resistant ayate will exfoliate skin like loofah. However, it can be machine-washed and lasts up to one year.

Hair-Care Tools

Taking good care of hairbrushes and other hair-care tools will help prolong their life and also help them work better. This is especially true of good-quality, natural-bristle brushes. Follow the manufacturer's instructions for best results. Do not immerse these brushes in water. Do not use detergents, ammonia, petroleum-based products, or shampoos to clean them, and do not blow-dry or machine-dry them.

"Dry" Clean Once a Week. After each use or at least once a week, use a comb to loosen any strands of hair that have become woven into the bristles. Insert the comb at the sides of the brush as near to the pad (where the bristles are attached) as possible, then push the comb through the bristles toward the center of the pad. Lift out the hair. Repeat from different points around the brush pad until all the hair is removed.

"Wet" Clean Once a Month. Once a month or so, wash your hairbrush. Do this more frequently if your brush regularly comes in contact with mousse, gel, or hair spray — or if you have oily hair. Don't wait until the pad and bristles are brown with oils or other residues.

What You Need
❏ Dishwashing liquid
❏ Cleaning brush or toothbrush reserved for cleaning hairbrushes

1. Fill the sink with warm water, add a drop or two of dishwashing liquid, and swish the water to make it sudsy.
2. Dry-clean the brush as usual (see above). Then dip a cleaning brush or toothbrush into the soapsuds and use it to gently scrub the hairbrush bristles from the pad to the tips. Clean the surface of the rubber pad with a light scrubbing action.
3. Rinse the brush quickly under cool running water, holding the brush vertically with the handle pointing up, to prevent water from entering the vent hole of the brush head.
4. Gently shake the hairbrush to remove any excess moisture, and allow it to air-dry on a hard surface, away from sunlight, with the bristles facing down.

Washing Combs (and Inexpensive Brushes). Once a week, wash combs and inexpensive nylon-bristle brushes as follows:

1. Fill the sink with warm water and add a few drops of dishwashing liquid or ½ tablespoon of ammonia.
2. If you're washing a brush, dry-clean it first, as described above. Drop the combs or brushes into the water and let them soak for 10 to 20 minutes.

3. Use a clean toothbrush to scrub the combs or brushes.
4. Rinse the combs or brushes under running water, and let them air-dry.

To clean brushes used on sensitive scalps and for cleaning baby combs and brushes, substitute 1 teaspoon of baking soda for the dishwashing liquid. Dissolve thoroughly in warm water and proceed as described on the previous page.

Cleaning a Blow-Dryer. Over time, lint and debris will collect in your blow-dryer, which can cause the dryer to overheat and/or reduce its performance. Most blow-dryers today are made with detachable filters for easy cleaning. If you use your blow-dryer daily, clean this filter once a month.

1. Unplug the dryer, twist off the plastic grid covering the back of the blow-dryer, and remove the screen underneath.
2. Use a soft toothbrush to brush away dust and hair that has collected on the screen. Then replace the screen and plastic grid.

A DIRTY CURLING IRON

One Challenge:

Burned-on hairspray and gel can make your curling iron unusable. Always unplug the curling iron and allow it to cool completely before cleaning it. Start by wiping the outside plastic surfaces with a damp, soapy sponge. Then choose one of these methods to clean the barrel.

Three Solutions . . .

1 Dampen a cotton ball or cotton cosmetic pad with rubbing alcohol or nail polish remover and use it to swipe the soiled area. Rinse by wiping the barrel again with a cotton ball or cosmetic pad dampened with warm water.

2 Sprinkle baking soda on a wet cloth, then wrap it around the dirty barrel. Let it sit for a few hours with the curling clamp in place. Then unwrap the cloth and wipe the barrel clean.

3 Make a paste of baking soda and water. Apply it to a scouring sponge, to remove the gunk. As a last resort to scrape off stubborn residue, gently wipe the barrel with a steel-wool soap pad. Wipe again with a damp cloth to remove the soap and other residue.

Toothbrushes

Old toothpaste in toothbrush bristles can harbor bacteria, so be sure to rinse your toothbrush well after each use. Some bacteria and viruses, including influenza and herpes simplex, can thrive for up to a week outside the body. For this reason, doctors agree that you should replace your toothbrush immediately after you've had a cold or the flu to prevent reinfection by the same germs. But do you need to disinfect your toothbrush periodically? You can if it makes you feel better, but you don't need to.

Following are guidelines from the National Center for Chronic Disease Prevention and Health Promotion on the everyday use and handling of toothbrushes.

- **Don't share.** Do not share toothbrushes. Those who share will increase their risk for infections, particularly if their immune systems are compromised. Label each person's toothbrush or use color coding for easy identification.
- **Apply toothpaste carefully.** When dispensing toothpaste, don't touch the tip of the toothpaste tube to your toothbrush; this helps avoid the transfer of bacteria from your brush to the tube.
- **Rinse well.** After brushing, rinse your toothbrush thoroughly with tap water to ensure the removal of toothpaste and debris.
- **Store upright.** Store your brush in an upright position to allow it to air-dry. If multiple brushes are stored in the same holder, keep the brushing ends separated.
- **Store in the open.** Do not routinely cover toothbrushes or store them in closed containers. Such conditions are more conducive to bacterial growth than the open air.

Nine Nifty Uses for Old Toothbrushes

Don't save every old toothbrush, but do set aside a few for special cleaning assignments. It's a good idea to wash old toothbrushes in the dishwasher to clean and disinfect them prior to reuse. Then put them to use to:

1. Clean garlic out of your garlic press.
2. Clean rinds and cheese from a hand grater.
3. Brush stain treatments into fabrics before laundering.
4. Gently scour around the base of bathroom and kitchen faucets.
5. Clean your contact lens case.
6. Clean jewelry.
7. Remove baked-on matter from toaster wires and racks.
8. Lift dust and debris from sliding-door tracks.
9. Clean a can opener blade.

- **Don't disinfect.** It is not necessary to soak toothbrushes in disinfectant solutions or mouthwash. This practice actually may lead to cross-contamination of toothbrushes if the same disinfectant solution is used for multiple toothbrushes. It is also unnecessary to use dishwashers, microwaves, or ultraviolet devices to disinfect toothbrushes. These measures may damage the toothbrush.
- **Replace regularly.** Replace your toothbrush every three to four months, or sooner if the bristles appear worn or splayed. A worn toothbrush does not clean teeth effectively.

Exercise Equipment

Home exercise equipment is easy to maintain. Spray "sweat" spots such as the seat and pads with a disinfectant cleaner after use, and then wipe them down with paper towels. If you don't use your equipment often, dust it occasionally with a damp cloth. To protect your flooring from sweat and scuff marks, place a washable mat or a carpet remnant that can be replaced every so often under your exercise equipment.

Treadmill Tips

Wear indoor-only shoes for your treadmill workout. Shoes that you also wear outdoors may track in sand and grit, causing unnecessary wear and tear on the belt. Lubricate any guide rods once or twice a year, according to the manufacturer's instructions.

Eyeglasses and Other Lenses

If you wear glasses every day, lens care should be a part of your daily routine. Experts advise cleaning lenses twice a day to prevent smudges and dust particles from damaging the surface and to ensure clear vision. But be sure to do it right! Never clean your glasses with a dry cloth. Always wet the lenses with water or a cleaning solution before wiping them. Even tiny particles can be abrasive when rubbed across the lens surface. Premoistened lens-cleaning tissues make it easy to clean your eyeglasses anywhere, but all you really need are a soft cloth and a little dishwashing liquid swished in a sink full of water. Follow these steps to clean your eyeglasses:

1. Immerse the eyeglasses in warm, soapy water.
2. Rub the lenses gently with your fingers.
3. Rinse to wash away dirt and oil.
4. Gently dry the lenses and frames with a soft, lint-free cloth.

Avoid using household cleaners, disinfectants, or soaps with creams to clean lenses. Do not dry lenses with a paper towel, tissues, old rags, or the tail of your shirt, which may have imbedded dirt or simply be too abrasive. You might get away without a scratch if you have glass lenses, but plastic lenses scratch more easily. Microfiber cloths are highly recommended. Originally designed to keep electronic manufacturing rooms clean, these super-soft, absorbent cloths gently remove dust and oils from your lenses. Wash the cloth weekly without fabric softener. While wet cleaning is preferred, you can also fog each lens with an exhale of breath and then wipe with a microfiber cloth for a quick clean.

Store glasses in a protective case when you're not using them, to keep them free of dust and also to prevent accidental damage to them. To avoid scratches, never lay your glasses lens-side down or put them in your handbag, tote bag, or sports bag without proper protection. Be aware that hairspray can damage lenses with anti-reflective coating; before spraying your hair, it's best to remove your glasses and put them in their case or cover them with a towel.

Contact Lenses and Storage Cases. Daily disposable lenses require no cleaning. Simply wear and toss as directed. Daily-wear hard and soft contact lenses should be cleaned, rinsed, and disinfected every time they are removed. Extended-wear contacts should also be cleaned daily. The following steps are general guidelines; it's best to follow the care and cleaning regimen recommended by your eye-care clinician.

1. Remove the lens from one eye.
2. Hold the lens in the palm of your hand. Put two or three drops of an approved cleaner on the lens. Rub well for 20 to 30 seconds.
3. Rinse off the cleaner with a sterile saline solution.
4. Repeat the above steps for the other lens.
5. Disinfect the lenses as directed by your eye-care clinician.

Lack of cleaning or improper care of your contact lenses increases the risk of developing an eye infection and can lead to more serious complications or even loss of vision. Always wash, rinse, and dry your hands thoroughly before handling your contacts. Handle lenses with your fingertips; avoid touching them with your fingernails. Do not use tap water or saliva to clean lenses. Do not reuse any lens-care solutions.

Store lenses in a lens case with fresh disinfectant solution. Many an infection has been traced to a dirty case. Rinse your storage case and leave it open to dry after use each day. Once a week, clean the storage case using a clean old toothbrush and contact lens cleaner. Every six months or so, replace your case.

Camera Lenses. Use a small ear syringe to blow dust particles off a camera lens with a small blast of air; do not use compressed air in a can, which might damage a delicate lens. If the lens appears dirty, breathe on it to create a mist, and then wipe the surface gently with a microfiber cloth or camera-lens-cleaning tissue. Do not wipe a dry lens, or you might scratch it. Also do not use chemically treated tissues or other solutions or solvents intended for cleaning eyeglass lenses. Always keep your camera lens capped when not in use.

Binocular Lenses. The Cornell Lab of Ornithology recommends the following procedure:

1. Lightly brush the lenses with a wad of lens-cleaning tissue or a soft camel's-hair brush to dislodge particles of sand and grit. Removing this debris prevents the lenses from becoming scratched during the cleaning.

2. Hold the binoculars upside down so that dirt will fall away from the lens surface. Fold a piece of lens-cleaning tissue so that it is at least four layers thick. This prevents oil from your fingers from soaking through the lens tissue and onto the lens surfaces. Gently wipe the lens surfaces with a circular motion. If there is an oily film on the lenses, put a drop of lens cleaner on the tissue and repeat the circular wiping movement.

3. Look for dirt on all the internal optics by holding the binoculars up to the light and looking into the objective lenses. If you see any, don't try to open the binoculars; you can easily disrupt their alignment. Although it's expensive, leave internal cleaning to the professionals; take your binoculars to a camera shop that also repairs binoculars.

Suitcases, Briefcases, and Handbags

Like anything else, luggage will have a longer life if it is cared for and stored properly. Leather briefcases and handbags require frequent conditioning to replace the natural lubricants lost during normal use. Soiling and odors can usually be resolved fairly easily.

Hard-Sided Luggage. Wash plastic luggage inside and out with a cloth or sponge dipped in a slightly soapy mixture of warm water and dishwashing liquid. Remove the soapy residue with a damp cloth. For stubborn stains, try applying a little bit of rubbing alcohol on the dry surface with a toothbrush. To keep the luggage looking like new, wax it with a silicone-based automotive wax or furniture polish.

Soft-Sided Luggage and Fabric Bags. Spot-clean soiled areas with a sponge or cloth dipped in slightly soapy water. It is not necessary to get the item soaking wet. You might also try using a laundry stain-removal spray or foam or an automobile mat and carpet cleaner. You may be able to toss unconstructed items such as tote bags and nylon bags into the washing machine on the delicate cycle, and hang them up to dry. Do not machine-dry fabric bags unless you want a smaller bag.

A Little Bit of History . . .

Suitcases were originally made from wooden boxes that were covered in cowhide, hand-stitched, and lined with silk. During World War II, while making camouflage for the army, Samsonite came up with the idea of using canvas to make suitcases. This revolutionary idea spawned a new, more affordable breed of luggage and put many of the earliest suitcase manufacturers out of business.

Smooth Leather Handbags and Briefcases.
Spray smooth leather bags and briefcases with leather protectant at the time of purchase to protect them from staining, drying, or cracking. To clean them, apply a cream leather cleaner with a soft cloth, following the instructions on the product label. You may be able to remove some marks and stains by gently wiping at them with a solution of 1 tablespoon of white vinegar in 1 cup of water. It's best to leave oil-based marks alone; they tend to disappear over time, as the leather uses the oils as moisturizer. After cleaning, apply leather conditioner liberally with a soft cloth, let it dry, and gently buff with a clean, soft cloth. Reapply leather protectant regularly to provide continual stain protection.

Odor Removal. Vacuum the inside of the bag. If it smells musty, lightly wipe the interior clean with a mixture of one part vinegar and five parts water to neutralize. *Note:* Vinegar may lighten some fabrics. Allow the bag to air for a few days, preferably in the sun or near an open window. An alternative to cleaning with the vinegar solution is to place a refrigerator box of baking soda in the bag to absorb the odor. Close the bag and leave it in a well-ventilated room for up to a week.

Storage Tips. Luggage will age more rapidly when it is exposed to extreme temperatures or humidity for extended lengths of time. If your luggage is stored in less-than-ideal conditions, make a note in your calendar to take it out of storage periodically. Opening the luggage and allowing it to air out regularly can help prevent the growth of mildew. It's also a good idea to clean your luggage when you bring it out of damp storage.

Leather luggage that has been stored in a dry environment needs conditioning on a regular basis to prevent it from drying out and cracking. Do not store leather bags in plastic bags, as the leather needs to breathe. To help an empty leather handbag retain its shape, you can stuff it with tissue paper before storing it.

Be sure that your luggage is completely dry before storing it.

Leather Shoes and Boots

It's inevitable that shoes and boots will start to look worn over time. But with regular cleaning and proper storage, leather footwear can look better longer and last longer, too. Ideally, leather shoes and boots worn often should be cleaned and polished often — at least once every four to six wearings or as needed. Shoes worn less often should be cleaned at least once each season.

Where do you take off your shoes when you come home? Keep a soft cloth handy in that spot so you can wipe off your shoes before putting them away. If your shoes are wet, wipe them off as soon as possible, allow them to air-dry naturally, and follow up with cleaning, conditioning, and waterproofing.

● EVERYDAY SOLUTION
Packing Shoes

When packing shoes for a trip, pull an old or worn sock over them to keep them from soiling other items.

- **To clean muddy boots and shoes.** Allow the boots or shoes to air-dry naturally, away from direct heat and light. Then bang the soles together to remove as much dirt as possible from them. Use a stiff nylon brush to remove the rest of the dirt from the soles as well as the uppers. Wipe away any remaining dirt with a damp cloth, and follow up with an application of leather cleaner (if needed) or just conditioner.
- **To remove salt stains.** Don't wait until the end of winter to clean salt off leather footwear. Salt appears as white line on your boots or shoes. If you notice white lines, sponge your boots or shoes with water immediately and allow them to air-dry. If the white lines reappear after cleaning, pour a little white vinegar on a damp cloth and wipe them away. Then dry with a soft cloth. Or apply salt-stain remover, available at shoe repair shops. Several applications of cleaner may be required to completely remove the white lines. When the leather is nearly dry, apply a small amount of leather conditioner to restore the leather's natural moisture and flexibility. Follow up with a full conditioning treatment after the leather has completely air-dried.

Store shoes in a spot that is dry (to prevent mildewing) and away from sunlight and direct heat (to keep leather from cracking and drying out). Experts recommend storing shoes and boots on "trees" designed to help footwear retain its shape. But that's not always practical, due to space or budget constraints. Instead, try stuffing the toes of your leather shoes with tissue or packing paper to prevent them from curling. Stuffing boots with paper or folded cardboard will prevent the tops from flopping over, which could cause damage to the leather over time.

Cleaning Smooth Leather. Spray new leather shoes with a leather protectant to help prevent stains, and respray them every few weeks. To clean smooth leather shoes:

1. Remove dirt and dust from the uppers with a damp cotton cloth.
2. Apply the leather cleaner of your choice, following the instructions on the product label, to loosen embedded dirt and stains. If the shoes are made of white leather and any scuff marks remain, wipe them away with a soft cloth moistened with rubbing alcohol.
3. If necessary, remove and wash the laces in a sink filled with warm, soapy water. Rinse and let air-dry.
4. Apply leather conditioner, following the instructions on the product label, to restore moisture to the leather. Polish if needed (see page 207).

SMART PURCHASE

Rather than buy an expensive little bottle of shoe leather cleaner, consider buying a larger bottle of leather upholstery cleaner, which you can use to clean all your smooth-leather belongings, including shoes, handbags, jackets, luggage, furniture, and automobile upholstery. *Note:* You'll still need to buy special cleaner for suede and nubuck leather.

Waterproofing. Water causes leather to lose its natural oils and become dry and stiff. Waterproofing helps prevent water penetration; it also protects against dirt, stains, and scuff marks. It's a good idea to waterproof boots, and other footwear if necessary, before the first wearing and regularly thereafter. Shoes and boots subjected to rain and snow should be waterproofed two to four times a year, depending on how often you wear them.

A number of stain- and water-repellent products are available for leather. Be sure that the product you choose is oil based; silicone formulas do not allow leather to breathe. Lanolin, the oil in sheep's wool, is a natural water repellent. Anhydrous lanolin, available at pharmacies, is a lubricating cream that comes in a tube and works well for waterproofing smooth leather. If your shoes combine leather and synthetic materials, such as boots with Gore-Tex lining, waterproof the leather parts as described below and use a silicone-based treatment for the synthetic parts of the shoe.

Whatever formula you choose, follow these simple steps for waterproofing:

1. Clean your boots or shoes (see above).
2. Coat each shoe liberally with the waterproofing formula.
3. Use a clean cloth to work the formula into the leather, especially into the welts at the midsole, the seams, and the stitching, where water is likely to seep in.
4. Allow your boots or shoes to dry overnight.

How To REMOVE MILDEW

Got mildew? Here's what to do with mildewed leather or fabric items such as luggage, handbags, and shoes.

1. Brush off as much of the mildew as you can with a dry sponge, cloth, or nylon-bristle brush. It's best to do this outdoors to avoid releasing mold spores in your home.
2. Use a soft white cloth or a sponge dampened with soapy water to wipe the item clean. Allow it to air-dry away from heat and sunlight.
3. If the item is made of leather, follow up with an application of leather conditioner, following the instructions on the product label.
4. If the mildew persists, try sponging the surface lightly with a mixture of equal parts of rubbing alcohol and water. Lightly wipe again with a sponge or cloth dampened with just water and let air-dry.
5. Leather items only: Finish with a treatment of leather conditioner.

Caring for Suede or Nubuck Leather. Do not use just any leather cleaner, conditioner, or waterproofing formula on suede or nubuck leather. Make sure you buy only products that are specifically recommended for these special leathers. It's a good idea to treat suede and nubuck leather with a stain and water repellent before the first wearing, and respray whenever water starts soaking in, rather than beading up on the leather surface. Also brush the leather regularly with a suede brush to keep shoes nappy and free of dust.

- **To remove stains.** You can remove most marks and stains by rubbing them with a pencil eraser. To remove oil stains, try sprinkling cornstarch or talcum powder on the spot, and leave it overnight to absorb the oil. After stain removal, brush the leather. For salt stains and other tough stains, and for best results in any situation, take your boots or shoes to a shoemaker or dry cleaner for professional cleaning.
- **To remove shiny spots.** To raise the nap on shiny spots, brush your boots or shoes or rub them gently with a terry-cloth towel.

Polishing. Choose a neutral shade of polish or a shade nearest to the color of your leather boots or shoes.

- **Wax polishes** are recommended for boots and shoes exposed frequently to rain and snow. Just be sure to condition the leather first, as wax polishes tend to dry out leather.
- **Cream and paste polishes** are best for covering scratches.

- **Liquid polishes and shoe wipes** are great in a pinch but are no substitute for a real polishing.
- **A natural alternative** to shoe polish is a little olive oil applied with a soft cloth.

Do not use shoe polish on jackets, handbags, or anything you wear or carry, or you will be wearing it on yourself.

Here's how to put a shine on your shoes:

What You Need:
- ❏ Newspaper
- ❏ Shoe polish
- ❏ Polish sponge or lint-free cloth
- ❏ Toothbrush
- ❏ Shoe brush
- ❏ Lint-free cloth or chamois cloth

1. Cover your work area with newspaper.
2. Remove the laces. Clean and condition the shoes (see above).
3. Apply polish to the leather, using a polish sponge or a lint-free cloth wrapped around your index finger. Spread the polish evenly from heel to toe, including the tongue, using a circular motion. Use a toothbrush to rub the polish into perforations and seams.
4. Allow the polish to dry for 10 to 15 minutes.
5. Slip one hand, palm down, into a shoe and pick it up. Use a shoe brush to rub the polish into the leather, using short back-and-forth strokes. Repeat with the other shoe.
6. Bring up the shine by polishing the shoes with a lint-free cloth or chamois cloth.

Preventing Smelly Shoes

- To freshen shoes after wearing them, sprinkle the insides liberally with baking soda; shake out the baking soda before putting the shoes back on. ***Helpful hint:*** Keep a box of baking soda in your closet for everyday use.

- Sprinkle table salt in canvas shoes to absorb moisture and odor. (But remember to shake out the salt before wearing the shoes!)

- Place cedar blocks in your shoes.

- Allow shoes to air before storing or rewearing them. A good rule of thumb is to avoid wearing the same pair of shoes two days in a row if possible.

- To remove odor from really smelly shoes, remove and wipe the insoles with a mixture of one part vinegar and five parts water. Also lightly wipe the inside of the shoe with the diluted vinegar solution. Allow to air-dry, preferably outdoors or near an open window.

- If odor is recurring problem with all or most of your shoes, treat your feet daily with an antiperspirant designed to help keep feet dry. You may also want to spray your shoes with a shoe disinfectant after wearing them, to kill the bacteria that can cause odor.

- Keep athletic shoes from smelling up a gym bag or suitcase by placing a fabric softener sheet or soap wrapper in each shoe. Additionally, when traveling, place each shoe in a plastic grocery bag and tie it up, to help prevent dirt and odor from transferring to other items in your suitcase.

Athletic Shoes and Fabric Shoes

Although it's a common practice to toss athletic shoes and canvas sneakers into the washing machine, it's not recommended. Machine washing may get the shoes clean, but the agitation breaks down the special construction of the shoe, thus shortening its life. It's best to follow the manufacturer's care instructions. *Helpful hint:* If you can't find the manufacturer's care instructions that came with your shoes, check the manufacturer's Web site.

Athletic Shoes. If you can't find cleaning directions or don't want to buy the special products that may be recommended, here's what you can do to wash any athletic shoe with canvas, leather, or nylon uppers.

1. Lay down newspaper over a work area near running water. Fill the dishpan or bucket with warm water.
2. Remove the shoelaces and insoles. Toss the laces into a laundry load of whites.

What You Need:

- ❏ Newspaper
- ❏ Dishpan or bucket
- ❏ Dishwashing liquid
- ❏ White or light-colored nylon scrubbing sponge
- ❏ Old nailbrush or toothbrush
- ❏ White paper towels
- ❏ Shoe polish (optional)

3. Dip the first shoe in the water just to wet it. Set it down on the newspaper.

4. Squirt a bit of dishwashing liquid on a nylon scrubbing sponge and use it to scrub the shoe inside and out. Use an old nailbrush or toothbrush to scrub stubborn dirt and stains.

5. Repeat steps 3 and 4 for the second shoe.

6. Dip both insoles in the water, and scrub them with the soapy sponge.

7. Immerse the shoes and the insoles in the water, swishing them around to remove most of the soap. Then rinse them clean under running water.

8. Stuff the shoes with white paper towels to help them retain their shape. Allow the shoes and insoles to air-dry naturally, preferably outdoors away from sunlight or near an open window.

9. When the shoes are dry, apply polish, if desired.

10. Reinsert the clean, dry laces and insoles.

How To

GET GRASS STAINS OUT

Grass stains are inevitable on white shoes, especially golf shoes, tennis shoes, and canvas sneakers. Here's what to do to get rid of them:

- *For canvas and nylon shoes*: Combine 1 tablespoon of ammonia, ½ cup of water, and a squirt of dishwashing liquid.

- *For shoes with leather uppers*: Combine ⅓ cup of white vinegar, ⅔ cup of water, and a squirt of dishwashing liquid.

Dip a toothbrush into the cleaning solution and use it to brush the stains away. Then wash the shoes as instructed on this page. If that doesn't remove the stain, try brushing it with a few drops of household ammonia mixed with 1 teaspoon of 3 percent hydrogen peroxide; rinse thoroughly afterward. If you prefer a store-bought solution, look for a grass-stain remover in the laundry-aids aisle of your supermarket; it will be shelved with the pretreatment formulas.

REMOVING GUM FROM SHOES

One Challenge:

It happens. One minute you're happily striding along, and the next minute you're hopping about on one foot with gum on the bottom of your shoe. What do you do?

Three Solutions . . .

1 Place your shoe in a plastic grocery bag, then press the sticky portion of the shoe into the side of the bag. Place the bag, with the shoe inside, in the freezer and allow the gum to freeze (at least 1 hour). Take the bag out of the freezer and pull the shoe away from the bag. The gum should stick to the bag, not the shoe.

2 Fill a zippered plastic bag with ice cubes and hold it directly on the gum until it freezes. Then pry the gum off the shoe with the edge of a putty knife.

3 Spray WD-40 on the gummy area. Wait 1 minute. Then wipe away the gum and the oily spray with a paper towel.

Canvas Sneakers. Spray the canvas with a fabric or leather stain protector before the first wearing and regularly thereafter to help prevent stains. If the shoes do get stained, pretreat the stains with a laundry stain-removal foam and wash as instructed above for athletic shoes. Shoe polish will also help protect your shoes.

Fabric Shoes. Protect cotton, linen, canvas, and other fabric shoes from stains by spraying them with a fabric or leather stain protector before the first wearing and regularly thereafter.

Use a professional shoe-cleaning product from a shoe repair shop to remove stains and soiling from fabric shoes, or have them professionally cleaned. Do not wash them.

Satin Shoes. Do not attempt to remove spots from or clean satin shoes; have them professionally cleaned.

Flip-Flops. You can toss flip-flops in the washing machine but not the dryer. Instead, allow them to air-dry.

Jewelry

Protect your jewelry investment by cleaning it regularly. But there is no one-fits-all cleaning solution for jewelry. What makes diamonds sparkle, for example, would ruin pearls. Ultrasonic cleaners are generally safe for cleaning all-metal jewelry as well as most diamonds, rubies, emeralds, garnets (except green garnets), sapphires, and tourmalines, but it could fracture other gems. Gemstones with any adhesive, such as inlay or foilbacks, also should not be put in an ultrasonic cleaner. The safest and gentlest way to clean most gems is with an old, soft toothbrush dipped in a mild solution of dishwashing liquid in warm water.

Check with your jeweler for the best way to clean different pieces. Following are some general guidelines.

Silver or Silver Plate. Mix a few drops of mild dishwashing liquid in 1 cup of warm water. Immerse the item in the cleaning solution, allowing the water to bead up on the surface of the silver. Then remove the item and pat dry with a soft cloth. To avoid scratching the metal, don't use a toothbrush to clean silver, or tissue paper or paper toweling to dry it. Use a silver polishing cloth to remove tarnish. If you use silver polish, be careful not to get it on any stones.

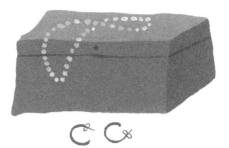

Exposure to air and light during storage will cause silver to tarnish. To prevent this from happening, store silver in a tarnish-preventing bag, or wrap it in acid-free tissue and store it in a zippered plastic bag. *Helpful hint:* Frequent wearing of silver or silver-plate jewelry slows the tarnishing process.

Gold or Platinum (No Gems). Polish the piece with a chamois cloth to keep the gold or platinum shiny. To remove tarnish, prepare a mixture of a few drops of mild dishwashing liquid and 1 cup of warm water or a mixture of ¼ cup of ammonia and 1 cup of water. Gently brush the gold or platinum with the cleaning mixture and an old, soft toothbrush, or let the piece sit in the cleaning mixture for 10 minutes. Rinse with warm water, and use a chamois or soft cloth to dry and polish the piece.

Diamonds, Rubies, or Sapphires. If the setting is gold or platinum, prepare a mixture of ¼ cup of ammonia and 1 cup of water. For gems set in silver, use a few drops of mild dishwashing liquid instead of ammonia. Pour the cleaning solution into a small bowl and gently drop in the piece. Use an old, soft toothbrush to dislodge dirt from around the setting, or let the piece soak for 10 minutes in the cleaner. It's very important to rinse the piece thoroughly with warm water. Then lay it on a tissue to dry.

It's also safe to clean these gems with rubbing alcohol. Fracture-filled stones should be cleaned with the soapy water, not the ammonia-based cleaner or rubbing alcohol.

Other Gemstones. As general maintenance, wipe the stones with a clean, soft, slightly damp cloth after wearing the pieces they are set in. Different types of gems require different care; check with your jeweler for the most appropriate method of cleaning your particular pieces.

Pearls. Wipe pearls with a soft cloth after wearing them, to remove traces of makeup, perfume, and lotion. Clean pearls individually by gently rubbing them with a soft cloth dampened in a solution of 2 cups of warm water and a few drops of a mild dishwashing liquid. Air-dry overnight. Store pearls in a chamois bag, or wrap them in tissue. If you wear a pearl necklace regularly, bring it to a jeweler for restringing once a year.

Costume Jewelry. Clean costume jewelry often in a solution of a few drops of mild dishwashing liquid in 1 cup of warm water. Dry thoroughly with a soft cloth.

Watches. Clean the exterior with a slightly damp cloth. Dry thoroughly with a soft cloth.

For Best Results

- Put jewelry on *after* applying makeup, perfume, hairspray, and lotions — not before.

- Remove jewelry before showering, swimming in a pool, or using a hot tub.

- Remove rings before using bleach and household cleaners, or wear gloves.

- Keep a dish handy to hold your rings when you remove them prior to cleaning or gardening.

- Do not clean jewelry with anything abrasive, such as toothpaste.

- For jewelry with more than one type of stone, use the gentlest cleaning method any of them requires.

- Use warm water when cleaning jewelry, to help break down dirt.

- Clean jewelry in a bowl, not the sink, to avoid accidental loss down the drain.

Part 4

Household Challenges

Why should household cleaning stop with only what we can see? What about the air we breathe and the water we drink? We know that a contaminated kitchen counter can adversely affect our health, but so can indoor air pollution and impure water. Shouldn't we know how to clean drains and when to clean the mechanical systems that heat and cool our home? Household systems are the heart of a healthy home, and they require regular cleaning checkups.

This section also addresses how to clean up after insects, rodents, and other unwanted houseguests — and how to keep them from coming back. And speaking of coming back, as the seasons go around, with them come seasonal cleaning chores. These are outlined in the last chapter, along with occasional cleaning strategies to help you prepare your home for a quick sale or get ready for holiday fun.

CHAPTER THIRTEEN

CLEAN AIR CHALLENGE

Clean air is a necessity for healthy living, especially since the majority of us spend more time indoors than outdoors. So, home cleaning should include cleaning indoor air. Studies have shown that the air in our homes can be even more polluted than the outdoor air in major cities. In fact, indoor air pollution represents a major portion of the public's exposure to air pollution. While having clean air can be a challenging goal, there are some plain and simple solutions for minimizing indoor air pollution covered in this chapter.

Indoor Air Pollution

Indoor air contains some of the same pollutants as outdoor air, but at lower levels. If you live near a heavily traveled roadway, incinerator, industrial plant, quarry, or large construction site, or in an area with high levels of outdoor air pollution, the obvious thing to do is keep your windows closed to prevent outdoor pollutants from

entering your home. You might also consider using portable air cleaners with a high-efficiency particulate air (HEPA) filter.

Most indoor air pollutants, however, are generated within the home. The U.S. Environmental Protection Agency (EPA) estimates that indoor air pollutant levels may be two to five times as high as the pollutant levels outdoors. Indoor air pollutants can include tobacco smoke, vapors from household products and building materials, various biological pollutants — such as bacteria, fungi, molds, viruses, and dust mites — and carbon monoxide and radon. These contaminants can be harmful in high concentrations. Additional pollutants can be generated by everyday activities such as cooking with gas, vacuuming, dusting, and using spray disinfectants, cleaners, and repellents. These activities all add particulate matter to the air, which can create health problems for many individuals — especially the very young and old and those with asthma or respiratory illness.

For best quality, the air in your home should be continually exchanged with fresh air. This is tricky with newer, more energy-efficient homes, which not only keep out heat and cold but also don't "breathe" like older homes that are not sealed as tightly. Ensuring proper ventilation is a good start in cleaning indoor air, particularly when you are using household cleaning products. If you can't open windows, whether because of outdoor pollutants or traffic noise or because your air conditioner is running, use ceiling and exhaust fans to facilitate the exchange of fresh air.

A heat recovery ventilator(HRV), also known as an air-to-air heat exchanger, is an energy-efficient ventilation alternative for homes with high humidity and substantial heating and cooling requirements. This ventilator exhausts stale air while bringing in a steady stream of fresh air that is heated or cooled to match room temperature. Smaller units can be wall- or window-mounted in rooms with ventilation problems; whole-house units are also available. An HRV can also help save on heating and cooling costs.

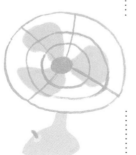

Dust and Biological Pollutants

Normal levels of dust in a home do not generally cause health problems. But high levels can result in allergic reactions ranging from nasal congestion to asthma. That's because house dust contains a whole slew of biological air pollutants, including viruses, bacteria, molds, mildew, pollen grains, pet dander, and dust mites.

In addition to keeping dust and other particulates in check with regular vacuuming, it's also important to monitor and control the level of moisture in your home. High relative humidity and damp surfaces encourage the growth of molds. Too much moisture in the air also creates a fertile breeding ground for dust mites. Sources of humidity are washing, bathing, cooking, unvented clothes dryers, and the simple act of people and animals breathing.

The best way to control humidity is with proper ventilation and dehumidifiers. Externally vented exhaust fans in bathrooms, kitchens, and laundry rooms can go a long way toward controlling moisture levels. Get in the habit of turning these exhaust fans on and off as needed. Or open a window to prevent the buildup of moisture. Cooling the air decreases its ability to hold moisture, but air-conditioning alone is generally not sufficient if you live in an area with high humidity. A dehumidifier is the best way to regulate humidity. Keep the relative humidity under 60 percent, and ideally between 30 and 50 percent.

For tips on preventing, controlling, and reducing exposure to dust, dander, mold, and pollen, see Allergies, Asthma, and Cleaning in chapter 2 (page 27).

Household-Products Pollution

Many common household products contain solvents and chemicals that emit potentially harmful gases during use — and even during storage. These products include paints, varnishes, and waxes as well as cleaning, disinfecting, cosmetic, craft, and hobby products. It's important to have excellent ventilation when you're using any of these products indoors, especially pesticides, solvents, and cleaning agents. Do not store opened containers of paints, varnishes, and similar materials inside your home. Buy these products in limited quantities for use as needed. Also, remove dry-cleaned items from their bags and allow them to air (outdoors if possible) before wearing or storing them, to reduce your exposure to perchloroethylene.

Building materials and furnishings are another major source of organic air pollutants. Formaldehyde, for example, is used in mattress ticking and to add permanent-press qualities to clothing and draperies. Formaldehyde is also widely used in the manufacture of building materials, including pressed-wood products used in paneling, flooring, cabinetry, and furniture. When choosing home furnishings and building materials, opt for natural materials such as wood and stone that are not manufactured with the use of adhesives. You can reduce your exposure to formaldehyde and other gases by increasing ventilation for the first few months in a new home or in a room with new furnishings. You also can reduce formaldehyde emissions with dehumidifiers and air-conditioning by controlling humidity and maintaining a moderate temperature. Coating pressed-wood products with polyurethane may also reduce formaldehyde emissions for a period of time. But do the coating outdoors if you can, or polyurethane fumes become the next problem! To be effective, any such coating must cover all surfaces and edges and must remain intact; if it chips or wears away, the formaldehyde will be released.

New carpets sometimes cause problems with air quality. The EPA suggests that new carpeting be unrolled in a well-ventilated area before it is installed. Open doors and windows during the installation to reduce your exposure to whatever chemicals may be emitted. During and after the installation, use window fans, room air conditioners, or exhaust fans to exhaust fumes to the outdoors. Keep them running for 48 to 72 hours after the new carpet is installed, after which time the fumes are reduced to minimal levels.

For Safety's Sake

- Avoid the use of aerosol products in your home.
- Do not use paint strippers and other strong chemicals in your home.
- Substitute nontoxic alternatives for cleaning and personal-care products.
- Use glues and other adhesives outdoors, or indoors only under very well-ventilated conditions.
- Do not store barbecue grills or their fuels in your living quarters or in an attached garage.
- Store solvents and pesticides outdoors.

Radon Pollution

Radon is a radioactive gas that results from the natural decay of uranium and is found in nearly all soils. Sometimes radon enters a home through well water, but most often it seeps up through the ground and into your home through cracks in the foundation, floor, or walls or around service pipes. You can't see, taste, or smell radon, but once it's in your home, the trapped gas decays into radioactive particles that can be trapped in your lungs when you breathe. Some facts to consider about radon:

- Nearly one in fifteen homes in the United States has a high level of indoor radon.
- The EPA estimates that about 21,000 annual lung-cancer deaths are related to radon exposure.
- Radon is the second leading cause of lung cancer, after cigarette smoking.
- Smokers and former smokers have 10 to 20 times the risk of nonsmokers for getting lung cancer from radon.

The U.S. Surgeon General and the EPA recommend that all homes be tested for radon. The testing is easy. It takes just a few minutes. And it's inexpensive. The EPA recommends conducting a short-term test, using a state-certified test kit available through mail order or at hardware stores, or hiring a trained contractor that provides testing services.

Testing should be conducted in the lowest lived-in area of the home, with the doors and windows shut. Follow the instructions on the test kit, and then send all the necessary materials to the lab specified on the package for analysis.

It generally takes a few weeks to get the results. If your result is a level of radon that is higher than is acceptable, you should follow up with a second short-term test or a long-term test, which will give you a better idea of the average radon level in your home, since it tends to vary from day to day and season to season. If the result of your initial short-term test is more than twice the acceptable level, follow up with another short-term test immediately.

If the test results indicate that you have a radon problem, take steps to fix it immediately. Check with your state radon office for the names of qualified or state-certified radon contractors in your area. The most common solution is to install a vent pipe system and special fans that pull radon from beneath the house and vent it safely to the outside. You may also need to seal cracks and holes in your home's foundation. Retest your home after the work has been done, to be sure that the radon levels have been reduced, and continue to retest every two years. It's always a good idea to test for radon before beginning any major structural renovation, such as converting an unfinished basement area into a family living space.

Q & A: Freshening Up

Q *Can plants control indoor air pollution?*

A Plants do remove carbon dioxide from the air. However, there is no evidence of plants having the ability to reduce indoor air pollutants in any significant way. Improving ventilation is a much more effective and practical means of cleaning indoor air.

Q *Should I have the ducts for my forced-air heating and cooling system cleaned?*

A Yes, no, and maybe. If you have allergies or an unexplained illness that you or your doctor thinks might be related to your home environment, you might want to consider having your ducts cleaned. If you see that your air ducts are contaminated with large deposits of mold or you smell a musty odor coming from the ducts, or if dust and debris are actually being released into your home from the registers, your ducts do need cleaning. Otherwise, the cleaning is probably not necessary. If you decide to hire a duct-cleaning service, plan to vacate your home during the cleaning process to protect yourself from exposure to dislodged pollutants and cleaning chemicals.

Q *What's the difference between an air cleaner and an air purifier?*

A An air purifier only purifies what's in the air. An air cleaner helps capture allergens that tend to float, such as pet dander.

Combustion Pollutants

Carbon monoxide (CO) is another silent killer. This toxic gas is produced by burning fuel. Potential sources of carbon monoxide in your home include room heaters, furnaces, fireplaces, gas ovens and ranges, and water heaters. It's important to keep these appliances in good working condition to avoid carbon monoxide poisoning. Surprisingly, each year nearly 300 people in the United States die from carbon monoxide poisoning in the home. Even more die from carbon monoxide produced by idling cars in the garage. Unborn babies, infants, elderly people, and people with anemia or with a history of heart or respiratory disease can be especially susceptible.

To protect yourself and your family, follow these tips from the U.S. Consumer Product Safety Commission and the EPA:

- Never burn charcoal indoors (even in a fireplace) or in a garage.
- Never let a car idle in the garage, even when the garage door is open.
- Never service fuel-burning appliances unless you have had the proper training and have the proper tools.
- Never use a gas range, oven, or dryer for heating. Borrow or purchase a portable space heater.
- Never operate an unvented gas-burning appliance in a closed room.
- Never ignore a safety device when it shuts off an appliance.
- Never ignore the smell of fuel.

- Don't sleep in a room with an unvented gas or kerosene space heater.
- Use only water-clear ASTM 1-K kerosene for kerosene heaters.
- Burn only seasoned hardwoods in stoves and fireplaces.
- Make sure fuel-burning appliances are properly installed.
- Read and follow the manufacturers' directions for the safe operation of all your fuel-burning appliances.
- If you have an oil or gas furnace or boiler, have it inspected and tuned up annually.
- Have all gas and kerosene appliances inspected once a year.
- Have all wood-burning appliances inspected once a year. If you use them for burning wood, have your chimney and flues cleaned at least once a year.

Carbon monoxide has no smell, no taste, and no color. Yet there are some clues that may help you detect a possible carbon monoxide problem. These include rusting or water streaking on a vent or chimney, a loose or missing panel on your furnace, loose or disconnected vent or chimney connections, loose masonry on your chimney, moisture inside your windows, and debris or soot falling from your chimney, your fireplace, or an appliance. Also notice any problems that could indicate improper appliance operation, such as a decrease in hot-water supply, your oil or gas furnace being unable to heat the house or running constantly, sooting on appliances, or an unfamiliar or burning odor.

> *When we realize we can make a buck cleaning up the environment, it will be done!*
>
> — Dennis Weaver

The most important thing you can do to prevent carbon monoxide poisoning is to properly use and maintain fuel-burning appliances. A carbon monoxide detector should be used only as a backup. Research the best detectors through Consumer Reports, the American Gas Association, and Underwriters Laboratories (UL). For the most reliable protection, do not buy a detector without UL certification.

Symptoms of carbon monoxide poisoning include dizziness, fatigue, headache, mental confusion, nausea, and shortness of breath. If you experience any of these symptoms while you're in your home and then feel better when you go outside, you may have carbon monoxide poisoning. Get fresh air immediately; open windows and doors for more ventilation. Turn off any fuel-burning appliances and leave the house. Seek medical attention immediately.

The Lowdown on Air Cleaners

The most effective strategies for improving air quality are to control the sources of specific pollutants and to ensure adequate ventilation by opening windows and doors and operating window or attic fans and outdoor-venting exhaust fans. Air cleaners may be useful as a secondary means of removing contaminants.

According to the Association of Home Appliance Manufacturers (AHAM), a portable air cleaner may significantly reduce the level of pollutants in a home. In one AHAM study, 57 percent of all air-cleaner owners said that air cleaners have had a positive effect on indoor air quality, and 32 percent said that cleaning indoor air led to an improvement in their health.

When buying an air cleaner, look for the clean air delivery rate (CADR) certification seal on the product packaging. The seal indicates that the air cleaner has been tested by an independent testing agency, and it tells you how well the air cleaner reduces pollutants such as tobacco smoke, pollen, and dust, as well as the size of the room it is suitable for. The higher the CADR number, the faster the unit filters air. You can then weigh the importance of other product features to find an air cleaner that fits your needs.

The Asthma and Allergy Foundation of America (AAFA) recommends that you talk to your doctor to find out whether air filtration would be beneficial for you, and if so, what type would be best. For people with allergies and asthma, a high-efficiency filter in the furnace used to condition the air in the whole house plus air cleaners with HEPA filters for individual rooms are ideal.

There are three general types of portable room air cleaners: mechanical air cleaners, electronic air cleaners, and ion generators.

- **Mechanical air cleaners.** Fan-driven air cleaners with HEPA filters essentially strain dust out of the air by forcing it through a special mesh that traps allergens as well as tobacco smoke. A portable air cleaner with a HEPA filter can remove 99.97 percent of airborne particles that are 0.3 of a micron or larger, including pollen, dust, and animal dander. Some of these air cleaners also include a carbon filter for removing odors. The gold standard of air cleaners, HEPA filters are particularly effective in reducing allergy symptoms when used in the bedroom of the allergy sufferer.
- **Electronic air cleaners.** Electronic or ionizer air cleaners use an electrical field to trap allergens by charging particles in the air. These particles are then attracted to a collection plate or to objects in a room, such as the walls, floors, or tabletops, where they can be easily removed through cleaning.
- **Ozone generators.** Ozone-generating air cleaners are not recommended. Not only do they do a poor job of removing allergens from the air, but these machines intentionally generate ozone at levels up to 10 times more than the acceptable standard. The sweet smell imparted is not a sign of cleaner air. Breathing ozone has the potential to cause a decrease in lung function and to aggravate asthma. Those with asthma and respiratory allergies are especially sensitive to ozone. The AAFA, other health-care officials, and government agencies recommend

against the use of ozone-generating machines in your home.

It's important to note that the fans in mechanical filters and, to a slightly greater degree, the ion chargers in electronic air cleaners do produce ozone, but as a by-product. Generally, the ozone by-product is within the acceptable limit of 50 parts per billion. However, some ionizers emit more ozone than others. The AAFA recommends that consumers ask for proof from the manufacturer that its product does not produce ozone at levels greater than 50 parts per billion before purchasing and using any type of air cleaner. Note that an EPA number on the product packaging does not imply EPA endorsement or suggest in any way that the EPA has found the product to be either safe or effective. It is simply establishes the identity of the facility that produces the product. The only seal with any credibility or reliability is the CADR seal.

Humidifiers

While air that is too moist can contribute to the growth of dust mite populations and mold, air that is too dry can be very uncomfortable and aggravate some respiratory problems. That's why many people choose to use humidifiers. There are four types of humidifiers: warm mist, cool mist, console, and ultrasonic. All are equally capable of adding moisture to a room, so your choice is more of a personal preference. A humidity level under 60 percent, but ideally between 30 and 50 percent, is recommended. To measure relative humidity in your home, you can purchase an inexpensive hygrometer at any hardware store. Whatever type of humidifier you choose, it is important to refill the tank with fresh water daily. Use distilled or deionized water in ultrasonic humidifiers to minimize particle formation.

- **Warm mist.** This type of humidifier uses a heating system to release into the room a warm, clean mist that tends to warm the room slightly. You can use some warm-mist humidifiers to introduce medication into the air to help relieve coughs and dry, scratchy throats. Use only medications approved by the humidifier manufacturer.
- **Cool mist.** A cool-mist humidifier has a filter that removes minerals and impurities from the water and then releases a cool, invisible mist that evaporates into the air.
- **Console.** Basically a cool-mist humidifier on a larger scale, the console humidifier will humidify multiple rooms, large areas, and sometimes the whole house.
- **Ultrasonic.** This humidifier produces a cool, soothing mist that you can see and feel. A water purification filter traps impurities to eliminate white dust.

Water contains minerals and sediment. These impurities are left behind in the humidifier and must be removed in order for your humidifier to function properly. The Consumer Products Safety Commission recommends that you clean your humidifier on a weekly basis, and more often if you have hard water. Always clean your humidifier at the beginning and end of each season. Be aware that bacterial and fungal organisms can be emitted from cool-mist and ultrasonic humidifiers that are not properly maintained.

Odor Patrol

- Clean toilets regularly.
- Change cat litter daily.
- Bathe dogs regularly.
- Spray an air sanitizer to eliminate odor-causing bacteria.
- Clean your refrigerator and freezer regularly.
- Sprinkle the insides of smelly shoes with baking soda.
- Put out a bowl of vinegar to absorb tobacco smoke and cooking odors.
- Use outdoor-vented exhaust fans when cooking.
- Hang up bath towels so that they will dry as quickly as possible.
- Spray upholstery and bedding with a fabric refresher.
- Use an air cleaner with a HEPA air filter and carbon filter.
- Use essential oils, sachets, or potpourri around your home.
- Avoid installing synthetic wall-to-wall carpeting; it tends to absorb odors.

Mist humidifiers should be cleaned at least once a week during regular use. Different types of humidifiers require different cleaning instructions. Following are general guidelines, but be sure to check your owner's manual for instructions specific to your make and model. Make sure that the humidifier is turned off and unplugged before you begin.

COOL MIST

1. Remove the filter pad and set it aside.
2. Descale the humidifier (see right).
3. Disinfect the humidifier (see right).

WARM MIST

1. Descale the humidifier (see right).
2. To clean the heating element, pour white vinegar into the base. Place the mist chamber down on the base. With the power off, allow the mist chamber to soak for at least 20 minutes.
3. Remove the power unit. With an old toothbrush, gently brush the mineral deposits away from the coils. Do not pick off the deposits or scrub them with a metal brush.
4. To rinse, pour cool water into the base and place the mist chamber on top of it. Allow the mist chamber to soak a few minutes, then wipe it with a soft cloth.

5. Disinfect the humidifier (see below). Do not run water through the mist chamber. Do not use any chemical substance to clean the heating element. Never operate the unit with vinegar in it.

DESCALING (Removing Mineral Buildup)

1. Fill the base and/or the water tank with 8 ounces (1 cup) of undiluted white vinegar.
2. Let the solution stand for 20 minutes. Periodically distribute the solution by shaking the tank or swishing the solution in the base. Clean all the interior surfaces of the base and/or the tank with a soft brush to remove scale.
3. When the 20 minutes are up, rinse the tank or base with clean water to remove scale and the vinegar.

DISINFECTING

1. Fill the base and/or water tank with water. Add 1 teaspoon of liquid chlorine bleach for each gallon of water in the base or tank.
2. Let the solution stand for 20 minutes. Periodically distribute the solution by shaking the tank or swishing the solution in the base.
3. When the 20 minutes are up, rinse the unit until the smell of bleach is gone.

courtesy of Honeywell Consumer Products

CHAPTER FOURTEEN

HOUSEHOLD SYSTEMS

We tend to take heating, air-conditioning, and plumbing systems for granted — until they don't work. Cleaning mechanical systems on a regular schedule can help prolong the life of your systems and minimize the need for costly repairs. The most difficult part about any of these cleaning chores is remembering to do them. Once you know what needs doing when, make a note on your calendar to do the tasks yourself or to schedule a professional to do them for you.

Cleaning and Clearing Drains

A clogged drain is a dirty drain. Kitchen drain clogs are most often caused by "plugs" of solid grease, embedded with food particles and other debris, that obstruct the free flow of water. To clear a tough grease clog that results in standing water in your kitchen sink, use a commercial drain opener with sodium hydroxide, which generates heat to melt the grease and break it down to simpler substances that can be rinsed away. Some drain-cleaning products also contain agents that produce gas, which provides agitation in the drain, a further help in moving the solids along. Clogged drains in bathroom tubs and sinks are often caused by hair, soap residue,

toothpaste, or a combination of these materials. On these problems, liquid drain openers containing sodium hypochlorite and sodium hydroxide can work well. Be very careful if you decide to use a commercial drain opener. These are very strong chemical cleaners that need to be used with extreme caution. Follow the label instructions exactly, and wear gloves to protect your skin and glasses to protect your eyes.

If the drain is only partially clogged, try clearing it with a less toxic approach. Sometimes just pouring boiling water down a partially clogged drain will clear it. If the clog is in a bathroom sink or tub, remove the strainer or stopper and any debris from around the drain opening.

What You Need:

❏ Plungers (one for sinks, one for toilets)

❏ Hand augers (one for tubs, one for toilets)

❏ Baking soda

❏ Vinegar

❏ Commercial drain opener

Using a flashlight, look down the drain to see whether a wad of hair is causing the obstruction. If so, reach in with a straightened coat hanger or a bottle brush and either push the hair down or pull it out. Then flush the drain with several gallons of hot water. If you can't see the obstruction, try using a plunger.

● **The plunger method.** Cover the drain opening with the head of the plunger. To create a vacuum between the plunger and the clogged drain, you need to "plug" other outlets to the drain. Stuff a rag into the overflow opening on a bathtub or sink, stop up the second sink of a double sink, or clamp off the dishwasher drain hose that goes to the garbage disposal. Then fill the sink or tub with enough water to cover the plunger head. Pump the handle of the plunger into the head several times and then quickly pull the plunger loose. Repeat as necessary. When the clog clears, flush the drain with scalding-hot water to clear any remaining debris.

● **The auger or snake method.** If the drain remains clogged after you've used the plunger, try using a hand auger, sometimes called a snake. A handy gadget to have, the auger consists of a cable, which you feed down into the drain

until it meets resistance, and a hand crank that lets you either push the obstruction further down the drain or snag and retrieve the obstruction. Once the drain is clear, flush it with scalding-hot water.

If you don't have an auger and the clog is in a sink, you can try removing and cleaning the sink trap, the S-shaped pipe that the drain feeds into. You'll need a plumber's wrench for this. Place a bucket underneath the trap, and then use the wrench to remove the trap pipe. Water and debris will drain into the bucket. Use a bent wire to pull out any debris from the waste pipe. After putting the trap back together, flush the drain with hot water. This last important step not only rinses the drain and pipes but also refills the trap

PLAIN & SIMPLE ORGANIZING TIPS

● Keep at least one extra filter on hand for your heating, cooling, and water-purification systems.

● Store all the supplies for your household systems in one central location.

● Keep all the operation and maintenance booklets for your household systems in a three-ring binder. File each booklet in a three-hole-punched sleeve, and store the binder in an accessible place.

● Create a log for recording the dates of cleaning, maintenance, and repair service for each of your household systems; tape the logs to each appliance, or store them in a household binder or file.

with water to prevent sewage gases from rising up through the drain.

Regular cleaning of drains, strainers, and stoppers can help prevent clogs. The simplest way to keep kitchen and bath drains clear is to add drain cleaning (see below) to your weekly cleaning routine. It's also important to avoid letting anything except liquids go down the drain. But never pour paint, paint thinners, or other chemicals down the drain. (See page 20 for disposal of hazardous waste.)

Following are plain and simple ways to keep your drains flowing freely.

Kitchen Drains. Avoid pouring grease down the drain. Liquid grease and oils solidify in cold pipes, where they trap food particles and cause drains to clog. Instead, pour grease into an empty metal can, allow it to harden, and throw the can away. Also, do not rinse coffee grounds down the drain; throw them out. Do not put any solid food products down drains that are not equipped with a garbage disposal. Do place a strainer over kitchen drains to prevent solid items from accidentally going down the drain.

To keep kitchen sinks clear, once a week pour ½ cup of baking soda into the drain, followed by 1 cup of white vinegar. Cover the drain for a few minutes and let it fizz. Rinse with a pot of boiling water.

Garbage Disposals. Always run cold water during and after running your disposal, to help solids move along and prevent clogs. Run hot water when you are disposing of greasy leftovers.

Do not put coffee grinds, corn husks, artichokes, onion skins, celery, and other high-fiber materials in the garbage disposal; they tend to cause clogs. Also do not attempt to grind bones.

To freshen your disposal, dump a cup or two of ice cubes down the disposal, along with a citrus-fruit rind, such as from a lemon, grapefruit, orange, or lime, turn on the water, and run the disposal. Or make and use vinegar ice cubes by combining 1 cup of vinegar with enough water to fill a tray.

Bathroom Drains. The most common cause of a drain clog in the tub or bathroom sink is hair. To keep bathroom sink and tub drains clear, as part of your regular weekly cleaning routine pour a pot of hot water down them (or stop up the drain, run some hot water into the tub or sink, and then open the drain so the hot water drains all at once). There are some simple things you can do to help prevent these clogs from forming:

Drain Cleaner

Unclog drains the natural way! Pour 1 pound of washing soda (you'll find it in the laundry aisle of the supermarket) in a bucket. Add 3 gallons of boiling water to dissolve it, and pour the mixture slowly, carefully, and directly into the drain.

- **Clean sink and tub stoppers.** Remove the pop-up stopper when you clean the sink or tub and rinse it off before replacing it. To remove an accumulation of soap scum on the stopper, wipe it down with a cloth or sponge dampened with white vinegar, or scrub it with an old toothbrush dipped in vinegar. On some sinks, the pivot rod under the sink must be removed to release the stopper, which makes regular cleaning a little more challenging and, let's be honest, somewhat impractical. In this case you may wish to simply clean in and around the stopper. Use a small wire brush to do a more thorough cleaning every so often. Or tuck a curly metal sponge around the stopper and push it down into the drain so that it is held in place. Leave it. Then, to clean the drain, all you have to do is pull out the sponge. Discard any hair that has collected and wash the sponge in the dishwasher before reinserting it into the drain. It's a nifty little trick.

- **Clean shower floor drains.** Periodically remove the strainer over the drain by unscrewing it from the drain opening. Bend a sturdy wire in half and use it to clear out accumulated hair and other debris from the drain. Before replacing the strainer, scrub it with an old toothbrush and a little white vinegar to remove soap scum.

Toilets. Don't use drain cleaner on a toilet clog. Commercial drain cleaners are designed primarily to dissolve grease, soap, and hair, and they won't help with a toilet clog. A clogged toilet is best tackled with a plunger, which will push the obstruction through the drain and allow for the free flow of water. Here's how:

1. If the toilet is overflowing, lift off the tank lid, pull up the float, and push down on the flapper at the tank bottom to stop the flush. Then turn off the water supply by closing the knob on the water line; it's usually located low on the wall behind the toilet.

2. Bail out the toilet until it is filled to half its normal level.

3. Cover the drain opening with the cup of the plunger to create a seal. Gently press the plunger handle down into the cup, release, and repeat until the water drains.

4. Pour a bucket of water in the toilet to make sure the bowl empties.

5. If you turned off the water supply, open it back up. Flush the toilet, and rinse the plunger in the flushing water.

6. If you can't clear the clog with a plunger, get out your toilet auger. Place the auger in the toilet with the upturned tip going into the drain. Push down on the auger as you turn the crank clockwise.

7. Once you feel the auger pass through the trap, crank counterclockwise to pull it back out.
8. Pour a bucket of water into the bowl to make sure it empties before you flush the toilet again.

After the clog is cleared, clean and disinfect your toilet bowl. Dip the plunger and, if you used it, the auger into the disinfectant solution or spray them with an all-purpose disinfectant cleaner, and allow them to air-dry. If the clogged toilet overflowed, you'll also want to clean and disinfect the outside of the toilet and the floor.

For Safety's Sake

- Never use a plunger or an auger during or after using a commercial drain cleaner, to avoid splashing the chemical on your skin, eyes, or clothing.
- Always try the least toxic method for cleaning clogs first.
- If you do use a commercial drain cleaner, wear gloves and glasses.

Water Systems

While your household drain system carries water away, other household water systems deliver water where you want it and how you want it — hot, soft, or pure. Annual cleaning of the components of this system, including your water heater, water softener, water purifier, and drip-irrigation system, should be part of your routine maintenance program to ensure that you get the highest quality and maximum efficiency from them. If you are uncomfortable or unsure of what to do, hire a licensed plumber or specialist to do the work for you.

Tank Water Heaters. Accumulation of sediment in the tank can reduce the efficiency of your water heater and shorten its life. Once a year, flush the tank to prevent the buildup of sediment (see the instructions on page 231). Flush twice a year if you have hard water. Flushing may also be the solution for operational problems with your hot water heater:

- **Noisy operation.** If your hot water heater is rumbling or sizzling or the water is produces is rusty or black, it may be due to sedimentation on the bottom of the tank or scale buildup on the elements. If you are a do-it-yourselfer, turn off the electrical power at the circuit breaker and turn off the water supply. Drain the tank and remove the access panel to the heating elements. Remove the heating elements, soak them in vinegar, and then scrape off the scale. You may need to replace the tank if sediment buildup is excessive.
- **Smelly water.** If your hot water begins to smell like rotten eggs, it could indicate bacteria formation inside the tank. Turn the water temperature up to 140°F (60°C) for several hours to kill the bacteria. If that does not solve the problem, it's possible that minerals in your water are reacting with the magnesium or zinc anode rod in the heater. Removing or replacing it with an aluminum rod may be the answer.

● **Water not hot enough.** If your gas hot water heater is not producing enough hot water, a burner orifice could be clogged. Shut off the gas, remove the access panel, and use a stiff wire or a needle to clean the burner ports. It's a good idea to clean the burner ports every year to ensure safe operation. Hire a professional if you are not comfortable doing this. A dirty burner orifice may also be the cause of a pilot light that won't stay lit, sooting on the heater, or a yellow (rather than a blue) flame. Another possible reason for lack of hot water is a blocked exhaust vent. Check the vent and clear it, if necessary. Also check the flue by placing your hand near the draft diverter. If you feel air flowing out, there is an obstruction that needs to be removed. As a preventive maintenance measure, keep the area above, below, and around the water heater free of objects and debris.

Water Softener Systems. If your home has a water treatment system for softening water, get familiar with the manufacturer's instructions for cleaning and maintaining it. Use only softening salts that are at least 99.5 percent pure. Nugget, pellet, or coarse solar salts are best. Do not use rock, block, granulated, or ice-cream-making salts, as they contain dirt and sediments that will cause maintenance problems.

The Water Quality Association recommends sanitizing your water softener once a year. Mix ¾ fluid ounce of household liquid chlorine bleach with 1 quart of water. Pour the mixture into the brine well. (Do *not* pour straight bleach into the well.) Then start the regeneration process to sanitize the system.

If your softener is not using up the salt you've placed in it, a hard crust or salt bridge may have formed in the salt storage area; that is,

How To FLUSH A HOT WATER HEATER

To clean or flush a hot water heater, attach a garden hose to the drain valve (the faucet located at the bottom of the heater). Run the open end of the hose to a floor drain or outdoors. Be aware that the water exiting the heater will be hot, so do not let it run onto your lawn or garden. Carefully open the drain valve; do not force it, especially if it is made of plastic, as it could break. Allow the water to drain for about 5 minutes. Then let the water fill a bucket. Allow the water to settle.

If the water is clear and there's no sediment on the bottom of the bucket, close the drain valve and remove the garden hose. If you do see sediment or if the water is discolored, continue flushing for another five minutes, and repeat the bucket test until the water is clear and free of sediment.

Note: If you have not been cleaning your tank on a regular basis, don't start now. The sudden flow of accumulated sediment can permanently damage your hot water heater!

there is an empty space between the water and salt. The salt needs to be dissolved in water to make brine. To break a salt bridge, take a broom handle and carefully push it down into the salt, working it up and down. If the handle strikes a hard object that is not the floor or sides of the tank, it's most likely a salt bridge. Carefully break the bridge with the handle. *Helpful hint:* In humid areas, it is best to fill the water softener system with less salt more often to prevent a salt bridge from forming.

Another reason why the water-softening system may not be using salt is a plugged nozzle and venturi. The venturi creates the suction that moves brine from the salt storage area to the resin tank during regeneration. If it becomes plugged with sand or dirt, the system will not work and you will get hard water. To clean, take apart the nozzle and venturi, wash their parts, and rinse the parts in warm water. If necessary, use a small brush to remove any iron buildup or dirt. Also check and clean the gaskets and other parts associated with the nozzle and venturi. Check your owner's manual for more complete instructions for your particular brand and model of water softener.

For Safety's Sake

If your water *suddenly* tastes or smells like rotten eggs, it's possible that sewage has gotten into your drinking water supply. Don't drink it. Call your local water supplier or have your well water tested immediately.

Drip-Irrigation Systems. Check the system periodically to make sure water is dripping from each emitter. If an emitter appears to be clogged, simply hold your finger over the end of its outlet for a few seconds and then let go. If the emitter still does not work properly, try gently cleaning it by inserting a broom bristle. If this does not unclog the emitter, replace it with a new one.

Water Purification Systems. Sources of tap water may include rivers, lakes, streams, ponds, reservoirs, springs, and wells. As water travels over the surface of the land or through the ground, it dissolves naturally occurring minerals and, in some cases, radioactive material. Removing all possible contaminants can be an expensive proposition and, in nearly all cases, would not provide greater protection of health.

However, some people may be more vulnerable to contaminants in drinking water than the general population. Immuno-compromised persons — such as persons with cancer undergoing chemotherapy, persons who have undergone organ transplants, people with HIV/AIDS or other immune-system disorders, some elderly people, and infants — can be particularly at risk of illness resulting from contaminants in their drinking water.

You should know what's in your water. Ask your local water supplier for copies of water treatment reports. If you have a well, have your water tested once a year for lead and bacteria. It's especially important to test well water if tests of your indoor air have detected the presence of radon. The risk of radon in your water is not so much from drinking it as it is from breathing in the vapors released into the air by showers and steam (see page 219). Radon, like lead, bacteria, and other contaminants, can be removed from the water supply at the point of entry or the point of use.

Even if the test results show that your water has no more than the allowable limits of contaminants, you may wish to consider installing a water purification system to clean up your drinking water or simply improve its taste, color, and odor. Some of the most common systems include the following.

- **Reverse-osmosis water filters.** Reverse osmosis is a comprehensive method of filtration that removes dirt, odors, chlorine, chemicals, lead and other metals, salts, nitrates, and fluoride from water. Reverse-osmosis units filter drinking water ahead of time and store it in a holding tank until the water is needed. Most units mount under the kitchen sink and usually come with a dedicated drinking-water faucet.

- **Water distillers.** Used in laboratories, distillation removes 99.9 percent of contaminants, including bacteria, viruses, and other microorganisms as well as metals, dirt and other sediments, and even radioactive particles. Water distillers boil water until it becomes steam, which is then condensed into pure, clean water.

- **Activated carbon filters.** The best choice for improving the taste of water, these filters attract and trap volatile chemicals such as chlorine, pesticides, and radon gas. The most convenient type attaches to the kitchen faucet via a diverter, which replaces the existing faucet aerator. The water filter can be turned on to produce drinking water and turned off when you want water for cooking or cleaning. Activated carbon filters are quite inexpensive.

- **Inline water filter.** Inline water-purification filters are installed directly in the cold-water pipe to treat and purify all household water, not just the water coming from one tap. With an inline filter, you get purified water flowing even through showers and outside faucets.

Be sure that the system you buy is proven to remove the contaminants that concern you most. Not all activated carbon filters remove lead, for example, and some reverse-osmosis filters don't remove chlorine. For a listing of units certified as safe and effective by NSF International, an independent nonprofit testing organization, as well as a list of the contaminants each unit removes, search NSF's database of certified products on the Internet (see Appendix B) for reliable information about water testing and treatment devices.

Also consider convenience and capacity when selecting a system. While distillers produce virtually contaminant-free water, it can take several hours to distill a gallon of water. Whatever system you choose, it's important to perform periodic maintenance, such as changing the filter or sanitizing the unit, as recommended by the manufacturer. This will ensure that you get the same water quality as you did when the system was new. Failure to perform the necessary maintenance can reduce water quality dramatically. Do not wait until your water tastes bad to do it. Most contaminants don't have a foul taste except in extreme quantities.

To obtain more information about water testing, contaminants, and potential health effects, contact your local water supplier or call the EPA's Safe Drinking Water Hotline (see Appendix B).

Septic Systems

Most people don't give much thought to what happens to household wastewater once it leaves the home. Do you know where your wastewater goes? About one in four homes in the United States is connected to a septic system. The rest are connected to sewer systems that direct wastewater to treatment facilities, where contaminants are removed before the water is released into storm drains. Eventually, all wastewater ends up in our groundwater, lakes, streams, and oceans. So it's important that this cleaning process takes place.

A septic system is like a mini wastewater treatment plant that collects, treats, and disposes of wastewater on-site so that it can percolate into the ground without clogging the soil or contaminating groundwater or surface water. The system consists of a tank and a leach field.

I try to take one day at a time — but sometimes several days attack me at once.

— Jennifer Unlimited

Wastewater enters the tank first. Solids remain in the tank, where they are broken down by bacteria. Liquid is funneled out of the tank into the leach field, where it seeps down into the ground. The bacteria in the tank and microorganisms in the soil remove disease-causing bacteria and organic matter from the wastewater, so that the end result is purified water that either enters the groundwater system or evaporates.

Septic-System Maintenance. Your septic tank requires regular cleaning; that is, solids that cannot be broken down by bacteria and should not be allowed to enter the leach field need to be pumped out. This is a job for professionals. The frequency of pumping depends primarily on the size of the tank and the number of people living in the home. For example, a 500-gallon tank connected to a home with four residents should be cleaned once a year, whereas a 1,000-gallon tank for the same number of people can go two and a half years between cleanings. You should clean your septic system a little more frequently if you use a garbage disposal. *Helpful hint:* Keep a record of any cleaning and maintenance done to your septic tank, including the date, the type of work done, who did the work, and how much it cost. Also keep the name and telephone number of your septic-system pumper handy in case of emergency.

A variety of additives are marketed to "improve" the performance of septic systems. However, at this time the EPA does not recommend the use of additives in your septic system, as the necessity and usefulness of these products has not been proven.

An improperly maintained septic tank can pollute surface and drinking water. Depending on the size of your family and the size of your tank, it may be a good idea to have your septic system inspected annually. Signs of a failing or failed septic system include sewage backup in drains or toilets, slowly draining sinks, tubs, and toilets, foul odors around indoor drains, repeated intestinal illnesses in household members, soggy areas on the ground above or near the leach field, or excessive growth of lush, green plants over the leach field even during dry weather. It is your responsibility as a homeowner to act immediately if you find any sign of a problem.

Preventing Problems. Be careful with what you put down the drain. Do not use toilets and drains for items such as cigarette butts, diapers, and sanitary products that should be disposed of in the wastebasket.

It is perfectly fine to dispose of household quantities of cleaning products such as detergents, bleaches, and disinfectants down the drain, regardless of where your wastewater goes. Basically, these products break down before they reach groundwater, or they become part of the sludge that is removed with other solids when the tank is pumped. However, neither septic systems nor community wastewater systems are designed to treat chemicals such as paints, solvents, oil, pesticides, or household hazardous wastes (see page 20). Do not flush or pour these products into drains or sewers; take them to a hazardous waste or recycling center. Some communities offer household hazardous waste collection days.

Heating and Air-Conditioning Systems

Have a qualified maintenance technician inspect and clean your heating and cooling equipment annually to keep it operating at peak efficiency and to prolong its life. Have your heating system, including any chimneys and flues, professionally inspected and cleaned prior to the start of the heating season. Have your cooling system cleaned prior to the start of the cooling season. Also have furnace-attached humidifiers cleaned and serviced once a year.

Apart from the annual cleaning, the most important thing you can do is to replace or clean any filters in your system on a regular basis, as recommended by the manufacturer of your equipment. Dirty filters reduce the efficiency of a system, which can mean more expensive heating and cooling bills. Some filters can be removed, washed, and replaced; others are replaced by new filters. Standard filters in forced-air heating and cooling systems are designed to keep the furnace and ductwork clean, but they do not improve indoor air quality. For that, you might want to consider installing a paper media filter or an electronic filter, either of which would sit between the main return duct and the blower cabinet. Paper media filters trap 99 percent of particles, including pollen, as small as 6 microns. Electronic filters capture 70 percent of particles as small as 0.3 microns, but to maintain efficiency, they must be washed every 30 days. The downside to these in-duct air filters is that the fan must be operating continuously for the filters to be effective, which can significantly increase your heating and cooling bills.

The cleaning routine for heating and cooling equipment is pretty simple:

- Vacuum return-air grills and warm-air vents regularly.
- Change or clean filters once a month during the heating and cooling seasons.
- Vacuum baseboard heater vents once a season using a brush attachment.
- Clean the chimney at least once a year if you burn wood regularly.
- If you burn wood, check your chimneys often for signs of creosote buildup (dry, flaky deposits or black, shiny deposits), and clean them when creosote is visible.
- Dust ceiling-fan blades at least once a month.

- Regularly dust and vacuum portable gas and electric space heaters.
- Clean any glass on fireplace doors periodically with a damp cloth or paper towel to remove ash dust or light brown stains. (Wait until the unit has cooled before cleaning it.)
- Wash the filters of window-mounted air conditioners in warm water and detergent every two weeks; dry thoroughly before replacing. Regularly vacuum the coils and clean the drain pans to prevent the growth of mold. Keep the condensing unit free of debris.

CHAPTER FIFTEEN

PEST CHALLENGES

It's nice to have company, except when your guest are insects and rodents that come to visit without any invitation — and then want to move in permanently. Not only are these residents unwelcome, but they litter your home with their nests, wastes, and dead bodies and often leave behind a path of destruction ranging from moth-eaten woolens and flea-bitten family members to serious health problems and structural damage to your home.

Pesticides versus Natural Methods

Roaches, mice, rats, termites, carpenter ants, ants, fleas, ticks, spiders, and silverfish are the ten most common household pests. According to the National Pest Control Association, every house in America has been visited by at least one of them in the past year. But they aren't the only messy houseguests that require cleaning up after. Houseflies leave germs on countertops, which then need to be disinfected. Pantry moths contaminate food supplies, which then need to be tossed out. Eliminating pests not only reduces cleaning time but also can improve the health of your home, not to mention your well-being.

You don't have to poison your home with pesticides and insecticides to get rid of rodents and insects. Understanding their behavior and changing yours is the key to control and prevention. When cleaning up pest problems, always start with the least toxic method. Look for natural methods to eliminate and prevent household pests before turning to chemical solutions. Simple home remedies include preventive measures such as putting away food and keeping floors and tables clean of crumbs. If there's nothing to eat, rodents are less likely to take up residency. Herbal solutions, such as the essential oils of peppermint or spearmint, can be used to repel insects. Nontoxic alternatives to pesticides also include a variety of traps and baits as well as ultrasonic technology, which uses high-frequency sound to drive rodents and insects away from your home without harming the human occupants.

Pesticides, particularly those used indoors, are poisonous not only to their targets but to humans and domestic animals as well. According to the National Safety Council's Environmental Health Center, the possible effects of exposure to pesticides include irritation to the eyes, nose, and throat; damage to the central nervous system and kidneys; and cancer. Pesticides should be used only to treat an infestation, not as a preventive measure.

If you feel you must use these chemical poisons, be sure to use them exactly as directed. Foggers, for example, require that you empty cupboards of food, remove toys, move out family members and pets, and thoroughly wash all usable surfaces and bedding when you return. Always read the product label for complete usage instructions. Other safety guidelines for pesticide use include the following:

- Do not use more than the recommended amount.
- Thoroughly ventilate the area after pesticide use.
- Safely dispose of unwanted or unused pesticides, following the disposal instructions on the product label.
- Store pesticides out of reach of children.
- Do not store pesticides in the living area of your home.
- Match the pesticide to the pest problem.

For Safety's Sake

It is illegal to use a pesticide in any manner other than as directed on the product label. For your health and safety and the safety of those around you, always read and follow the directions precisely.

You might think that your only exposure to household pesticides is the exposure you receive during use. But studies have shown that the amount of pesticides in a home is often greater than can be explained by recent pesticide use. Other possible sources of pesticide residue include contaminated soil that's been tracked inside, dust that floats in from outside, and stored pesticide containers. It's important to know that children are much more susceptible than adults to possible health hazards from pesticide use. This is especially true for young children, who spend a lot of time playing and crawling on the floor, where pesticides are commonly applied.

For answers to questions about pesticides and to request EPA publications on pesticides, call the National Pesticide Telecommunications Network (see Appendix B). For alternative options for controlling different kinds of pests in your home, yard, and garden, contact your local cooperative extension service.

General Prevention

Prevention is the best policy against household pests. Most insects and rodents prefer to live outdoors, but they will often seek food, water, and shelter in your home, especially in the colder months. The best preventive measures are to:

- Remove food and water sources.
- Make your home uncomfortable for pests.
- Employ barriers to keep pests out.

Following are some simple things you can do to prevent unwelcome intruders from making your home their own.

- **Clean regularly.** Frequent cleaning removes crumbs and other food sources that attract pests. Cleaning also disturbs pests' habitat, which generally forces them to seek shelter elsewhere. Clean spilled food immediately, especially in kitchen and pantry areas. Store dried foods in airtight containers. Clean trash bins regularly (see the Q&A sidebar on page 142) and make sure they have tight-fitting lids.
- **Seal out pests.** Inspect your home for places that have or could become entryways for insects and rodents. Keep pests out with tight-fitting doors, windows, and screens. Check door sweeps (the rubber or bristled flaps sometimes secured at the bottom of doors to create a tight seal between the doors and their frame); install or replace them if necessary. Check window screens and repair any rips. Seal cracks and crevices around windows and doors and in siding with silicone caulking. Be sure that any vents to the outdoors have screens in them.
- **Reduce excess moisture.** Insects thrive on moisture, so it's important to repair leaking roofs, chimneys, and pipes. Keep your gutters cleaned out, and make sure your attic and crawl spaces have good ventilation to prevent the buildup of moisture. Also replace or repair all water-damaged wood.
- **Keep your foundation clear.** Keep the perimeter of your home free of leaves, wood, mulch, compost, and heavy vegetation. Trim back shrubs, trees, and grass that can bring insects in contact with your home or provide dark, dank hiding places near your foundation. If the pests are living that close, they'll soon be moving in.
- **Clean up indoor clutter.** Keep clutter to a minimum, especially in garages, sheds, basements, and other storage areas. Otherwise, insects and rodents are likely to take up residence because they can settle in unnoticed. Also rid your home of newspapers, magazines, and paper bags, which can become hiding and nesting places. For storage, choose lidded plastic boxes over cardboard boxes. If you do you use cardboard boxes, keep them off floors, preferably on shelves.
- **Go high-tech.** Many people swear by electronic pest-control devices that plug into the wall. These devices emit a high-pitched noise that is undetectable to humans, dogs, and cats but may deter spiders and other insects. Just be sure to get one that is "tuned" for the type of critter you are trying to chase away.

Rodent Control

Tracks and droppings are sure signs of a rodent infestation. You might also see gnawed cables or electric wires or damaged walls, floors, and doors. The sight of even one mouse or rat is

How to Keep Mice from Moving In

- Seal any hole larger in diameter than a pencil in your walls or floors. Stuff all cracks and holes, especially those around gas and water pipes, with steel wool to seal out mice and other rodents.

- Store pet food in rodent-proof containers.

- Get rid of trash, discarded tires, and other clutter that may serve as rodent nesting sites.

- As an early warning system, place glueboards in strategic locations, such as in attics, in crawl spaces, and behind appliances. Check them at least monthly, or more often if there's been recent activity.

- If you have woodpiles in your yard, make sure they are 100 feet or more from the house, and elevate the wood at least 12 inches off the ground.

- You might try getting a cat. Even if the cat does not kill mice or rats, it might discourage them from moving in.

cause for action, because rodents reproduce rapidly; two mice can produce 2,500 heirs in as little as six months. Also, rats and mice carry disease in the fleas and ticks that infest them, and contaminate food with their urine and feces.

A mouse can pass through cracks and holes as small as a nickel; rats can squeeze into holes as small as a half-dollar. Try to determine how these rodents are getting into your home by sprinkling talcum powder on the floor in the suspect areas. Footprints or tail marks will indicate activity. The garage is a favored entry point, particularly if it houses birdseed, pet food, trash bins, or other sources of food. A cluttered garage also provides lots of hiding places for mice, which tend to be shy creatures. Seal up points of entry that you find, clean up all clutter in those areas, and put all food in airtight containers.

Poisons are not recommended for getting rid of rodents, for two important reasons: 1) the rodents often die and decay inside walls or under the house, resulting in a smell you really don't want to live with, and 2) the poisons are hazardous to children and pets. Instead, deploy mousetraps, glueboards (spring-loaded traps baited with peanut butter), or live traps. After trapping an animal in a mousetrap or on a glueboard, dispose of the trap and rodent in a plastic bag and put it in the trash. If you choose to use live traps, release the rodent at least 100 feet from your home, and make doubly sure it can't get back in by sealing it out (see the sidebar on this page).

Wash countertops, cabinets, drawers, and other durable surfaces that may have come in contact with rodents, using a solution of detergent and water, and then disinfect them.

Take precautions when cleaning up mouse droppings to avoid exposing yourself to a virus that can be deadly. Hantavirus is a respiratory illness that is spread by infected deer mice through their droppings, urine, or saliva. Symptoms include fever and body aches, which progress to breathing problems and even death. If you have an extensive mouse problem, check with your local health department for advice on the safest way to handle the situation. The following are general guidelines to go by:

- Do not sweep or vacuum mouse droppings; this potentially can stir the virus up into the air.

- Dampen the droppings with disinfectant and then either mop or wipe them up with paper towels and a solution of water, detergent, and disinfectant. Double-bag and seal the paper towels before disposing of them.

- Wear rubber, latex, or vinyl gloves when you are cleaning up droppings. Before removing the gloves, wash your hands with disinfectant and then in soap and water; discard the gloves, and then wash your hands again with soap and water. If you are working in an area with poor ventilation, also wear a dust mask.

Flying Intruders

It's bad enough when you have to swat away flying insects outdoors. Indoors, they're not just annoying but also potentially destructive.

Indian Meal Moths. These pests, also known as pantry moths, enter the home through infested grains and other dried foods, including flour, spices, cereals, nuts, dried fruit, snack foods, birdseed, and pet food. Carefully inspect dried foods and packaging seams for webbing or larvae, which are sure signs of infestation. Discard infested food immediately in a closed container or an outdoor trash can, and vacuum up any of it that may have spilled on your shelves. If swat-

ting does not eliminate any remaining moths that are flying around, use sticky traps designed to attract pantry moths.

Prevention:
Pour dried food into sealed plastic bags or other clear, airtight containers that allow you to visibly inspect for infestation.

Clothes Moths. It's the *larvae* of the clothes moth, not the adults, that feed on wool, fur, silk, feathers, and other animal-based materials. They prefer to feed in dark, undisturbed areas, such as closets, attics, and boxes in which fabrics are stored for long periods of time. Items commonly infested include anything made of wool, down pillows and comforters, natural-bristle brushes, and stuffed toys.

If you find damage that you think may have been caused by clothes moth larvae, check all of the aforementioned commonly infested items carefully for signs of infestation, such as holes in fabrics, live or dead moths or larvae, webbing, or cocoons. If you do have an infestation, vacuum the area thoroughly, especially dark, out-of-the-way corners in closets. You can kill off larvae by placing infested clothing outdoors in bright, hot sunlight. Or place the infested items in polyethylene bags, squeeze out the excess air to prevent condensation, and put the bags in the freezer for three days. Do not treat infested clothing with insecticides. Infested furniture, on the other hand, will probably need to be fumi-gated by a licensed pest-management professional. If you take any infested clothing to the dry cleaner, notify the cleaner that you have a moth problem so your clothing can be segregated from other clients' clothing.

Prevention:

- Cleaning is the best prevention. Keep closets and dresser drawers clean.
- Store only laundered and dry-cleaned fabrics — perspiration, perfume, and some stains attract moths.
- Vacuum carpets and upholstered furniture regularly, especially if you have pets, since pet hair is "good eating" for moth larvae. Pay special attention to areas where pet hair may accumulate, such as along baseboards and underneath furniture. Use your vacuum's crevice tool to clean in corners and hard-to-reach areas.
- Avoid storing natural fabrics in areas with high humidity; moths love dark, heated, humid environments. Consider leaving a light on in closets that have previously had moth infestations.

For Safety's Sake

Inhaling mothball vapors can be dangerous. Mothballs are meant to kill moths, eggs, and larvae in containers that are airtight, so that none of the harmful vapors are released. Naphthalene, the active ingredient in mothballs, is a suspected human carcinogen that may damage eyes, blood, liver, kidneys, skin, and the central nervous system. If you store clothing with mothballs, wash it before wearing it, to avoid exposure through your skin. Keep mothballs out of reach of small children.

- When you're storing fabrics in tightly sealed trunks, garment bags, boxes, or chests, store mothballs, cedar wood, or cedar chips with them, following the instructions that come with them. Replace or rejuvenate cedar with cedar oil every few months. Or store your fabrics with moth-repellent sachets made of dried lemon peels or dried lavender and cedar chips.

Flies. The housefly is a danger to the health of family members and pets, because it can carry and spread germs from the material it breeds in, feeds on, or walks on. That material can include manure and rotting garbage. So if a fly lands on food, consider it contaminated. Aerosol sprays can be used to knock down adults but will not solve the problem. Eliminating flies requires eliminating their breeding sites. Common breeding sites include fermenting organic material, trash cans, recycling bins, dirty mops, floor drains, and sink overflow drains. Find the source and then clean it thoroughly. After the area is cleaned, maintain that state of cleanliness. Use flyswatters and flypaper to eliminate adult flies.

Prevention:
- Wash trash and recycling receptacles regularly.
- Keep garbage in sealed trash bags.
- Place a few sprigs of fresh basil in fruit bowls to keep flies away from your fresh produce, or place a potted basil plant nearby. Another good spot for a potted basil plant is just outside the kitchen door. Sprigs of fresh lavender, eucalyptus, or mint will work also.

The methods of control discussed above work for common houseflies as well as fruit flies, drain flies, blowflies, cluster flies, and others.

Creepy Crawlers

Crawling insects most often come in search of food and water. Send them marching with the following cleaning regimes.

Ants. When they find a food source, ants generally follow an established trail to get there and bring the food back to their colony. When that food source is in your home, effective ant control begins with finding that trail and following it back to the point of entry. Common points of entry include windows, doors, drains, and switch plates.

The most popular home remedy for deterring ants is white vinegar. Mix a solution of equal parts of white vinegar and water and carefully pour or spray it around the ants' point of entry. Another natural deterrent is to sprinkle a line of cayenne pepper or ground cinnamon all around the point of entry; ants will not cross this line. You can try tracing the ant trail back to the outdoor colony and spot-treating it with an insecticidal spray or dust. If you must use pesticides indoors, avoid sprays. A safer approach is to bait ants and let them destroy themselves by taking the bait home to share with their fellow ants. Once you have determined the point of entry, just set delayed-action bait in the ants' line of travel. The ants will take the bait back to their nest, and eventually the nest will accumulate a toxic dose, which will eliminate the entire colony.

Prevention:

- Be sure to wipe up crumbs and sticky spots from counters, tables, and floors.
- Do not allow dishes to soak in the sink overnight; ants will find them.
- Put sugar in an airtight container, and put your honey jar in a zippered plastic bag.
- Wash trash and recycling receptacles regularly.
- Wash your kitchen counters and floors with a solution of equal parts of white vinegar and water.
- Vacuum up dead insects on your windowsills. They attract foraging ants, who may in turn be attracted to the numerous cracks and crevices around window casings that are ideal nest sites.

Carpenter Ants. These large black or brown ants gnaw through dead or decaying wood and are capable of doing severe structural damage to your home. If you see live carpenter ants in your home in winter or a swarm of flying ants in the spring, there's a good chance you have an infestation. Also be on the lookout for cobwebs containing dead carpenter ants and the sawdust they create. While dead "swarmers" can be vacuumed up, there are no effective home remedies for eliminating carpenter ants. The use of chemicals is required to minimize the risk of damage to the structural timbers of your home. An alternative to spraying or dusting is to use a bait that the ants will take back to their nest. If the ants don't

take the first bait you put out, try another brand. A reputable pest-management professional can perform a thorough inspection to locate the nest and determine the best treatment.

Prevention:

- If you have wood siding or trim on the exterior of your home, make sure that it does not come in direct contact with soil.
- Store firewood away from your home.
- Keep all trees and bushes trimmed back so they do not touch your house.
- Indoors, do not allow wood to become excessively damp, as rot and fungus make wood a vulnerable location for nests. For the same reason, repair rotted wood as soon as possible.

Termites. If you see winged termites emerging from tree stumps or woodpiles near your home, it does not mean that your home is infested. However, if you see them emerging from the base of a foundation wall or adjoining porch, you most likely have a termite problem. Often, though, you can have an infestation without ever seeing a termite. Look for other indicators, including earthen (mud) tubes on foundation walls that contain small creamy-white worker termites traveling between their underground colonies and your home. You might also notice wood that is hollowed out along the grain, with bits of dried mud or soil lining the hollows.

Getting rid of a termite infestation requires the services of a termite treatment professional who is trained in the use of special equipment and liquid pesticides. Do not attempt to do it yourself.

Prevention:
- Do not stack landscape timbers, firewood, or wood mulch anywhere near your house.
- Have your home inspected regularly for termites.

Scorpions. Although scorpions prefer to live outdoors, buildings in new developments may have scorpion visitors because construction work has destroyed the animals' natural habitat. If they do get inside, scorpions are likely to hide under damp towels, washcloths, and sponges in the kitchen and bathroom. A live scorpion can be captured by placing an inverted glass jar over it and sliding a piece of cardboard underneath to trap it. Release the scorpion into a jar of soapy water to kill it. (Scorpions cannot climb on glass.) While the sting of a scorpion is not likely to kill you, it can be very painful. It should be noted, however, that some types of scorpions are more venomous than others and that children are at greater risk of developing an acute reaction.

Prevention:
- Remove scorpions' food sources: grasshoppers, spiders, and other insects. Put on work gloves and remove woodpiles, rocks, loose boards, and any other debris from the immediate vicinity of your home.
- Seal any cracks or crevices where scorpions may be getting inside.

- Cover weep holes (drainage holes) in windows and sliding doors with fine-mesh aluminum screening (available from hardware or lumber stores).
- Use window screening to cover the open ends of drainpipes.

It's not a good idea to spray the perimeter of your building with pesticide; not only is this approach ineffective, but it may be harmful to children, pets, and wildlife.

Spiders. The simplest way to eliminate spiders is to disturb them often enough that they decide to move elsewhere. Removing cobwebs makes adult spiders more vulnerable and removes egg sacs, which will prevent another generation of spiders from taking up residence. Of course, not all spiders are web spinners; some are ground dwellers. Consider placing glue traps on either side of entrances where doors are opened frequently, as this is where they are likely coming in. Don't bother with general insecticide sprays; they are not effective against spiders.

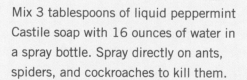

make your own

Nontoxic Bug Spray

Mix 3 tablespoons of liquid peppermint Castile soap with 16 ounces of water in a spray bottle. Spray directly on ants, spiders, and cockroaches to kill them.

Prevention:

- Regularly vacuum windows and windowsills, curtains, registers, corners of rooms, storage areas, basements, and other seldomly used areas to remove spiders and their webs.
- Vacuum frequently behind and under furniture, wall hangings, and stored materials.
- Store cardboard boxes off the floor and seal them with packing tape to keep out spiders.
- Avoid storing newspapers and magazines in the basement, attic, or garage, as these will attract spiders.
- Outdoors, sweep cobwebs and nests from doorways, lights, windows, and shrubs. Also sweep your foundation every so often.
- Eliminate sources of standing water; they will attract mosquitoes, a food source for spiders.

Cockroaches. As is the case for other insect pests, a good cleaning will go a long way toward preventing trouble with cockroaches. However, sanitation alone will not handle the problem. As disgusting as it sounds, roaches often "ride" into homes in grocery bags and food packaging. So even the cleanest homes can get them. Following are a few ideas for getting rid of these unsavory characters:

- **Catnip.** Catnip is a natural cockroach repellent. Simmer catnip in a small amount of water to make a tealike solution. Spray it around baseboards, on table legs, in cabinets, and under the lips of counter. Note that this might not be the best solution if you have a cat!
- **Beer bread.** Place a slice of bread in a coffee can with enough beer to thoroughly soak the bread. Lay the can on its side and leave it overnight in a popular cockroach "visiting" area. Empty the can in the morning and repeat as often as needed.
- **Bleach.** If cockroaches are coming into your home through a drainpipe, pour one capful of bleach into the drain and close it up overnight.
- **Poisons and traps.** The EPA recommends that you try using poison baits, boric acid, and traps before resorting to pesticide sprays. Good places to place sticky traps include under the refrigerator, dishwasher, and sink. To determine more specifically where to place traps, turn on a light at night and watch where the roaches run and hide.

ALLERGY ALERT

Allergens found in cockroach feces and saliva can cause allergic reactions or trigger asthma symptoms in some individuals. A recent study funded by the National Institute of Environmental Health Sciences and the National Institute of Allergy and Infectious Diseases showed that cockroach allergens appear to worsen asthma symptoms more than other known triggers. The best prevention is a clean house.

If you do spray, spray only the infested area, and do not spray where you prepare or store food or where young children play, crawl, or sleep. Make sure there is plenty of fresh air when you spray, and after spraying, thoroughly air out the room.

Prevention:

- Clean up all food crumbs and spilled liquids right away.
- Wash dishes as soon as you are done using them.
- Wipe and dry your kitchen counters and sinks before going to bed.
- Store food in sealed containers.
- Store trash in containers with tight-fitting lids, and remove trash daily. Wash trash receptacles regularly.
- Fix plumbing leaks and other moisture problems.
- Seal cracks or openings around or inside cabinets.
- Keep counters, sinks, tables, floors, and all other surfaces clean.
- Empty and wash your kitchen cabinets and drawers periodically.
- Keep your bathroom clean and dry.
- Be wary of bringing into your home used furniture, TVs, and other appliances, since they may harbor cockroaches.

Silverfish. Dark, damp, cool conditions in the kitchen, bathroom, laundry room, and basement are apt to lure silverfish. Silverfish are also attracted to attics that supply plenty of food in the form of paper insulation and storage boxes.

If you have a lot of silverfish, you have most likely had an infestation for some time, as silverfish lay small quantities of eggs and mature slowly. Fast-moving and most active at night, these flat, silvery gray, small, soft, wingless insects are often found in sinks and bathtubs — once they crawl in, they cannot crawl out. Given this fact, one way to capture silverfish is to wrap the outside of a glass jar with tape, sticky side out, and place the jar near the primary activity area. Once silverfish crawl inside the jar — and they crawl all over the place, so they'll find the jar readily enough — they will be trapped. You can then drown them in soapy water. You also can physically remove silverfish and their larvae with frequent vacuuming, especially by vacuuming cracks and crevices with your vacuum's crevice attachment.

Sanitation alone is only somewhat effective at controlling infestations because silverfish tend to hide in protected places, such as between wall partitions or in books and papers. In some cases, you may need to resort to the use of insecticides to stop them from damaging book bindings, wallpaper, and other paper items and dry goods.

Prevention:

- Eliminate the moist conditions that attract silverfish by repairing leaky plumbing and lowering your home's humidity with a dehumidifier. Also ventilate closed rooms and attics to control humidity.
- Keep the areas around your kitchen and bathroom plumbing free of moisture and food particles.

- Store cereal and other dry food in sealed containers.
- In addition to starchy foods and molds, silverfish feed on paper, glues and pastes, and natural fabrics such as cotton, linen, rayon, and silk. Remove unneeded papers, boxes, books, and clothes from storage to eliminate these pests' food sources and hiding places.

Earwigs. Really more of a garden pest, earwigs are sometimes driven indoors by hot, dry weather. They are likely to be attracted to paper and fiber products stored in moist basements, bathrooms, or kitchens.

Physically remove live or dead earwigs by sweeping or vacuuming. You can also try trapping earwigs: Spray a newspaper lightly with water, roll it up, and secure the roll loosely with a rubber band. Leave it overnight in an area where you have seen earwig activity. The earwigs will be attracted to the newspaper for the food and moisture it provides. Kill the earwigs by dropping them into boiling water, burning the newspaper, or squashing them. Or dump the earwigs and traps in a sealed container in the trash.

Earwigs don't really do much damage, so the use of insecticides indoors to get rid of them is generally unwarranted. If you do use insecticides, restrict the application to earwig-infested areas or suspected hiding places.

Prevention:
- If earwigs are consistently finding their way indoors, look for and seal up possible entry points, which usually are damp areas in the foundation, such as near a drain spout or beneath an air conditioner, where it drips.
- Keep the perimeter of your home dry and clean, and remove hiding places such as ground cover, mulch, or leaf litter around your foundation and doorways.
- Replace white outdoor lights with yellow sodium vapor lights, which are less likely to attract earwigs and other insects.

Fleas. If you are not averse to using insecticide on your pets, the most popular and effective method of flea control is a commercial topical application, which can prevent the need to fumigate your home. As fleas jump on your pets, they die. These products are far more effective than flea sprays and powders.

You can also manually remove fleas from your pet's body with a flea comb, though this can be very time-consuming, especially if you

make your own

Flea Spray

Citrus sprays can be effective at killing and discouraging fleas. Score and slice a lemon, place it in a bowl, and pour 1 cup of boiling water over it. Allow to sit overnight, and then spray or sponge the citric solution onto your pet.

have a large dog or multiple pets. If you want to give it a try, concentrate on combing the areas where fleas congregate, usually around the neck in cats and on the lower back and belly in dogs. Use the back of your fingernail to crush "captured" fleas against the comb, or shake them into a glass of soapy water to kill them.

To remove fleas from your house, vacuum frequently to get rid of flea eggs and larvae. After vacuuming, sprinkle flea powder into your vacuum cleaner bag, and then seal the bag and place it in the outdoor trash. If you do need to use a flea bomb or fogger, remove yourself and your pets from the house and be sure to wash water bowls and food dishes afterward.

Prevention:

- Generally, a healthy pet does not attract as many fleas as an unhealthy pet, which is why it's important to feed your pets a good diet and to ensure that they get regular exercise.
- Insecticidal flea collars provide the most effective flea control — if you put them on your pets *before* you see fleas. Herbal flea collars also can be helpful in discouraging fleas, perhaps more so for cats than for dogs.
- If fleas are problematic where you live, bathe your cats and dogs frequently with herbal pet shampoos that incorporate the essential oils of eucalyptus, citronella, cedar, or other flea-repellent herbs.
- Though not as effective as insecticides, natural flea (and tick) deterrents include brewer's yeast, garlic, and apple cider

vinegar. Brewer's yeast and garlic come in pill form that you can give to your pet, following the manufacturer's instructions. To give your pet vinegar, daily add 1 teaspoon of vinegar to 1 quart of drinking water per 40 pounds of pet weight.

- Wash pet bedding frequently, in hot water.

Hiring a Pest Management Professional

While you may be able eliminate some pest infestations, others are more effectively controlled by a licensed and certified pest management professional. If you are unsure or uncomfortable about the use of pesticides, it's always best to seek professional help.

Shop Around. Ask your friends, neighbors, or business associates for the names of firms with which they have had positive experiences. Get written estimates from several companies. Ask them to outline the cost of the labor and materials as well as what they are going to do and how long it will take. Base your selection on the value of their service, not the price.

Be wary of special deals and high-pressure sales tactics. Look for knowledgeable and competent professionals who take the time to help you understand your pest problem and what to do about it, including what steps you can take to prevent future problems, as well as any possible nonchemical alternatives. Avoid companies that want to apply pesticides on a fixed schedule without regard to the extent of your pest problem. Unnecessary or excessive use of pesticides can lead to needless chemical exposure to humans, pets, and the environment.

Check References. Before hiring a pest control company, check on the firm's reliability with the Better Business Bureau (www.bbb.org) and your local chamber of commerce. Choose a pest control company that has a good reputation in the community — one that has been in business in the same area for several years and depends on the satisfaction of its customers. Make sure the company is bonded, licensed, and certified. As an extra safety measure, call your local pesticide bureau to find out whether any complaints have been filed or any enforcement actions taken against the company.

Ask the company whether it is affiliated with any professional organizations. Membership in a professional organization reflects a commitment to integrity and responsibility. Professional associations usually offer members opportunities for training on the latest developments in technology, safety, research, and regulations. They also require members to follow the best pest-management practices.

Ask to See a License. Ask for proof that the company's salesperson or technical representative holds a commercial pesticide applicator's license. Although the applicator of pesticides is required to hold a license, the person making recommendations for pesticide use should also be trained and certified. It is important to use only licensed applicators whenever possible (not all states require licensing). An individual who holds a commercial applicator's license or certificate has demonstrated a basic knowledge and an understanding of the principles of pesticide use. Applicators are generally required to carry their current license with them while using any pesticide. You should ask to see the license of anyone who intends to apply pesticides on your property. If an applicator is unable or unwilling to show you his or her current license, do not allow the work to proceed.

Ask for a Written Contract. The pest control company you choose should provide you with a written contract. Make sure that the contract says the pest control company will inspect your home before applying any pesticide. They should know and understand your particular pest problem before recommending a treatment program. Ask the company to outline its plan for dealing with your problem and describe why and where the applications will take place. Remember, pesticides can be poisonous to you and your family. As much as possible, educate yourself before signing a contract.

Following are some other contractual matters to consider:

- **Types of pesticides.** The contract should state which products will be used for each application. If you do not understand the delineation of pesticide use on the contract, ask for further explanation. Do not agree to anything until you are satisfied with what is to be done. Always ask whether lower-risk pesticide alternatives are available.

- **Safety concerns.** The contract should note any special safety concerns, including family members with allergies and health problems, infants, the elderly, pregnant women, and pets. The choice of pesticides and/or other aspects of the pest-control strategy must reflect these concerns. You may want to include a statement that permits you to reject unwanted chemicals.

- **Extent of application.** Do not sign contracts that call for periodic spraying. Agree only to a fixed contract that is effective for a specific period of time.

- **Precautions to limit exposure.** The contract should note any special precautions you should take to reduce your exposure to the pesticides that will be applied. Should you be out of the house during and after the application? For how long? What about drying time or ventilation? What should you expect after the application? Will there be any odors or visible residue?

- **Legalities.** Make sure that all blanks in the contract are filled in. In addition to the contractor's name, address, phone number, and license number, the contract should include a statement that the contractor is responsible for insuring his employees against possible injury on the job. It should also include a warranty or guarantee with all conditions spelled out. For example, if a problem comes up during or after the treatment, what is the company obligated to do to resolve the problem?

When the work is finished, the contractor may request your signature on a completion certificate. Before signing, inspect the job carefully to see that the work has been done to your satisfaction. Do not sign the completion certificate if you have a valid complaint about the work. Ask to speak to a supervisor.

CHAPTER SIXTEEN

SEASONAL & SPECIAL OCCASIONS

Regular care and cleaning of your home and belongings can prevent expensive repairs and help your home and belongings last longer and maintain their value. To follow through on this concept, in addition to weekly or biweekly cleaning, it's important to implement monthly, seasonal, and annual cleaning schedules. Use the strategies and checklists in this chapter as a guide to cleaning seasonally as well as for occasional events, such as holidays and preparing your home to sell.

Monthly Cleaning Chores

Each week, add a couple of monthly chores to your regular cleaning routine. Or write monthly cleaning tasks on individual sticky notes and attach them to your calendar in the appropriate week; when you've completed a task, move its sticky note ahead to the following month's schedule as a reminder. In time, the monthly tasks will become part of your routine and you will no longer need the reminders.

- In the cooling season, change any air-conditioning filters.
- In the heating season, change any furnace filters.

- Vacuum baseboard heaters, heating ducts, and vents.
- Wash throw rugs.
- Vacuum upholstered furniture.
- Vacuum under sofa cushions.
- Clean ceiling fans.
- Wipe smudges and spills off cabinet doors.
- Sweep patios, walkways, and the garage floor.
- Run ice cubes through the garbage disposal to clean its blades.
- Wash and disinfect trash cans and recycling bins.
- Clean the oven.

Once Every Season

Some cleaning chores require doing at least every few months. One way to remember to do them is to use the first day of each new season as a reminder. Allow one full day or 8 hours spread over a week to complete these tasks. Use the checklist below as your guide for what needs to get done. An even simpler strategy is to clean things as needed; for example, clean the oven when you notice that it is getting dirty.

- Clean the kitchen exhaust hood and filter.
- Clean the top of your refrigerator and kitchen cabinets.
- Remove cobwebs from open beams, overhangs, and storage areas.
- Flip your mattress and rotate it so that what was the head is now the foot. Vacuum what is now the sleeping side of your mattress. If possible, air the mattress outdoors in the sunshine to kill dust mites.

PLAIN & SIMPLE ORGANIZING TIPS

- At the end of each season, donate any clothes and shoes for that season that you didn't wear.
- Make seasonal cleaning easier by first donating or selling items you no longer use or need.
- Clean items before putting them in storage so that they are ready to use when you remove them.
- Store all seasonal items together.

• EVERYDAY SOLUTION
Cleaning Smoke Detectors

Let the change of daylight saving time (or Halloween and Easter) be your cue to check and clean smoke detectors. Wipe the outside casing of each detector clean, and then open the detector and vacuum the inside. When you put the detector back together, test it. Every other time you clean the detectors (once a year), replace the batteries.

- Wash all pillows, blankets, comforters, bedspreads, mattress pads, and bed skirts.
- Straighten dresser drawers.
- Clean light fixtures inside and out.
- Clean and condition all your leather furnishings.
- Condition and polish wood furniture, paneling, and cabinets.
- Empty and vacuum out kitchen cupboards and drawers.
- Erase smudge marks and fingerprints on painted walls, especially around light switches and doorknobs.
- Take down shower curtains and wash them.
- Wash curtains and draperies.
- Remove and launder slipcovers.
- Clean carpets (twice a year, or more often if needed).
- Remove mineral deposits from showerheads.
- Clean all household drains, if you have not been doing this weekly.
- Add fresh mothballs or fresh cedar products to storage boxes.

For Safety's Sake

The Home Safety Council warns that cleaning activities may increase your risk of injury from falls, poisonings, and other hazards. Following these simple safety steps can greatly reduce your risk of injury from cleaning your home, garage, and yard.

- When cleaning, decluttering, or reorganizing, reduce the risk of falls by keeping stairs, steps, landings, and all floors clear of clutter.

- Carry only loads you can see over, and keep one hand free to hold on to banisters and railings.

- Tuck away telephone and electrical cords so that they are not in the path of traffic.

- In homes with children, make sure toys and other items are always safely put away when they're not in use.

- If you need to climb, use a stepladder or safety ladder. When using a ladder, don't stand above the rung designated as the highest safe standing level. For a stepladder, the highest safe standing level is the second rung from the top, and for an extension ladder, it's the fourth rung from the top. Before using a ladder, make sure its rungs are dry and the ladder is securely positioned on a flat surface.

- When cleaning out cabinets, read all product and medication labels carefully, and separate those whose labels say "Caution," "Warning," or "Danger." To prevent accidental poisoning or overdose, lock up these products and medications, out of the sight and reach of young children. Get rid of any products and medications whose expiration date has passed.

- Follow safety recommendations when using harsh products, such as wearing gloves and masks. Do not mix products together, because their contents could react, with dangerous results.

- Never use gasoline as a cleaning solvent, and never use or store gasoline in your home, even in tiny quantities. Because its vapors can readily ignite, gasoline can present a serious fire hazard and is too dangerous to use for any purpose other than as a motor fuel.

- Buckets are often used for cleaning and present a serious drowning danger to young children. Never leave a bucket or any standing water unattended, and store all buckets and barrels empty and upside down.

courtesy of the Home Safety Council

Once a Year: The Big Clean

Spring is the traditional time to conduct a thorough home cleaning — an annual ritual that dates back to the late nineteenth and early twentieth centuries. Between woodstoves, coal-burning stoves, and kerosene and oil lamps, homes were so sooty and smelly by the end of winter that there was no choice but to wash everything come spring. It was not uncommon to see all the contents of a home spread out in the yard as homemakers toiled away to remove dirt and grime from every crevice.

Today, an annual spring cleaning isn't something that *must* be done. And *when* you do it is not so important as *how* you do it. You can spend a whole day or weekend or week doing your "spring" cleaning, or you can incorporate annual cleaning chores into your regular cleaning schedule by selecting several tasks to complete each month. Make it a family affair: Get the kids to help, and enjoy the satisfaction that comes from working together as a team. When the work is done, plan to celebrate with popcorn and a movie or a trip to the park.

- Clean bookshelves and books.
- Clean out your financial files. Shred and discard any papers you no longer need to keep. Transfer old documents that you need to save, such as tax returns, to archive boxes.

- Move heavy furniture and large appliances so you can vacuum behind and underneath them.
- Change the water filter in your refrigerator, if it has one.
- Vacuum the refrigerator coils.
- Vacuum out dust from inside your central vacuum system, using a regular vacuum cleaner.
- Clean the clothes dryer exhaust duct and damper and the space under the dryer.
- Flush the water heater to remove accumulated sediment.
- Have all major appliances serviced according to the manufacturers' recommendations.
- Wash any walls that need it.
- Unclutter your home room by room.

Seasonal Cleaning Chores

With every season comes a new list of cleaning chores specific to that season. Here are some "to do" lists that you can adapt to your own lifestyle.

In the Spring. About the time you turn off the heat for the season, or when the muddy season has come and gone, is the right time to get going on your spring cleaning. Take advantage of the extra hours of daylight to tackle some of these outdoor projects.

- Replace heavy winter bedding with lighter sheets, bedspreads, comforters, or quilts.
- Launder all winter bedding before putting it into storage.
- Put winter clothing and accessories into storage.
- Collect and tag unwanted items for a summer garage sale.
- Wash windows inside and out.
- Roll up large area rugs and vacuum the floor that had been underneath them.
- Clean gutters and drainpipes.
- Clean any salt residue from the garage floor; sweep and then damp-mop.

- Clean the burner tubes on your gas grill before using it.
- Scrape and wash moss and debris off the roof.
- Remove debris from gutters and downspouts.
- Wash the driveway, patios, and sidewalks.
- Wash the exterior of your home.
- Clean the tracks of any sliding doors.
- Scrub mildew from decks, porches, and siding.
- Look for signs of pest damage; treat your home if necessary.
- Inspect for plumbing leaks and other moisture problems.
- Open your pool (see the sidebar on page 258).
- Clean and waterproof winter boots and shoes.

In the Summer. Summertime often means more cleaning time. The kids spend their days coming in and out, tracking in water from the pool as well as freshly mown grass and asphalt on their shoes. Dry weather and open windows also allow more dust to make its way into your home.

- If you have kids, assign light housekeeping chores and summer yard chores to them.
- Unclutter children's closets and drawers; donate any clothes and shoes they have outgrown.
- Hold a garage sale to get rid of unwanted or unneeded items.
- If you have a pool, clean it regularly throughout the season.

- When you go to the beach, empty beach bags upon your return to prevent wet towels from mildewing and food crumbs from attracting insects.
- Scrub mildew from decks, porches, and siding.
- Look for signs of pest damage.
- Inspect for plumbing leaks and other moisture problems.

In the Fall/Winter. Plan to do outdoor cleaning jobs on one of those beautiful fall days when the air is crisp and the sun is warm. Save indoor fall cleaning for a rainy day.

- Clean and store patio furniture, outdoor tools, and the lawn mower.
- Clean, sand, and condition the wood handles on your outdoor tools.

Out-of-Season Storage Tips

- Always launder or dry-clean clothes and bedding before storing them. Perspiration, odors, and stains on natural fabrics attract clothes moths like a bright light in the dark. See page 241 for more information on preventing clothes moths.
- Store clothing in sealed boxes or bags. Further protect clothes from insect and rodent damage by adding moth repellent (mothballs, cedar wood, or cedar chips) to boxes or bags before sealing them up. Plan to wash any fabrics that come in direct contact with mothballs before using them again.
- Label all your containers.
- Store boxes of same-season items together.
- If you are short on storage space, use vacuum-seal bags to reduce the volume of fabric material by up to 75 percent. Some of these bags come specially designed with a hanger for suits, coats, and other bulky items, allowing you to maximize closet storage space.
- Clean and waterproof leather shoes and boots before putting them away. That way, they're ready to wear when you need them. Store leather footwear in a large plastic lidded box or sealed trash bag to keep them free of dust while they're in storage.
- Clean and dry outdoor furniture before storing it for the winter. Cover the furniture with plastic sheeting, seal the sheeting with tape or staples, and put the furniture in a dry basement, garage, or shed. Or store the furniture against an outside wall or under a porch, and cover it with a tarp that is firmly secured against inclement weather. Store outdoor cushions separately, in sealed plastic garbage bags in a dry location.

- Clean and store children's summer toys; donate or sell any items they no longer use.
- Remove, wash, dry, and store or replace window screens.
- Clean and store your barbecue grill.
- Drain and put away garden hoses.
- Check your snow-removal equipment to make sure it is in working order.

- Put up holiday lights; it's easier to do this in the fall than it is in the middle of winter, when it might be cold and icy underfoot.
- Buy sand, salt, or whatever other ice-treatment product you use for cleaning driveways, sidewalks, and steps.
- If you burn wood, have the chimney and flues professionally cleaned.

Opening and Closing Your Pool

If you're lucky enough to have a pool in your backyard, you also have a little extra to do in the way of seasonal chores every spring and fall.

TO OPEN YOUR POOL

1. **Remove the cover.** Drain any water off the pool cover, directing it to drain away from, and not into, the pool. Sweep off the cover, and then clean and store it in a dry place that's protected from the sun.
2. **Fill the pool.** Generally, the fill line is in line with the middle of the skimmer opening.
3. **Check your equipment.** Make sure everything is clean and in working order.
4. **Clean up.** Give your pool a good brushing and vacuuming. Skim any debris out of the water.
5. **Test and balance the water chemistry.** See the sidebar on page 147 for complete details.

TO CLOSE YOUR POOL

1. **Balance the water.** Test the pH, total alkalinity, and water hardness, and adjust as needed.
2. **Run the filter.** Depending on the state of your water, you may need to run it anywhere from 24 to 48 hours.
3. **Clean up.** Vacuum and brush the pool. Clean out the skimmer baskets and traps.
4. **Prepare equipment.** Follow manufacturer's instructions for lowering the water level, shutting off the filter pump, and draining the pump, filter, heater, hoses, and all other applicable equipment. If needed, use an antifreeze formulated for pools.
5. **Remove the floater.** The use of a floating cartridge while your pool is covered can result in damage to your vinyl liner.
6. **Winterize the water.** Add a winter shock product and an algicide to prevent algae growth.
7. **Replace the cover.** Covering your pool keeps unwanted debris from getting into it; it also keeps valuable chemicals from getting out. A good cover will save many hours when it's time to open your pool next season.

courtesy of Omni Pool Products

- Have the furnace or boiler cleaned.
- Clean or replace humidifier elements.
- Wash windows inside and out.
- Roll up large area rugs and vacuum the floor that had been underneath them.
- Wash and put away summer clothes and blankets.
- Scrub mildew from decks, porches, and siding.
- If you have a pool, clean, drain, and cover it.
- Clean gutters and drainpipes.
- Look for signs of pest damage.
- Inspect for plumbing leaks and other moisture problems.
- Check the attic to make sure it has adequate ventilation.

Preparing to Sell Your Home

Cleaning is the most important thing you can do in the process of preparing your home for sale. A dirty home not only is a real turnoff for prospective buyers but also plants a seed of doubt about how well you've maintained and cared for your home. According to a survey conducted by the Soap and Detergent Association, the cleanliness of a home may have the biggest influence on a potential home buyer's first impression of it. Respondents ranked cleanliness, with 51 percent of the vote, at the top of the list of what makes the biggest impact when walking into a home for the first time, above scents/odors, style of decor, furnishings, and

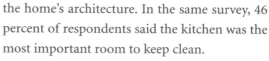

the home's architecture. In the same survey, 46 percent of respondents said the kitchen was the most important room to keep clean.

Realtors agree that cleaning is the simplest thing you can do to help your home sell faster at top dollar. So before you even put your home on the market, start cleaning and decluttering. Allow yourself a few weeks to a few months get your home ready to show. Then be prepared to spend extra time every day to keep it that way. Consider hiring a cleaning service to do the thorough cleaning or to help with maintenance. You may also want to consider hiring a landscaper to clean up your yard or a professional organizer to help with uncluttering and organizing your home.

Declutter Every Room. Remember, you're trying to sell your home, not your stuff. Uncluttering will make every room look larger. Pare down your furnishings to the bare essentials. Clear every horizontal surface — countertops, tables, and shelves — and then put back just one or two accent pieces or functional items. Less furniture and fewer knickknacks will make it easier to keep your home clean for prospective buyers. Also be sure to declutter closets, cupboards, and shelves to make them look more spacious and accommodating. Don't use these places to stash stuff! Buyers will want to open every door. Donate or sell what you don't use, and find a home — possibly in storage — for everything else. Disposing of items now will make your move easier and quicker when the time comes, and perhaps even cheaper, if you are paying by the pound. If you have years of accumulated junk to clear out, consider renting a large, roll-off trash container or dumpster.

Start Packing Now. Remove photographs, trophies and awards, collectibles, religious artifacts, knickknacks, and other personal items that might get in the way of new owners seeing your home as their own. Pack and store all extraneous furnishings and personal belongings. Also pack up valuables and anything that could be broken or stolen. Consider short-term rental of a storage unit for things you plan to move to your next home, including seasonal decorations, sports equipment, and other items that may currently be stored in your basement, attic, or garage. Having less stuff in these storage areas will make them look bigger, which is more appealing to buyers. One option for renting a storage unit is to rent a portable storage unit from a moving company that will deliver the unit to your home and then take it away and store it until you are ready to move.

Clean from Top to Bottom, Inside and Out. Once you get the clutter out of the way, give your home a thorough cleaning. Start by washing the windows inside and out. Shampoo your carpets or have them professionally cleaned. Then, working in one room at a time, clean all surfaces, from ceiling fans and light fixtures to walls and floors. Wipe windowsills and ledges, wash window coverings, clean scuffs and marks from the floors and walls, and polish the floors. Clean the grout of tiled surfaces; regrout if necessary. Clean the interior of your oven and refrigerator.

If you have the time, a fresh coat of paint can go a long way toward a cleaner look. And don't forget to beautify your entryway: sweep sidewalks, remove cobwebs and debris, and wash the door and lighting fixtures to help your home make a good first appearance. Also mow the lawn, trim the bushes, and remove all trash and clutter from the yard.

Maintain Cleanliness. Once you've thoroughly cleaned and organized your home, it's important to maintain it in that state until you sell it. Following is a checklist for daily cleaning:

- Clear the front yard of debris and toys.
- Keep the front door and entryway clean and free of clutter.
- Put away clothing and personal items.
- Make the beds and straighten up the bedrooms.
- Wipe down bathroom counters and sinks after every use.
- Clean the toilet.
- Use a squeegee on the shower door and walls to prevent water marks.
- Wipe down kitchen counters, sinks, and appliances after every use.
- Wash dishes immediately after using them, or put them in the dishwasher.
- Spot-clean windows and mirrors as necessary.
- Scoop and dispose of dirty cat litter.
- Spray an odor neutralizer to eliminate unpleasant scents.
- Don't just put things down; put them away.

- Keep a basket or lidded plastic box handy for quick pickups of clutter; store it in a closet, under a bed, or in an out-of-sight but accessible place.
- Make your kitchen sink and appliances shine.

Helpful hint: Keep disposable cleaning wipes handy for quick touch-ups on a moment's notice.

Use Good Scents. Smoking, cooking, and pet odors can be a real turnoff to prospective buyers. Avoid smoking in your home during the selling process. Remove lingering smoke and unpleasant cooking odors by setting out a bowl of vinegar or using an odor eliminator spray. Bowls of potpourri can lend a nice fragrance to a room, but avoid the use of heavily scented air fresheners, which may not appeal to everyone and may even make a visitor wonder what you are trying to cover up. You might also consider using freshly scented cleaning products to deodorize your home. One simply scent-sational strategy is to bake a loaf of bread, chocolate-chip cookies, or cinnamon rolls prior to a potential buyer's visit. If you like this idea but you're short on time, buy frozen, ready-to-bake items or simmer some cinnamon potpourri.

How To REMOVE SMOKE ODOR

Smoke odors are the most difficult odors to eliminate, because the smoke particles are so small, they penetrate everything. To get rid of the odor, you need to clean every surface.

Walls and ceilings. Use a cleaning solution with ammonia to wash the walls and ceilings. Also clean light fixtures and ceiling fans. Make your own cleaner with 2 gallons of hot water, ½ cup of borax, and 1 tablespoon of sudsy ammonia (or 1 tablespoon of regular ammonia with ½ teaspoon of dishwashing liquid). You may need to repaint the walls and ceilings after washing. If so, you can use a stain-blocking sealer as a primer to prevent nicotine particles from penetrating through the paint.

Carpets and floors. Shampoo or steam-clean carpets. When dry, sprinkle carpets with baking soda and allow it to sit overnight. Vacuum carpets in the morning. If the nicotine has penetrated the padding, you may need to replace the carpet and padding. Scrub linoleum, tile, and wood floors with cleaners appropriate to floor type (see chapter 4).

Heating systems. Have heating and cooling system ductwork professionally cleaned. Hire a chimney sweep to clear smoke odor.

As much as possible, open windows and use fans to ventilate the area. To help absorb lingering odor, place bowls of vinegar throughout the house. Leave them out overnight or longer, as needed.

Cleaning for a Move

Moving in? Moving out? Either way, you've probably got some cleaning to do. Try to schedule your move so that you have time to clean the new place *before* you move in your belongings, and clean the old place after it's empty. If the two locations are nearby, you may be able to do the pre-move cleaning a day or two beforehand and the post-move cleaning on moving day or a day or two afterward if you still have access to the old place. If you have to do the pre-move and post-move cleaning on the same day, do as much cleaning as you can before moving out. Then, on moving day, you might just need to clean floors. Then schedule your move so that you have time in the morning to do a quick cleaning at the new place. You may want to consider hiring a professional cleaner at one or both ends of your move to reduce moving time and labor.

It's always a good idea for renters to inspect their new home before moving in so that the landlord can be notified of any problems. You might want to take photographs prior to moving in to document any pre-existing stains on carpets or other damage so that you will not be held liable when you move out. At the end of the contract period, renters are generally expected to do a thorough cleaning before getting back their security deposit.

When moving out, remove everything from your home and then clean. Following are a few do's and don'ts to keep in mind:

- Do toss old magazines, catalogs, and junk mail. Don't even give it a second thought, because you will be getting more at your new place.
- Do not transport hazardous waste. Give away or dispose of all hazardous goods, flammables, pesticides, paints, aerosols, and old batteries before moving.
- Check all closets, drawers, and cupboards for forgotten items.
- Take out the trash.
- Do not remove lightbulbs from the sockets or you won't be able to see to clean!
- Leave behind a kitchen chair or small stepladder so you can clean ceiling fans, the tops of built-in bookcases, upper shelves of kitchen cabinets, windows, and any other hard-to-reach places.
- Leave all the cleaning supplies you will need, including a vacuum.

The move-out cleaning should be a deep cleaning of everything in the living space: floors, baseboards, windows, walls, doors, sinks, toilets, showers and tubs, mirrors, remaining appliances (stove and refrigerator), countertops, shelves, and bathroom and kitchen cabinets. To make sure you clean every last inch, work in one room at a time and then close doors as you finish. Depending on how long you've lived in your home; the final cleaning could take days. Allow more time than you think you will need, and enlist the help of friends and family.

Cleaning a Dorm Room

Trying to keep a small communal living space clean can be a real challenge, especially for freshman students who are used to having parents do their laundry and clean house. It's a good idea to send students off with a few cleaning skills and essential cleaning supplies (see sidebar). Daily cleanup is as simple as making the bed, putting dirty clothes in a basket, and tossing out the trash.

A word of advice to students: Don't wait until you are out of underwear to do laundry. Do get in the habit of dusting and sweeping weekly or as often as needed. Dorm dwellers may be able to borrow a vacuum cleaner from the residence hall.

Wherever they live, students are responsible for the cleanliness of their "homes." In a dorm environment, responsibility is limited to the dorm room. In suite and apartment living situations, cleaning responsibilities extend to bathrooms and kitchens as well. Cleaning should be a shared responsibility of all roommates. It's important to decide who will do what, especially in a suite or an apartment with a shower and toilet to clean and dishes to wash.

Any issues that arise, such as dirty laundry piling up on every horizontal surface, should be addressed immediately. One way to cope with differences in cleaning styles — neat freak versus slob — is to have each roommate carve out personal space, generally the area around his or her bed, desk, and closet. Develop and agree to some guidelines such as "We confine our messes to our own personal domains" and "We empty the garbage every Sunday night."

College Cleaning Supplies

Don't forget to pack some basic cleaning tools and supplies for your dorm room. Following is a checklist of suggested items:

- Laundry basket or bag
- Laundry detergent, fabric softener sheets, and stain treatment
- Small change purse or empty film canisters to carry quarters for washers and dryers
- Iron and small ironing board
- Wrinkle-releasing spray (optional)
- Paper towels
- All-purpose disinfectant cleaner spray or wipes
- Air deodorizer
- Garbage bags
- Broom, carpet sweeper, or electrostatic dust mop

Apartment and suite residents will need additional supplies, such as:

- **For toilets,** toilet brush and toilet bowl cleaner
- **For the rest of the bathroom,** basin, tub, and tile cleaners, sponges, glass cleaner for mirrors
- **For dishes,** dishwashing liquid, dishwasher detergent if there's a dishwasher, dishcloths or sponges, dish towels, dishpan, and rubber gloves (optional)

Special-Occasion Cleaning Strategies

It's hard enough to organize and shop for holidays and special occasions, let alone clean your home for overnight and party guests. But a little advance planning and organization can make the difference between a stressful and a stress-free experience. Remember that the real reason for the season or event is to celebrate and enjoy. And the simplest way to avoid the pressure of preparing for holidays is to start early. Don't create unnecessary stress by leaving your cleaning to the last minute.

• **Decide now how clean you need to be.** Your home doesn't need to be spotless unless you think it does. If you are hosting an evening event, you can dim the lights to hide dust. Or, if you want to greet the holiday with an immaculate home but don't have the time to do it right, consider hiring a professional cleaning service. *Helpful hint:* Save the carpet shampooing for after the holidays, so that accidental spills won't be so upsetting.

• **List all the necessary chores.** Make a checklist of all the cleaning chores that need to be done in preparation for the upcoming holiday or special occasion. In front of each chore, put an estimate of the time it will take to complete that task. That way, if you have a spare hour, you can look for a task that you could accomplish in that time. Some things, such as polishing silver and cleaning a guest room, can be done a month or more in advance. Dedicate one day each weekend for tackling preholiday cleaning jobs such as cleaning guest rooms and bathrooms and decluttering and organizing kitchen cabinets.

• **Do only what needs doing now.** Leave big projects like cleaning the walls for spring cleaning. If you're cleaning in preparation for Passover, don't worry about dust and cobwebs; focus your efforts on removing *chametz* from your home. (*Chametz* refers to bread, noodles, spaghetti, custard cereals, beer, and all malt products; removing *chametz* includes removing all crumbs of these products.)

• **Make room.** Make room for holiday food by cleaning out your refrigerator and pantry. Donate unneeded or unwanted pantry items to a local food bank.

• **Enlist other family members.** Getting your children involved with holiday cleaning will teach them how to organize and tackle big jobs while also getting them in the spirit of the holiday.

EVERYDAY SOLUTION
Freshening Table Linens

To freshen table linens after they've been in storage, without relaundering them, run the linens through the dryer with a damp white towel or washcloth and a fabric-softener sheet. Or use a wrinkle-releasing spray, as directed on the product label. To dewrinkle and freshen more delicate, more elaborate, or dry-clean-only fabrics, use a home dry-cleaning kit.

- **Finish early.** Pretend the holiday or special occasion starts one day earlier than it actually does. Then you can enjoy a day of rest before the festivities begin.

Last-Minute Strategies. If you have only one day to clean, concentrate your efforts on the public areas of your home: the kitchen, bathrooms, living areas, and entryways. If you have only a few hours, make your kitchen and bathroom sparkle. Guests will assume you keep this standard for the rest of your home also.

- Clean toilets, sinks, mirrors, and bathroom floors.
- Clean the tub and shower, or simply close the curtain.
- Put out fresh hand towels for guests.
- Empty the kitchen and bathroom trash cans and wastebaskets.
- Unclutter kitchen countertops and wipe them clean.
- Wash the kitchen floor.
- Go around the house with a laundry basket and toss in it any clutter; stash the basket in an out-of-sight location.
- Close doors to rooms that are off-limits to guests.
- Dim the lights for an evening party.
- Consider holding the party outdoors.

Post-Party Work. You can make the chore of cleaning up after a party easier by implementing a few simple strategies.

- Consider treating your upholstered furniture and carpeting with a stain-resistant coating to make it easier to clean up accidental spills.
- Use decorative disposable plates, utensils, and glasses and paper napkins; invest in good-quality products that are less likely to break or leak.
- Place trash containers in multiple strategic locations. Put extra trash bags at the bottom of each trash container so that when a bag is full, you can take it out and have a new one at the ready immediately.
- Keep cleaning supplies handy for quick cleanups; recommended items include a cordless vacuum for crumbs, a wet mop for spills, paper towels, and your favorite all-purpose cleaning solution.
- If you have food laid out, have receptacles handy for things like nutshells, shrimp tails, and toothpicks.
- Do not allow stains to sit on furniture, carpets, or clothes overnight.
- Prohibit smoking or allow smoking outdoors only; provide ashtrays.
- If guests ask what they can do to help, assign the task of picking up trash, removing empty dishes from the food-serving area, or wiping up the drink-serving area and tossing empty bottles.
- Accept all offers to help clean up after the party.

REMOVE CANDLE WAX

- **From upholstery and carpeting.** Freeze the gum or wax by applying ice or a commercial freezing product in an aerosol can. Shatter the material with a blunt object and vacuum up the chips before they soften. Then, if needed, follow the instructions for removing oil-based stains on page 66.

- **From tablecloths.** Place ice on the wax to make it brittle, and scrape off what you can with a credit card. Then place a brown paper bag over the wax and place another brown paper bag under the fabric. Iron the top bag with a medium-hot iron until all the wax has been transferred to the bag. Replace the dirty bag with a clean bag as needed until all the wax residue has been removed.

- **From wood.** Place ice on the wax to harden it, use a credit card to gently scrape off what you can, and remove any remaining residue with a cloth moistened with cream furniture wax.

- **From glass votive holders.** Put the candleholder in the freezer for several hours, and then pry at the wax inside with a butter knife. It should pop right out. Wash the votive in hot, soapy water to remove any wax residue. (Putting a little bit of water in the bottom of the votive before placing the candle inside will prevent the wax from sticking.) If the cloth is stained, apply a nonflammable spot remover formulated specifically for grease, oil, or tar, and then launder as usual.

Appendices

LAUNDRY SOLUTIONS

LAUNDRY STAIN REMOVAL CHART

After pretreating and washing a stained item, always check to make sure the stain has been removed before putting the item in the dryer. Dryer heat can permanently set some stains. If the stain remains, pretreat and wash again.

courtesy of The Soap and Detergent Association

Stain	Treatment
Adhesive tape, chewing gum, or rubber cement	Apply ice or cold water to harden the surface; scrape away residue with a dull knife. Saturate the stain with a prewash stain remover or cleaning fluid. Rinse, then launder.
Baby formula	Pretreat or soak the stain using an enzyme presoak product. Soak for at least 30 minutes and up to several hours for aged stains. Launder.
Beverages (coffee, tea, soft drinks, wine, alcoholic beverages)	Sponge or soak the stain in cool water. Pretreat with a prewash stain remover, a liquid laundry detergent, a liquid detergent booster, or a paste of powder laundry product and water. Launder using liquid chlorine bleach, if safe for the fabric, or all-fabric (oxygen) bleach. *NOTE:* Older stains may respond to pretreatment with or soaking in an enzyme presoak product.
Blood (fresh)	Soak in cold water (do not use hot water, as it will set the stain). Launder. *NOTE:* If the stain remains after washing, rewash using a bleach safe for the fabric.

Stain	Treatment
Blood (dried)	Pretreat or soak in warm water with an enzyme presoak product. Launder. *NOTE:* If the stain remains, rewash using a bleach safe for the fabric.
Bodily fluids	Pretreat or soak in an enzyme presoak product. Launder using liquid chlorine bleach, if safe for the fabric, or all-fabric (oxygen) bleach.
Brown or yellow discoloration from iron, rust, or manganese	Use a rust remover recommended for fabrics; launder. *NOTE:* Do **not** use liquid chlorine bleach to remove rust stains, because it may intensify the discoloration.
Candle wax	Scrape off surface wax with a dull knife. Place the stain face-down between clean paper towels and press with a warm iron. Replace the paper towels frequently to absorb more wax and to avoid transferring the stain to the surface below. Sponge any remaining stain with prewash stain remover or cleaning fluid; blot with paper towels. Let dry, then launder. *NOTE:* If any color remains, rewash using liquid chlorine bleach, if safe for the fabric, or all-fabric (oxygen) bleach.
Chocolate	Pretreat or prewash in warm water with an enzyme presoak product or a prewash stain remover. Launder. *NOTE:* If the stain remains, rewash using a bleach safe for the fabric.
Collar or cuff soil	Pretreat with prewash stain remover, liquid laundry detergent, or a paste of powder detergent and water. Then launder.
Cosmetics	Pretreat with prewash stain remover, liquid laundry detergent, or a paste of powder detergent or laundry additive and water. Or rub with bar soap. Then launder.

Stain	Treatment
Crayon (a few spots)	Treat like candle wax (above), or dampen the stain and rub with bar soap. Launder using the hottest water considered safe for the fabric.
Crayon (on a whole load of clothes)	Wash with hot water using laundry soap and 1 cup of baking soda. *NOTE:* If color remains, launder using liquid chlorine bleach, if safe for the fabric. Otherwise, pretreat or soak in an enzyme presoak product or all-fabric (oxygen) bleach, using the hottest water considered safe for the fabric, then launder again.
Dairy products	Pretreat or soak the stain, using an enzyme presoak product. Soak for at least 30 minutes or several hours for aged stains. Launder.
Deodorant, antiperspirant (light stain)	Pretreat with liquid laundry detergent. Launder.
Deodorant, antiperspirant (heavy stain)	Pretreat with prewash stain remover. Allow to stand for 5 to 10 minutes. Launder using an all-fabric (oxygen) bleach.
Dye transfer	When white fabrics have picked up color from other fabrics in the wash, use a packaged color remover, following the label directions. Then launder. *NOTE:* If the dye remains, launder again, using liquid chlorine bleach, if safe for the fabric. For noncolorfast fabrics, soak in all-fabric (oxygen) bleach, then launder.
Egg	Pretreat or soak the stain, using an enzyme presoak product. Soak for at least 30 minutes, or several hours for aged stains. Launder.
Fabric softener	Dampen the stain and rub with bar soap. Rinse out, then launder.
Fruit, juice	Wash with a bleach safe for the fabric.

Stain	Treatment
Grass	Pretreat or soak in an enzyme presoak product. *NOTE:* If the stain persists, launder using liquid chlorine bleach, if safe for the fabric, or all-fabric (oxygen) bleach.
Grease, oil (light stain)	Pretreat with prewash stain remover, liquid laundry detergent, or liquid detergent booster. Launder using the hottest water considered safe for the fabric.
Grease, oil (heavy stain)	Place the stain facedown on clean paper towels. Apply cleaning fluid to the back of the stain. Replace the paper towels under the stain as necessary to soak up the residue. Let dry, rinse, and then launder using the hottest water considered safe for the fabric.
Ink	Try one of the following pretreatments, and then launder the stained item: 1) Pretreat using a prewash stain remover. 2) Sponge the area around the stain with denatured alcohol or cleaning fluid. Place the stain facedown on clean paper towels and apply alcohol or cleaning fluid to the back of the stain. Replace the paper towels as needed to soak up the liquid. Rinse. 3) Place the stain over the mouth of a jar or glass, holding the fabric taut. Drip denatured alcohol or cleaning fluid through the stain so the ink will drop into the container as it is being removed. Rinse thoroughly before laundering. *NOTE:* Some ballpoint, felt-tip, and liquid inks may be impossible to remove, and laundering may in fact set some types of ink.
Mildew	Launder the stained item using a bleach safe for the fabric and the hottest water recommended for the fabric. *NOTE:* Badly mildewed fabrics may be damaged beyond repair.
Mud	Let the item dry, then brush off as much mud as possible. Pretreat with a paste of powder detergent and water, liquid laundry detergent, a liquid detergent booster, or, for heavy stains, an enzyme presoak product. Launder.

Stain	Treatment
Mustard	Pretreat with a prewash stain remover. Launder using liquid chlorine bleach, if safe for the fabric, or all-fabric (oxygen) bleach.
Nail polish	You can try removing the stain with nail polish remover (but do not use on acetate or triacetate fabrics). Place the stain face-down on clean paper towels. Apply nail polish remover to the back of the stain. Replace the paper towels frequently to soak up the liquid. Repeat until stain disappears (if it does). Rinse and launder. *NOTE:* Nail polish may be impossible to remove.
Paint (water based)	Rinse the fabric in warm water while the stain is still wet. Launder. *NOTE:* Once the paint is dry, it cannot be removed.
Paint (oil based or varnish)	Try to remove the paint, using the same solvent recommended on the label of the paint can for use as a thinner. If you don't have that solvent on hand, use turpentine. Rinse. Pretreat with a prewash stain remover, bar soap, or laundry detergent. Rinse again, and then launder.
Perfume	Pretreat with a prewash stain remover or liquid laundry detergent. Launder.
Perspiration	Treat with a prewash stain remover, or rub with bar soap. If the perspiration has changed the color of the fabric, apply ammonia to fresh stains or white vinegar to old stains; rinse. Launder using the hottest water considered safe for fabric. *NOTE:* Stubborn stains may respond to being washed in an enyzme presoak product or all-fabric (oxygen) bleach in the hottest water considered safe for the fabric.
Pine resin	Sponge cleaning fluid into the stain; let dry. Mix equal amounts of liquid laundry detergent and ammonia; soak the stain in the solution. Launder using liquid laundry detergent.

Stain	Treatment
Scorch	Launder using liquid chlorine bleach, if safe for the fabric. Or soak in all-fabric (oxygen) bleach and hot water, then launder. *NOTE:* Badly scorched fabrics may be damaged beyond repair.
Shoe polish (liquid)	Pretreat with a paste of powder detergent and water. Launder.
Shoe polish (paste)	Scrape the residue from the fabric with a dull knife. Pretreat with a prewash stain remover or cleaning fluid; rinse. Rub detergent into the dampened area. Launder using a bleach safe for the fabric.
Tar	Scrape the residue from the fabric with a dull knife. Place the stain facedown on paper towels. Sponge with cleaning fluid. Replace the paper towels frequently to absorb more tar and to avoid transferring the stain to the surface below. Launder in the hottest water considered safe for the fabric.
Tobacco	Dampen the stain and rub with bar soap; rinse. Pretreat or soak in an enzyme presoak product. Launder. *NOTE:* If the stain remains, launder again using a bleach safe for the fabric.
Typewriter correction fluid	Let the stain dry thoroughly, then gently brush off the excess with a clothes brush. Send the item to a professional dry cleaner and describe the type of stain.

LAUNDRY CHALLENGES AND SOLUTIONS

The majority of laundering questions that arise today have to do with poor cleaning results, poor soil and stain removal, residues of lint and scum, and fabric damage. Here are the typical problems, with causes and treatments most likely to solve them. Ways to prevent problems from occurring are also given.

courtesy of The Soap and Detergent Association

Grayness overall

Cause	Solution	Preventive Measures
Insufficient amount of detergent	Rewash with an increased amount of detergent and/or use a detergent booster or bleach.	Use a sufficient amount of detergent.
Wash-water temperature too low	Rewash in hotter water.	Wash in the hottest water considered safe for the fabric.
Transfer of soil	Rewash with an increased amount of detergent and in the hottest water considered safe for the fabric. Use bleach that is safe for the fabric.	Separate heavily soiled items from lightly soiled ones. Use a sufficient amount of detergent, a bleach safe for the fabric, and the hottest water considered safe for the fabric.

Transfer of color

Cause	Solution	Preventive Measures
Incorrect sorting	Do not dry items. Quickly rewash with detergent and a bleach safe for the fabric. Severe damage may be permanent.	Sort carefully by color. Separate white or colorfast white-background prints, colored pastels in solids and prints, medium and bright colors, and dark colors.

Uneven Stain Removal

Cause	Solution	Preventive Measures
Insufficient use of detergent after treatment with a prewash stain remover	Treat the entire item with prewash stain remover, or soak in a concentrated solution of a liquid laundry detergent. Rewash with an increased amount of detergent and in the hottest water considered safe for the fabric.	Use a sufficient amount of detergent, and wash in the hottest water considered safe for the fabric.

Yellowing (from buildup of body soil)

Cause	Solution	Preventive Measures
Insufficient amount of detergent	Rewash with an increased amount of detergent, and/or use an enzyme presoak product, detergent booster, or fabric-appropriate bleach.	Use a sufficient amount of detergent.
Wash-water temperature too low	Rewash in hotter water.	Wash in the hottest water considered safe for the fabric.
Treating synthetic fabrics as "delicate," thus giving them short, gentle, cool washes	Wash in hot water, at least 130°F (54°C), using a permanent-press cycle (with a cooldown that lowers the water temperature before the first spin). Increase the amount of detergent, and/or use a detergent booster or fabric-appropriate bleach.	Launder frequently with a laundry detergent and in water at at least 100°F (38°C).
Handwashing synthetic fabrics with a light-duty detergent	For extremely discolored synthetics that cannot be bleached with liquid chlorine bleach, soak in a product containing enzymes or a detergent booster. Or treat with a color remover by soaking according to package directions. Then launder.	

Yellowing/fabric discoloration

Cause	Solution	Preventive Measures
Use of liquid chlorine bleach on silk, wool, or spandex items	Yellowing cannot be removed.	Do not use liquid chlorine bleach on silk, wool, or spandex items.

Blue stains

Cause	Solution	Preventive Measures
Failure of a blue coloring agent in detergent, laundry aid, or fabric softener to dissolve or disperse	If caused by a detergent or powdered laundry aid, add 1 cup of white vinegar to 1 quart of water in a plastic container. Soak item for one hour in the solution; rinse and launder.	Add the laundry product first, then the clothes, before starting the washer.
	If caused by fabric softener, rub the stain with bar soap, then launder.	Dilute the fabric softener before adding to the wash or rinse cycle or to the dispenser.

Yellow or brown stains (rust)

Cause	Solution	Preventive Measures
Iron and manganese in the water supply	To restore a discolored load of white clothes, use a rust remover recommended for fabrics. Follow the package directions. Repeat if necessary. Then launder. Do not use liquid chlorine bleach to remove rust stains; it may intensify the discoloration.	Use a nonprecipitating water softener in both the wash and the rinse waters to keep the iron in solution. For an ongoing problem, install an iron filter in your water supply system.
Iron in water pipes or water heater	Same as above.	Before washing, run the hot water for a few minutes to clear the lines. Flush the water heater occasionally.

From: _____
_____
_____

BUSINESS REPLY MAIL

FIRST-CLASS MAIL   PERMIT NO. 10   N. ADAMS MA

POSTAGE WILL BE PAID BY ADDRESSEE

STOREY PUBLISHING
PO Box 206
North Adams MA 01247-9919

We'd love your thoughts . . .

Your reactions, criticisms, things you did or didn't like about this Storey book. Please use space below (or write a letter if you'd prefer — even send photos!) telling how you've made use of the information . . . how you've put it to work . . . the more details the better! Thanks in advance for your help in building our library of good Storey books.

Book Title: _____

Purchased From: _____

Comments: _____

Pamela B. Art
President, Storey Publishing

_____

_____

_____

_____

Your Name: _____
              (Please Print)
Mailing Address: _____

E-mail Address: _____

☐ You have my permission to quote from my comments and use these quotations in ads, brochures, mail, and other promotions used to market Storey books.

To order this book or any Storey title CALL 800-441-5700 or visit our web site at www.storey.com

Signed _____ Date _____

e-mail: feedback@storey.com | website: www.storey.com | Printed in United States | 12/05

Storey

Poor soil removal

Cause	Solution	Preventive Measures
Insufficient amount of detergent	Rewash with an increased amount of detergent.	Use a sufficient amount of detergent.
Wash water temperature too low	Wash in hotter water.	Wash in the hottest water considered safe for the fabric.
Overloading of washer	Rewash, with fewer items in a load.	Wash fewer items in a load. Sort clothes by color, fabric, and amount of soil. Use the proper water level for the size of each load.

Greasy, oily stains

Cause	Solution	Preventive Measures
Insufficient amount of detergent to hold the soil in solution until the end of the wash cycle	Treat with a prewash stain remover or a liquid laundry detergent and rewash.	Use a sufficient amount of detergent.
Wash water temperature too low	Rewash in hotter water.	Wash in the hottest water considered safe for the fabric.
Undiluted liquid fabric softener	Rub fabric softener stains with bar soap; launder.	Avoid pouring fabric softener directly on fabrics. Dilute rinse-cycle fabric softener before adding it to the final rinse.
Added fabric softener in too small a load.	Rub fabric softener stains with bar soap; wash.	Add a few bath towels to the dryer load to provide proper tumbling action.

Residue or streaks of powder, particularly noticeable on dark or bright colors

Cause	Solution	Preventive Measures
Undissolved powder detergent	Rewash; add detergent to the water first; then add the clothes and start the washer.	Always add detergent before adding your clothes.
In hard water, some powder detergents can combine with minerals in the water to form a residue	Combine 1 cup of white vinegar and 1 gallon of warm water in a plastic container. Soak the item in the solution, rinse, and launder.	Launder in the hottest water considered safe for the fabric. Do not overload the washer. Or use a liquid laundry detergent or a nonprecipitating water softener with a powder detergent.

Fabrics are stiff, colors are faded, and/or fabrics experience increased wear and abrasion

Cause	Solution	Preventive Measures
In hard water, some powder detergents can combine with minerals in the water to form a residue	Combine 1 cup of white vinegar and 1 gallon of warm water in a plastic container. Soak the item in the solution, rinse, and launder.	Use a liquid laundry detergent or use a nonprecipitating water softener with a powder detergent.

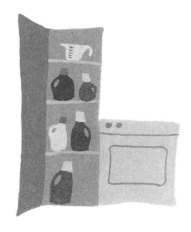

Lint on clothing

Cause	Solution	Preventive Measures
Improper sorting; mixing items that give off lint, such as sweaters, bath towels, and flannels with synthetics, corduroys, velours, and other napped fabrics	To help remove severe lint deposition, hand-pat the dry item, using masking or transparent tape. Rewash, using a fabric softener in the final rinse. Dry in the dryer.	Wash items that give off lint in separate loads from synthetic or napped fabrics. Turning lint collectors inside out may help. Wash very heavy lint shedders, such as blankets, chenille bedspreads, or rugs, alone.
Tissues in pockets	Remove tissues and rewash items.	Empty all pockets before laundering.
Overloading of washer or dryer	Rewash, breaking up the laundry into smaller loads.	Wash and dry fewer items in a load. Use the proper water level for the size of each load.
Insufficient amount of detergent	Rewash with an increased amount of detergent.	Use a sufficient amount of detergent.
Clogged washer lint filter	Clean the washer lint filter and rewash.	Clean the filter after each use.
Overdrying in a dryer, which creates a buildup of static electricity in synthetic fabrics	Rewash, using a fabric softener in the washer or dryer or using a detergent containing a fabric softener in the wash.	Use fabric softener to reduce static attraction of lint to synthetics. Remove items from the dryer while they are slightly damp.
Dryer lint screen is full	Rewash clothes. Clean the lint screen before drying them.	Clean the lint screen after each use.

Pilling

Cause	Solution	Preventive Measures
Some synthetic and permanent-press items have a natural tendency to "pill."*	Lint may be attracted to the little balls. To remove the lint, use a lint brush or a roller with masking or transparent tape.	Pilling cannot be prevented completely. It is a natural characteristic of some synthetic and permanent-press fabrics. Use a fabric softener in the washer or dryer to lubricate the fibers. When ironing, use a spray starch or fabric finish on collars and cuffs.

*This happens because when fibers break off the surface, they ball up and cling to the surface rather than breaking away like natural fibers. This is due to abrasion from normal wear and is commonly found on socks, sweaters, collars, cuffs, underarm areas, or any other portion subjected to abrasion.

Holes, tears, or snags

Cause	Solution	Preventive Measures
Incorrect use of liquid chlorine bleach	Irreversible condition.	Never pour liquid chlorine bleach directly on clothes. Use the bleach dispenser in the washer, or dilute with at least four parts of water before adding to the wash water. For powdered bleach, follow package directions.
Unfastened zippers, hooks, and belt buckles that snag synthetic knits	Irreversible condition.	Fasten zippers, buckles, hooks, and eyes before adding items to the washer. Turn synthetic knits inside out before putting them in the washer.
Rips, tears, and broken threads in seams	May be irreversible if rips, tears, and seams cannot be mended.	Mend any visible damage before washing, especially open seams that will fray and become difficult to mend.
Overloading the washer	May be irreversible if holes, tears, and snags cannot be mended.	Wash fewer items at a time so that the load can circulate freely. Use the proper water level for the amount of clothes being washed.
Sun degradation	Irreversible condition.	Check items like curtains for sun degradation before washing them, by gently pulling the fabric to determine its condition. If the fabric seems sturdy enough to wash, use the gentle cycle.

Color loss or color fading

Cause	Solution	Preventive Measures
Unstable dyes used in garments. Most common with neon and fluorescent colors, as well as bright reds, greens, blues, purples, pinks, black, and peach. Full-strength application of laundry pretreatment products may remove some or all of the color. Sometimes even rubbing with water will cause these colors to bleed or fade.	Color loss or fading due to unstable dyes may be irreversible. If the instructions on the garment-care label were correctly followed, return the garment to the store where it was purchased and ask for a refund or replacement.	Read and follow instructions on garment-care labels. To be safe, always test pretreatment products on an inconspicuous area of the garment, and test the item for colorfastness before washing. Wash new items separately the first few times to remove excess dye.
Water too hot for colored fabrics	Irreversible condition.	Read and follow the instructions on garment-care labels. Do not wash items in water hotter than what is considered safe for the fabric.
Improper use of bleach	Irreversible condition.	Test item for colorfastness before using any kind of bleach. As a precaution, use an all-fabric (oxygen) bleach.
Undiluted bleach applied directly to fabric	Irreversible condition.	Do not pour undiluted bleach directly on clothes. Follow the directions on the product label for correct use.

Wrinkling of synthetic or permanent-press fabrics

Cause	Solution	Preventive Measures
Failure to use correct cycle	Rewash, using the permanent-press cycle on the washer and dryer, if available. If not, for the washer, use warm wash water and a slower or shorter spin speed, followed by a cold rinse. For the dryer, use a high temperature setting, followed by 10 minutes of air drying. Remove items from the dryer as soon as it stops, and hang or fold them.	Same as solution.
Failure to remove items promptly from dryer at end of cycle	Rewash, removing items from the dryer as soon as it stops; hang or fold them immediately.	Same as solution.
Overdrying	Put the clothes back in the dryer. Set the control for 15 to 20 minutes on the permanent-press or timed cycle. The heat and cooldown period will remove the wrinkles.	Reduce drying time and remove items when there is still a trace of moisture in them; hang or fold them immediately.
Overloading of washer and/or dryer	Rewash, breaking up the items into smaller loads.	Do not overload the washer and/or dryer. Use fabric softener.

Shrinking

Cause	Solution	Preventive Measures
Overdrying	Irreversible condition.	Reduce drying time and remove clothes when there is still a trace of moisture in them. Remove knits, especially those made of cotton, while they are still slightly damp. Stretch them back into shape and lay them flat to finish drying.
Residual shrinkage	Irreversible condition.	Many knits and woven fabrics can shrink when laundered. Allow for this when purchasing. Also, check the quality of the item.
Agitation of woolen items	Irreversible condition.	Keep agitation in both the wash and the rinse cycles to a minimum. Use slow agitation or soaking for washing and rinsing. Regular spinning does not contribute to shrinkage and will speed up drying.

FURTHER RESOURCES

Carpet-Cleaning Tips and Referrals

The Carpet and Rug Institute
P.O. Box 2048
Dalton, GA 30742-2048
706-278-3176
www.carpet-rug.com
Information on selecting and cleaning carpets.

Institute of Inspection, Cleaning and Restoration Certification
2515 East Mill Plain Boulevard
Vancouver, WA 98661
360-693-5675
www.iicrc.org
Referrals to certified carpet cleaners in your area.

Shaw Floors
P.O. Drawer 2128
616 E. Walnut Avenue
Dalton, GA 30722-2128
800-441-7429

Fabric Care Tips

International Fabricare Institute
14700 Sweitzer Lane
Laurel, MD 20707
800-638-2627
www.ifi.org
Information about dry cleaning and fabric care tips.

National Cleaners Association

252 West 29th Street

New York, NY 10001

800-888-1620

www.nca-i.com

Information about dry cleaning
and fabric care tips.

Natural Household Cleaners

Arm & Hammer Baking Soda

Church and Dwight Co., Inc.

P.O. Box 7468

Princeton, NJ 08543

800-524-1328

www.armhammer.com

The Web site offers ways to use baking soda
as a cleaning and deodorizing agent.

Pure Liquid Gold

7527 Spruce Street

Concrete, WA 98237

360-826-4389

www.pureliquidgold.com

The Web site offers household uses for grapefruit
seed extract as a cleaner and disinfectant.

ReaLemon/Mott's Inc.

900 King Street

Rye Brook, NY 10573

800-426-4891

www.realemon.com

The Web site describes ways to use lemon juice as
a household cleaning agent.

Salt Institute

700 North Fairfax Street, Suite 600

Fairfax Plaza

Alexandria, VA 22314-2040

703-549-4648

www.saltinstitute.org

See the Web site for surprising uses for salt as a
cleaner and deodorizer in and around the home.

The Vinegar Institute

5775 Peachtree Dunwoody Road

Building G, Suite 500

Atlanta, GA 30342

404-252-3663

www.versatilevinegar.org

Household hints and tips for using vinegar
as a cleaner, sanitizer, and deodorizer.

Organizing and Decluttering

AuctionDrop

48233 Warm Springs Boulevard

Fremont, CA 94539

866-DROP-IT-OFF (866-376-7486)

www.auctiondrop.com

An eBay drop-off service in partnership with
the UPS Store.

Clutterers Anonymous

P.O. Box 91413

Los Angeles, CA 90009-1413

310-281-6064 (recorded meeting information)

www.clutterersanonymous.net

A fellowship of individuals who share experience,
strength, and hope that they may solve their com-
mon problem with clutter and help others recover.

Clutterless Recovery Groups, Inc.

c/o Mike Nelson

2421 South Conway Avenue, #764

Mission, TX 78572-1560

512-351-4058

www.clutterless.org

A nonprofit organization run by clutterers for clutterers, with online support groups.

Collective Good

4508 Bibb Boulevard, Suite B-10

Tucker, GA 30084

770-856-9021

www.collectivegood.com

Refurbishes and distributes cell phones to your choice of charities.

Craigslist.org

Online bulletin board for posting giveaway items to your local community (postings can be found under "For Sale").

Direct Marketing Association

Mail Preference Service

P.O. Box 643

Carmel, NY 10512

To reduce junk mail, write to this address and request that you be removed from marketing lists. Include your name (with various spellings) and address.

Dress for Success

Offices Worldwide

www.dressforsuccess.org

Find a collection center in your area for this organization, which distributes career clothing to economically disadvantaged women looking for jobs.

Freecycle.org

Online bulletin boards for posting giveaways to people in your local area.

LiveDeal

www.livedeal.com

Free online postings of items for sale to local and national buyers.

Messies Anonymous

5025 Southwest 114th Avenue

Miami, FL 33165

www.messies.com

Online self-help groups and other helpful resources.

National Association of Professional Organizers (NAPO)

4700 West Lake Avenue

Glenview, IL 60025

847-375-4746

www.napo.net

Online referrals from the largest national association of professional organizers in the world to professional organizers in your local area.

National Cristina Foundation

500 West Putnam Avenue

Greenwich, CT 06830

203-863-9100

www.cristina.org

Provides refurbished computers to people with disabilities, students at risk, and economically disadvantaged individuals.

**National Study Group on
Chronic Disorganization (NSGCD)**

P.O. Box 1990

Elk Grove, CA 95759

916-962-6227

www.nsgcd.org

Online resources and referrals to professional organizers specializing in helping the chronically disorganized.

Professional Organizers in Canada

www.organizersincanada.com

Internet-based organization with referrals to professional organizers in your area.

Professional Organizers Web Ring

www.organizerswebring.com

Internet-based organization with online discussion forums and referrals to professional organizers in your area.

reBOOT Canada

136 Geary Avenue, Suite 110

Toronto, ON M6H 4H1

Canada

416-534-6017

www.rebootcanada.ca

Refurbishes and distributes computers to charitable organizations to increase access to technology.

TechSoup.org

435 Brannan Street, Suite 100

San Francisco, CA 94107

415-633-9300

www.techsoup.org

Accepts computer donations; connects nonprofits to donated and discounted computer products.

Pests and Pesticides

**National Pesticide Telecommunication
Network (NPTN)**

800-858-PEST (800-858-7378)

www.nptn.orst.edu

A cooperative effort of Oregon State University and the United States Environmental Protection Agency that provides information about pests and pesticides via its Web site and hotline.

National Pest Management Association, Inc.

9300 Lee Highway, Suite 301

Fairfax, VA 22031

703-352-NPMA (703-352-6762)

www.pestworld.org

Referrals to pest-management professionals in your area.

Safety and Environmental Issues

Earth 911

7301 East Helm, Building D
Scottsdale, AZ 85260
877-EARTH911 (877-327-8491)
www.earth911.org
Information about environmentally friendly recycling and disposal.

Environmental Protection Agency

National Service Center for Environmental Publications
P.O. Box 42419
Cincinnati, OH 45242
800-490-9198
www.epa.gov/ncepihom
Information about indoor air quality, mold, pesticides, and more.

Environmental Protection Agency

Safe Drinking Water Hotline
4606M, 1200 Pennsylvania Avenue NW
Washington, DC 20460
800-426-4791
www.epa.gov/safewater/hotline/index.html
Information about drinking-water and ground-water programs authorized under the Safe Drinking Water Act.

Home Safety Council

1725 Eye Street NW, Suite 300
Washington, DC 20006
202-349-1100
www.homesafetycouncil.org
Safety guidelines for use in and around your home.

Indoor Air Quality Information Clearinghouse

P.O. Box 37133
Washington, DC 20013
800-438-4318
www.epa.gov/iaq/whereyoulive.html
Information about indoor air quality and the relationships to asthma, mold, radon, and secondhand smoke.

National Safety Council's Radon Hotline

800-SOS-RADON (800-767-7236)
24-hour recording with information about radon.
800-55-RADON (800-557-2366)
Hotline to speak to a live specialist during normal business hours.

NSF International

P.O. Box 130140

789 North Dixboro Road

Ann Arbor, MI 48113-0140

800-673-8010

www.nsfconsumer.org

Information about water testing and water treatment devices.

Partnership for Food Safety Education

655 15th Street NW, 7th Floor

Washington, DC 20005

800-SAFEFOOD (800-723-3366)

www.fightbac.org

Information on cleaning to prevent food-borne bacteria.

The Soap and Detergent Association

1500 K Street NW, Suite 300

Washington, DC 20005

202-347-2900

www.cleaning101.com

Extensive information about laundry, dishwashing, and household cleaning products, as well as reports on environmental and human safety issues.

Index

INDEX

OTHER STOREY TITLES
YOU MIGHT ENJOY

Organizing Plain & Simple, by Donna Smallin. Organizing expert Donna Smallin brings sanity back to your household with this treasure chest of clutter-control advice. Smallin's room-by-room, tried-and-true organizational techniques ease the burden of managing your money, house, time, family, and life's big changes. 320 pages. Paperback. ISBN 1-58017-448-5.

Unclutter Your Home, by Donna Smallin. Here are hundreds of tips, techniques, and ideas for organizing the worthwhile, getting rid of the obsolete, and making time for what really matters, like friends, family, and personal growth. 192 pages. Paperback. ISBN 1-58017-108-7.

The One-Minute Organizer Plain & Simple, by Donna Smallin. These 500 simple and painless quick fixes offer solutions to the busy person's daily battle with clutter, both physical and mental, one minute at a time. 256 pages. Paperback. ISBN 1-58017-584-4.

Keeping Life Simple, by Karen Levine. These 380 practical tips and inspiring thoughts will help you reduce clutter, focus on what really matters, and enhance life's everyday moments. 384 pages. Paperback. ISBN 1-58014-600-3.

Feng Shui Dos & Taboos, by Angi Ma Wong. In a fun, A-to-Z format, Angi Ma Wong suggests more than 350 feng shui practices, principles, and tips. 416 pages. Paperback. ISBN 1-58017-308-X.

Every Woman's Quick & Easy Car Care, by Bridget Kachur. This user-friendly guide is your complete Auto Mechanics 101. Any woman with an open mind and a willing hand can follow these simple, step-by-step tutorials. 288 pages. Flexibind. ISBN 1-58017-451-5.

The Woman's Hands-On Home Repair Guide, by Lyn Herrick. Fix it yourself and save money in the process with this essential handbook written by a woman for women. These basic home repair rules include step-by-step instructions for fixing and renovating all the things that can go wrong around the house. 208 pages. Paperback. ISBN 0-88266-973-7.

*These books and other Storey books are available whereever books are sold,
or directly from Storey Publishing, 210 Mass MoCA Way, North Adams, MA 01247,
or by calling 1-800-441-5700. www.storey.com*